D1272942

ALSO BY JONATHAN SACKS

Arguments for the Sake of Heaven: Emerging Trends in Traditional Judaism

Celebrating Life: Finding Happiness in Unexpected Places

The Chief Rabbi's Haggadah

Community of Faith

Covenant and Conversation: A Weekly Reading of the Jewish Bible: Genesis, the Book of Beginnings

Crisis and Covenant: Jewish Thought After the Holocaust

The Dignity of Difference: How to Avoid the Clash of Civilizations

Faith in the Future: The Ecology of Hope and the Restoration of Family, Community, and Faith

From Optimism to Hope: Thoughts for the Day

The Home We Build Together: Recreating Society

The Koren Sacks Siddur

A Letter in the Scroll: Understanding Our Jewish Identity and Exploring the Legacy of the World's Oldest Religion

Morals and Markets

One People?: Tradition, Modernity, and Jewish Unity

The Persistence of Faith: Religion, Morality and Society in a Secular Age

The Politics of Hope

Radical Then, Radical Now: The Legacy of the World's Oldest Religion

To Heal a Fractured World: The Ethics of Responsibility

Tradition in an Untraditional Age

Will We Have Jewish Grandchildren?: Jewish Continuity and How to Achieve It

Future Tense

Future Tense

JEWS, JUDAISM, AND ISRAEL IN THE TWENTY-FIRST CENTURY

RABBI JONATHAN SACKS

SCHOCKEN BOOKS, NEW YORK

 Published in the United States by Schocken Books, a division of Random House, Inc., New York, and in Canada by Random House of Canada Limited, Toronto. Originally published in Great Britain as *Future Tense: A Vision for Jews and Judaism in the Global Culture* by Hodder & Stoughton, a Hachette U.K. company, London, in 2009.

Schocken and colophon are registered trademarks of Random House, Inc.

Library of Congress Cataloging-in-Publication Data
Sacks, Jonathan, Rabbi [date].
Future tense : Jews, Judaism, and Israel in the twenty-first century / Rabbi Jonathan Sacks.
p. cm.
Includes bibliographical references.
ISBN 978-0-8052-4269-0
1. Judaism—21st century. 2. Jews—Identity. 3. Faith (Judaism). 4. Judaism—History—Modern period, 1750–. 5. Israel and the diaspora. 6. Judaism—Relations—Christianity. 7. Judaism—Relations—Islam. 8. Christianity and other religions—Judaism. I. Title.
BM565.S216 2009 296.09'05—dc22 2009049771
www.schocken.com

Printed in the United States of America
First American Edition
2 4 6 8 9 7 5 3 1

Contents

Prologue 1

1. Story of the People, People of the Story 11
2. Is There Still a Jewish People? 25
3. Jewish Continuity and How to Achieve It 49
4. The Other: Judaism, Christianity and Islam 71
5. Antisemitism: The Fourth Mutation 89
6. A People That Dwells Alone? 113
7. Israel, Gateway of Hope 131
8. A New Zionism 155
9. The Jewish Conversation 181
10. Torah and Wisdom: Judaism and the World 207
11. Future Tense: The Voice of Hope in the Conversation of Humankind 231

Epilogue 253
Notes 265
For Further Reading 279

Future Tense

Prologue

'Yesterday,' said the fabled politician, 'we stood at the edge of the abyss, but today we have taken *a giant step forward*.' Jewish history can sometimes feel like that: danger, followed by disaster. It does today.

Sixty years after its birth, the state of Israel is deeply isolated. It faces missiles from Hezbollah in the north and Hamas in the south, two terrorist groups pledged to Israel's destruction. It has fought two campaigns, Lebanon in 2006, Gaza in 2008–09, whose outcome has been inconclusive. In the wings is Iran and the threat of nuclear weapons. Rarely has its future seemed so fraught with risk.

At the same time it has faced a chorus of international disapproval for its attempt to fight the new, ruthless terror that takes refuge among civilian populations. If it does nothing, it fails in the first duty of a state, to protect its citizens. If it does something, the innocent suffer. It is a conundrum to perplex the most inventive mind and trouble the most thoughtful conscience.

The existence of the state of Israel would, thought Theodor Herzl, put an end to antisemitism. Instead, Israel has become the focus of a new antisemitism. The emergence within living memory of the Holocaust of a new strain of the world's oldest hate is one of the most shocking developments in my lifetime.

Were these the only problems facing the Jewish people, they would be formidable. But there are others that weaken from within. There is the crisis of Jewish continuity. Throughout the Diaspora on average one in two young Jews is, through outmarriage, assimilation or disaffiliation, choosing not to continue the

Jewish story; to be the last leaf on a tree that has lasted for four thousand years.

There is the eclipse of religious Zionism in Israel and modern orthodoxy in the Diaspora, the two forms of Judaism that believed it was possible to maintain the classic terms of Jewish life in the modern world. Jews are either engaging with the world and losing their Jewish identity or preserving their identity at the cost of disengaging from the world. There are continuing divisions within the Jewish world, to the point that it is difficult to speak of Jews as one people with a shared fate and a collective identity.

This book is about all these issues, but it is also an attempt to get beneath them. For there is something deeper at stake, something fundamental and unresolved about the place of Jews, Judaism and Israel in the world. 'A picture held us captive,' said Wittgenstein, speaking about philosophy. The same, I believe, is true of Jews. An image of a people alone in the world, surrounded by enemies, bereft of friends, has dominated Jewish consciousness since the Holocaust. That is understandable. It is also dangerous. It leads to bad decisions and it risks becoming a self-fulfilling prophecy.

Jews need to recover faith—not simple faith, not naïve optimism, but faith that they are not alone in the world. The former Soviet dissident Natan Sharansky, imprisoned for his wish to leave and go to Israel, tells the story of how his wife, Avital, gave him a Hebrew book of Psalms to sustain him in the hard years ahead. The Russians confiscated it and he fought for three years to have it returned. Eventually it was.

Sharansky knew little Hebrew, but he treated the book as a code to be deciphered, which he eventually did. He recalls the moment one line yielded its meaning, the verse from Psalm 23: 'Though I walk through the valley of the shadow of death I will fear no evil for you are with me.' It was an epiphany. He felt as if someone had written those words directly for him in that place, that time. He survived, won his freedom, and went to Israel. He carries the book with him to this day.

Sharansky is a living symbol of the Jewish people through time. Often enough they too lost their freedom, but as long as they felt 'I will fear no evil for you are with me', they had an inner resilience that protected them from fear and despair. It was not a naïve faith, but it was awesome in its power. Jews kept faith alive. Faith kept the Jewish people alive. Faith defeats fear.

Fear, on the other hand, generates a sense of victimhood. Victims feel themselves to be alone. Everyone is against them. No one understands them. They have two choices: either to retreat within themselves or to act aggressively to defend themselves. Victims blame the world, not themselves. For that reason, it is a self-reinforcing attitude. Victims want the world to change, forgetting that it may be they who have to change. The victims' fears may be real, but victimhood is not the best way to deal with them.

Fear is the wrong response to the situation of Jews in the contemporary world. It is easy, surveying the news day by day, to believe that they are the worst of times, but in some ways they are the best. Never before in four thousand years of history have Jews enjoyed, simultaneously, independence and sovereignty in Israel, and freedom and equality in the Diaspora.

The very existence of Israel is as near to a miracle as we will find in the sober pages of empirical history. Israel has had to face war and terror, but it has transformed the Jewish situation by the mere fact of its existence as the one place where Jews can defend themselves instead of relying on the all-too-often-unreliable goodwill of others. At the same time Jewish life in the Diaspora is flourishing, culturally, educationally, even spiritually, in ways that would have been unimaginable a century ago.

In truth, these are not the worst of times, nor the best of times, but the most challenging of times. Jews today are in a position they have rarely if ever been in before in four thousand years of history. They face the world, in Israel and the Diaspora, on equal terms or, at least, on Jewish terms. What terms are they?

That is the question I address in this book. My argument is

that we are in danger of forgetting who Jews are and why, why there is such a thing as the Jewish people, and what its place is within the global project of humankind. In the past Jews lived through catastrophes that would have spelled the end of most nations: the destruction of Solomon's temple, the Babylonian exile, the Roman conquest, the Hadrianic persecutions, the massacres of the Crusades, the Spanish expulsion. They wrote elegies; they mourned; they prayed. But they did not give way to fear. They did not define themselves as victims. They did not see antisemitism written into the fabric of the universe. They knew they existed for a purpose, and it was not for themselves alone.

Jews, whether in Israel or elsewhere, need to recover a sense of purpose. Until you know where you want to be, you will not know where to go. So this book is not just about the problems facing Jews, Judaism and Israel in the twenty-first century. It is also about the larger question of who Jews are, and why.

I have been intimately involved in all the problems about which I write: the fight against antisemitism, the strengthening of Jewish continuity and, within a Diaspora context, the defence of Israel in the media, academia, non-governmental organisations (NGOs) and British and European politics. My role has been a small one, one voice among many, and it has been a privilege to work with people and organisations, Jewish and non-Jewish alike, who have done so much more.

Yet I have felt something missing from these efforts. That is no one's fault. It is the price paid for immediacy and involvement. What I sensed missing is the larger picture, the historical perspective, the connection of the dots into a portrait that would show us the *who* and *what* and *why* of the Jewish situation against the broad backdrop of the human and historical landscape. There is a line in the Bible more often quoted by non-Jews than Jews: 'Without a vision, the people perish' (Prov. 29:18). Yet it is Jews who should be listening to that verse. They were a people of vision whose heroes were visionaries. That much must never be lost.

In the heat of the moment, people do what they did last time. They revert to type. They choose the default mode. In the present instance, that is the wrong reaction. Things change. The world in the twenty-first century is not what it was in the twentieth or nineteenth. Borders that, a few decades ago, seemed to guarantee Israel's safety are no defence against long-range missiles. Secular nationalism of the kind that dominated the Middle East after the Second World War is not the same as religiously motivated terror, and cannot be negotiated in the same way.

The old antisemitism, a product of nineteenth-century European romantic nationalism, is not the same as the new, however old the recycled myths. You cannot fight hate transmitted by the Internet in the way you could fight hate that belonged to the public culture. Tell Britons about the rise in antisemitism and, for the most part, they look at you with blank incomprehension. They don't read it in their newspapers; they don't see it on their television screens. How are they to know that their next-door neighbour may be inhaling it from a website of whose very existence they are unaware?

Under pressure, people do the predictable. Moses did so once, and it cost him his entry into the Promised Land. The people wanted water. God told Moses to take a stick, speak to the rock, and water would appear. Moses took the stick, hit the rock, and water flowed. Then God said, in effect, 'You didn't do what I told you. You cannot enter the land.'

The story has perplexed almost everyone who has ever read it. So large a punishment for so small a sin? Besides which, what actually was the sin? What we forget is that an episode almost exactly the same had happened before, shortly after the Israelites crossed the divided Red Sea. Then God had told Moses to take a stick and hit the rock, which is what he did. On this second occasion he followed precedent. He did what he had done before. We can imagine his thoughts: 'God said, "Take a stick." Last time that meant, "Hit the rock," so this time too I will hit the rock.'

There was one salient difference: a matter of forty years. The first time he was leading a people who, a few days previously, had been slaves. Now he was leading their children, a generation born in freedom. Slaves understand that with a command comes a stick. Free men and women don't respond to sticks but to words. They need leaders who speak, not strike. Moses, the man who led a generation for forty years out of slavery, was not the man to lead a free people across the Jordan.

Responses right in one age may be wrong in the next. That applies to Jews and Judaism today. I am troubled by the predictability of Jewish reactions, as if the past were still casting its shadow over the present. Today Jews are not victims, not powerless, and do not stand alone. Or, to put it more precisely, thinking in such terms is counter-productive and dysfunctional. Antisemitism is not inevitable, nor is it even mysterious. Nor is there a law of nature that says that Jews must quarrel with other Jews, frustrate each other's efforts and criticise each other mercilessly, acting as if they were still in the wilderness wondering why they ever left Egypt.

The world has changed and Jews must change, the way they always changed, going back to first principles and asking about the nature of the Jewish vocation, 'renewing our days'—in that lovely Jewish paradox—'as of old'.

This is a book I was reluctant to write. There have been so many written in the past few years: about Israel, the new antisemitism, Jewish continuity and the like. I have not sought lightly to add to their number. What I have tried to do is sketch the big picture, the larger vision, and to set it before what I hope will be a new generation, not just of readers but of leaders. I have tried to ask the great questions—who Jews are and what is being asked of them at this time—and whether my answers are persuasive or not, the questions are real and will not go away.

I believe that time-horizons within the Jewish world—indeed, within the West generally—are too foreshortened. We think about yesterday, today and tomorrow while the enemies of Jews and freedom are thinking in decades and centuries, as Bernard Lewis has often argued. In a battle between those who think short and those who think long, the latter win in the long run almost by definition. Tactics are no substitute for strategy; tomorrow's headlines are not the verdict of history. Jews have been around for two-thirds of the history of civilisation. That is long enough to know that Jewish life needs something more prophetic than crisis management.

So I have tried, in the following chapters, to set the present in the wider context of past and future, and immediate problems in terms of ultimate ideals. My argument will be that we have lost our way and need to recover the classic terms of the Jewish story. That story is not about antisemitism or about Israel as a nation surrounded by enemies. It is not about Jews destined to live alone, at best misunderstood, at worse the perennial target of hate. It is about faith, an unusual faith in which God summoned a people and charged them with becoming his partners in creating lives, and in Israel a society, that would become a home for the divine presence. That faith inspired not only Jews but also Christians and Muslims, whose religion grew in Jewish soil, as well as others who respected the Jewish love of family, community, education, tradition, the pursuit of justice, the passion for argument and the Jewish sense of humour that can laugh even in the face of tragedy.

I believe that this is not accidental. *Judaism was never meant for Jews alone.* It contains a message for all humanity, and much in the twenty-first century will depend on whether this message or a different one prevails. Judaism belongs to the human conversation, and we must take the trouble to share our ideas with others, and let others share theirs with us. For a long time—most of history—this was simply not possible. The world was not interested in what the Jews had to say. Either they were there to be converted or assimilated, or they were 'the other' to be reviled. That has changed, for two reasons.

First, liberal democracies allow space for a multiplicity of voices. We all have a right to speak, and to do so in our own person. That is the glory of liberal democracy. Second, because of the existence of the state of Israel, Jews can speak on equal terms. No longer need they be haunted by the trauma of homelessness.

These are not minor changes. They mean that Jews must go back to the beginning and to the Hebrew Bible and ask again what it is to be Jewish, part of a singular people in a plural world, conscious at one and the same time of the uniqueness of identity and the universality of the human condition. What is it to be true to your faith and a blessing to others regardless of their faith? That is the Jewish question.

The problems confronting Jews in the twenty-first century are formidable, but they confront others as well. Israel faces terror, but so does every free society after 9/11. Jews face hatred and prejudice. So do Muslims, Hindus and Sikhs in Britain, Christians in Nigeria, Buddhists in Tibet and Chinese in the Philippines. Jews worry about whether their children and grandchildren will carry on their traditions. So does every religious minority in the diverse democracies of the West. Having written books about Jewish continuity, I have been consulted by British Muslims on Islamic continuity and by Hong Kong Chinese on Confucian and Taoist continuity.

It took a non-Jewish writer, the Catholic historian Paul Johnson, in his magisterial *A History of the Jews,* to state the obvious. The Jews, he writes, were 'exemplars and epitomizers of the human condition'. They seemed to present 'all the inescapable dilemmas of man in a heightened and clarified form'. The conclusion he reaches is that 'It seems to be the role of the Jews to focus and dramatize these common experiences of mankind, and to turn their particular fate into a universal moral.'[1] Our uniqueness is our universality.

Jews are not alone in the challenges they face. The world is going through a whirlwind of change, the pace of which it has rarely seen before. In the months while I was writing this book, from the summer of 2008 to the beginning of 2009, the entire global financial structure collapsed. One economy after another went into recession. There was a tragic terrorist attack in Mumbai. Israel conducted a controversial campaign in Gaza. Antisemitic attacks in Britain reached their highest levels since record-keeping began twenty-five years ago. Never before have events in one place had such rapid repercussions everywhere. We find ourselves, in Matthew Arnold's graphic phrase, 'wandering between two worlds, one dead, the other powerless to be born'.

It is at this historic moment, more perhaps than at any previous juncture of the Jewish past, that God's words to Abraham, summoning him to a life through which 'all the families of the earth will be blessed', resonate most loudly. Jews are the world's oldest—until recently, the world's only—global people. They are the people who rebuilt their lives after the Holocaust, the greatest crime of human against human. Israel is the nation that, under almost constant attack for sixty years, has sustained a free and democratic society in a part of the world that never knew such things. The time has come for Jews to let go of their fears and lay hold again of their historic strengths.

These are controversial propositions, but I do not advance them lightly as academic speculations untested by experience. To the contrary, they are conclusions to which I have been driven as a result of personal involvement in all the issues I address. I have applied them in the field, and they work. I have examined them in the light of our sacred texts, and they cohere.

It is my considered view that, in this tense and troubled century, Jews must take a stand, not motivated by fear, not driven by paranoia or a sense of victimhood, but a positive stand on the basis of the values by which our ancestors lived and for which they were prepared to die: justice, equity, compassion, love of the stranger, the sanctity of life and the dignity of the human person without regard to colour, culture or creed. Now is not the time to retreat into a ghetto of the mind. It is the time to renew that most ancient of biblical institutions, the covenant of human solidarity, made in the days of Noah after the Flood. Without compromising one iota of Jewish faith or identity, Jews must stand alongside their friends, Christian, Muslim, Buddhist, Hindu, Sikh or secular humanist, in defence of freedom against the enemies of freedom, in affirmation of life against those who worship death and desecrate life.

We are entering, said Alan Greenspan, an age of turbulence. The antidote to fear is faith, a faith that knows the dangers but never loses hope. Faith as I understand it is not certainty but the courage to live with uncertainty, the courage Natan Sharansky discovered in his prison cell, the courage that led Jews to rebuild their lives and their ancestral home after the Holocaust, the faith that led generation after generation to hand on their way of life to their children, knowing the risks involved in being Jewish yet never ceasing to cherish the privilege of the challenge. The Jewish people are ancient but still young; a suffering people still suffused with moral energy; a people who have known the worst fate can throw at them, and can still rejoice. They remain a living symbol of hope.

I

Story of the People, People of the Story

> God created man because God loves stories.
>
> *Elie Wiesel*

> Jews have always had stories for the rest of us.
>
> *Andrew Marr*

In 1876, the greatest English writer of her time, Mary Ann Evans, better known as George Eliot, published what was to be her last novel.[1] It was called *Daniel Deronda,* and it was what would have been called a Zionist novel, had the word 'Zionist' existed at the time. The main character in the novel is a young woman, Gwendolen Harleth, yet the fact that Eliot called the book *Daniel Deronda* shows that for her it was the story of the eponymous hero, Daniel himself, that constituted the heart of the book.

Deronda, an Englishman whom Gwendolen meets, had once saved the life of a young woman, Mirah Lapidoth, who was about to drown herself in the Thames. Mirah was Jewish, the first Jew Deronda had met. His interest in Jews kindled, Deronda wanders around London visiting Jewish sites and comes to meet a learned scholar, Mordecai, who earns his living repairing jewellery. Mordecai becomes Daniel's mentor in the history and practises of the Jews. Mordecai is a member of a debating society called The Philosophers and it is there that Daniel hears him defend Jewry as a living people and Judaism as a living faith, evidently a controversial view in those days and that place. Though both, he concedes, are exhausted, only one thing is needed to revive them: the restoration of Jews to their sovereignty and their land. ' "Looking towards a land and a polity," ' he says, ' "our dispersed people in all the ends of the earth may share the dignity of a national life which has a voice among the peoples of the East and the West." '

Mordecai tells Daniel he has a mission, to be part of this project. But he is ill, his health is failing. He tells Daniel that perhaps they had been brought together because Daniel himself is fated to be the carrier of this mission, and hints that he may be Jewish himself. Daniel has not until now known who his mother was. He asks his guardian, who tells him that he had kept her name from Daniel at her request. He travels to meet his mother, a Russian princess living in Genoa, and eventually she confides in him that she had been born a Jew, a fate from which she had fled. This was the reason she had kept her identity hidden: she did not want her son to suffer because of his birth. Knowing now who he is, Daniel is drawn to Mordecai's dream. The novel ends with him taking his leave of Gwendolen and setting out for the Promised Land: ' "The idea that I am possessed with is that of restoring a political existence to my people," ' he tells her, ' "making them a nation again, giving them a national centre, such as the English have, though they too are scattered over the face of the globe." '

It was an extraordinary decision on George Eliot's part to dedicate her last great work to the Jewish dream. She had no Jewish connections. She spent years of study immersing herself in the literature of and about the Jews. She even learned Hebrew as part of her preparation. She knew her theme would not be popular, and that her championing of the Jewish cause would bring her negative reviews. 'The Jewish element', she wrote in her journal, was 'likely to satisfy nobody'. There had been no recent event to bring the fate of the Jews to public notice. The Damascus Blood Libel lay thirty-six years in the past, the Russian pogroms five years in the future. The word 'antisemitism' had not yet been coined.

Yet the fate of the Jews clearly engaged her and it formed the subject of the last essay she wrote before she died. It was called 'The Modern Hep! Hep! Hep!'—the reference was to the cry of the Crusaders in the Middle Ages as they were about to massacre

Jews. The suffering of this people spoke to her. So too did its contribution to civilisation. Jews, she said, were 'a people whose ideas have determined the religion of half the world, and that, the more cultivated half'. She was astonished that they had kept their self-respect despite the contempt in which they had been held in Christian Europe. The question she posed was whether Jews had leaders, 'some new Ezras, some modern Maccabees', who would re-establish the people as a nation in their own land, creating there 'a centre of national feeling, a source of dignifying protection, a special channel for special energies which may contribute some added form of national genius'.

Somehow, at the end of her life, George Eliot identified with the Jewish story, its pains and persecutions, and above all its unwritten chapter, prophesied twenty-five centuries ago: the return to Zion. It was as yet barely a dream, a vision, a hope, but as George Eliot knew, Jews were a people of hope.

'I've Seen the Promised Land'

Ninety-two years later, on 3 April 1968, an African-American leader delivered a sermon in the Mason Temple Church in Memphis, Tennessee.[2] Still a young man—he was thirty-nine at the time—he was nonetheless famous throughout the world. In 1964 he had been awarded the Nobel Peace Prize. His name was Martin Luther King Jr.

The biblical story of the exodus from slavery to freedom and the long journey across the wilderness to the Promised Land had long inspired African-Americans in their struggle for civil rights. In the nineteenth century they had sung their own version of Exodus 5:1:

> Go down, Moses,
> Way down in Egypt's Land.
> Tell ol' Pharaoh,
> Let my people go.

Dr. King lived and breathed that story. His speeches were full of quotations from the Hebrew Bible. It was a story that gave him hope, and through it he gave his fellow African-Americans hope.

At the climax of the most memorable of all his public addresses, the 'I have a dream' speech delivered before the Lincoln Memorial in Washington in August 1963, he quoted at length from Isaiah 40:4–5, the passage Jews read on the 'Sabbath of Consolation': 'I have a dream that one day every valley shall be exalted, every hill and mountain shall be made low, the rough places will be made plain and the crooked places will be made straight and the glory of the Lord shall be revealed and all flesh shall see it together.' He added, 'With this faith we will be able to hew out of the mountain of despair a stone of hope.'

By 1968, though, the mood among the Civil Rights Movement was tense. Many were impatient with King's slow pace and progress. The more militant believed that only violence would achieve their goals. Others thought the whole idea of racial integration was wrong. Colour would always divide. King, they thought, was pursuing an impossible dream. Knowing of the opposition he faced, King sensed that his life was in danger. It was this premonition that led him, that night, to end his speech with extraordinarily prophetic words.

He reminded his audience of the last day of Moses' life. Moses knew that he would not himself be able to cross the Jordan, to which he had led the people for forty years. God granted him one last gift: not entry into the land but a glimpse of it from afar, from a mountain-top on the other side of the river. Moses' life had not been in vain. He had taken the people almost all the way, but it would be a new generation who would complete the journey.

These were almost the last words Dr. King spoke that night: 'We've got some difficult times ahead. But it doesn't matter with me now. Because I've been to the mountain-top . . . And I've looked over. And I've seen the promised land. I may not get there with you. But I want you to know tonight that we as a people will get to the promised land.' It turned out to be the last day of his life too.

The next day he was assassinated. Forty years later, an African-American, Barack Obama, was elected President of the United States for the first time. He had begun his campaign by writing a book to which he gave a significant title: *The Audacity of Hope*. Hope needs audacity. That is what Martin Luther King Jr. had: the courage to stay with his dream even though he knew it was too much for some, too little for others, and too civil for the extremists; even though he sensed he would not be there to see it come true. He knew what the rabbis knew: 'It is not for you to complete the task, but neither are you free to stand aside from it.' He had led African-Americans along the biblical journey, and a generation later they reached the promised land. The Jewish story is the West's meta-narrative of hope.

The World Turned Upside Down

'These are the times', wrote Thomas Paine, 'that try men's souls.'[3] Certainly these times are trying Jewish souls. A decade ago, as the Christian millennium approached, many—I was one—believed Jews were entering a new and quieter phase in their history. Israel was in full pursuit of peace. Antisemitism was at an all-time low. Jews had achieved unprecedented prominence in most of the societies in which they lived. The Jewish voice was listened to with respect.

Then the world turned upside down. The peace process foundered, to be replaced first with an intifada, then with an almost ceaseless wave of suicide bombings, then with missile attacks from Lebanon in the north, Gaza in the south. Israel found itself surrounded not just by enemies—that much it has always known—but by terrorist groups, themselves funded by and proxies for states, committed to Israel's destruction as a matter of non-negotiable religious conviction.

Nor was the attack merely physical: it was political as well.

Israel found itself at the receiving end of a vastly ramified, international campaign of delegitimation, instigated by non-governmental organisations, academics and sections of the media, becoming the only nation among the 192 making up the United Nations to find its very right to be and to defend its citizens called into question.

Alongside this and intimately related to it came the return of antisemitism: the world's oldest hate in the world's newest dress. Jews found themselves assaulted in the suburbs of Paris and the streets of Manchester. Synagogues were desecrated, Jewish cemeteries vandalised, Jewish schools firebombed, Jewish students intimidated on campuses. All this had happened after decades of determination, in the form of anti-racist legislation and education, to ensure that the hate that led to the Holocaust should never happen again.

None of this, perhaps, should have been surprising. One of the advantages of being a people with four thousand years of history is that wherever Jews find themselves, they have been here before. 'Hello darkness my old friend,' sang Simon and Garfunkel in the 1960s, in an authentic reflex of Jewish memory. Yet I belong to a generation born after the Holocaust but old enough to remember events like the Six Day War. We hoped, we believed, that Jews had finally moved from darkness to light. We were wrong.

These are serious, disturbing problems. Perhaps the most serious of them all is the loss of Jews in the Diaspora through assimilation, outmarriage and the gradual attenuation of Jewish ties, and the loss of a sense of purpose, even identity, within Israel itself. When Jews in the past had a sense of purpose, nothing could defeat them. When they lacked it, they found ingenious ways of almost defeating themselves.

The Wrong Story

This is a book about the challenges facing Jews, Judaism and the state of Israel in the twenty-first century. But it is not a conventional book. My concern is not simply to analyse the problems, though I try to do that. My belief is that many, perhaps most, Jews within Israel and outside have forgotten the Jewish story: the journey from slavery to freedom, darkness to light, exile to the Promised Land, a journey of faith sustained by faith. In its place has come another story, so often recited, so often seemingly confirmed by events, that it has come to seem *the* Jewish story.

It goes like this: Jews have been persecuted throughout the ages. They were in Christian Europe from the eleventh to the twentieth century. They are now in the predominantly Muslim Middle East. To be a Jew is to be hated and to defy that hate. As one twentieth-century Jewish theologian, Emil Fackenheim, put it: Jews are commanded to stay Jewish in order to deny Hitler a posthumous victory.[4] Jews are, in the biblical phrase, 'the people that dwells alone' (Num. 23:9).

This book is a challenge to that narrative. First, it *isn't* the Jewish story. The facts may be true, but the narrative is wrong. Second, it risks becoming a classic case of a self-fulfilling prophecy. Believing themselves to be alone, Jews will find themselves alone. Third, it leads to a set of attitudes utterly inconsistent with classic Jewish self-understanding. It turns Jews into victims. It renders them passive-aggressive. It makes them distrust the world, which can lead to other- or self-hatred. Fourth, it generates policies that are self-destructive. Fifth, it demoralises at the very time when the Jewish people need strength. Sixth, it will lead Jews to leave Judaism. Seventh, it deprives Jews and humanity of the very thing that constitutes the Jewish message to humanity: the Jewish story, told and lived, whose theme is the audacity of hope.

In thrall to the other narrative, that Jews are the people fated to dwell alone, Jews try to fight antisemitism alone. Israelis tend to believe that with the exception of the United States, the state of Israel is alone. The greatest Jewish thinker of the twentieth century, Rabbi Joseph Soloveitchik, wrote a famous essay titled *The Lonely Man of Faith*.[5]

I disagree with all these propositions. Jews cannot defeat antisemitism alone. Israel cannot survive alone. In Judaism the man and woman of faith are not alone. To the contrary: *emunah,* the Jewish word for faith, is about the redemption of solitude, the antithesis of being alone. All these attitudes are understandable given the terrible history of the twentieth century, but they are misplaced given the circumstances of the twenty-first. Those who take refuge in solitude compound their problems rather than solve them. The single most important challenge facing the Jewish people, in Israel and the Diaspora, is to recover the Jewish story. It inspired George Eliot. It inspired Dr. King. The time has come for it to inspire Jews.

Redeeming Evil

This is not Pollyanna-ish optimism. No Jew who knows Jewish history can be an optimist. It is, rather, realism pure and simple. As the first Prime Minister of Israel, David Ben-Gurion, said, 'In Israel, to be a realist you have to believe in miracles.' For Jews faith is as necessary as life itself. Without it the Jewish people would simply not have survived.

In 2001, after the Oslo peace process had broken down and the suicide bombings had begun, I told the then Israeli ambassador: 'In the past, Israel's enemies have tried to put it in a military crisis and failed. Then they tried to put it in a political crisis and failed. Now they are about to put it in a *spiritual* crisis, and they may succeed.'

That, ultimately, is what twenty-first-century terror is about, and Israel has been its most consistent target. The suicide bombings brought war from the battlefront to the buses of Haifa, the shops of Tel Aviv and the restaurants of Jerusalem. There were times when Jewish parents sent their children on the school bus not knowing whether they would see them alive again. The missiles of Hezbollah and Hamas placed two-thirds of Israel—the north and south—within their range. As I write, there are seven-year-old children in Sederot who have known safety only in a bomb shelter. The delegitimation of Israel among some media, academic and NGO circles has left its people feeling abandoned and alone. The aim is to intimidate and create despair, and it needs immense resources of faith and courage not to be affected. That is the spiritual crisis.

It is also the peculiar power of terror in the global age. It is not merely that terror deliberately attacks innocent civilians and etches everyday life with fear. It is rather that it takes the virtues of the open society and exploits them as vulnerabilities. One particularly poignant example came in the terror attacks on Mumbai in November 2008. Among the victims were a young rabbi and his wife, Gavriel and Rivkah Holzberg.

They were members of a group known as Chabad, or Lubavitch Hassidim. I did not know them personally, but they and I had been inspired by the same man, Rabbi Menachem Mendel Schneerson, the Rebbe of Lubavitch. He had done something no Jew had ever done before. He had sent emissaries throughout the world, wherever there were or could be Jews. Their role was to keep an open house and offer hospitality to strangers. That is what the Holzbergs had done. It is possible—so went several news stories at the time—that they had given food and lodging to the people who subsequently murdered them.

I knew the Rebbe of Lubavitch. I am a rabbi today because of him. For years I wondered what led him to his extraordinary project. Judaism is not a missionary faith, nor had rabbis engaged in outreach to isolated or estranged Jews. Eventually I came up with a hypothesis, and it remains the only satisfying explanation I have heard. Rabbi Schneerson, a Jewish mystic, believed in the idea of *tikkun,* that by our acts we can redeem a fractured world and rescue fragments of divine light from the heart of human darkness.

But he had lived through the Holocaust, in which almost the entire world of the Jewish mystics of Eastern Europe was destroyed. How do you redeem evil of that magnitude? I believe that he had come to the conclusion that if the Nazis had hunted down every Jew in hate, he would send his disciples to search out every Jew in love. That is what inspired me to become a rabbi.

After the tragedy of Mumbai, I began to ask myself whether such gestures are still possible in an age of terror. In Genesis 18, Abraham welcomed strangers and discovered that they were angels. The Holzbergs had welcomed strangers and found that they were murderers. Does terror show that openness is mere vulnerability? The answer must be 'no'. The Jewish way, of which the Rebbe was a supreme exemplar, is to rescue hope from tragedy. However dark the world, love still heals. Goodness still redeems. Terror, by defeating others, ultimately defeats itself, while the memory of those who offered kindness to strangers lives on.

The Will to Power Versus the Will to Life

Thousands of books have been written about terror since the collapse of the Israeli-Palestinian peace process and the events of 9/11. They deal with the methods of terror, the politics of terror, the psychology of suicide bombers, the nature of religious extremism and the end-of-days martyrdoms intended to bring about the final reign on earth of the god who is said to command holy war. What I have not yet encountered is a book about the strength of hope needed to defeat terror by the simple act of refusing to be terrified.

Leaders of Al Qaeda, Hamas and Hezbollah never tire of repeating the mantra that they are bound to win in the great confrontation that will shape the twenty-first century, because 'You love life, while we are unafraid of death.' That precisely demarcates the spiritual battleground of our time. Moses said at the end of his life:

> This day I call heaven and earth as witnesses against you that I have set before you life and death, blessings and curses. Now choose life, so that you and your children may live. (Deut. 30:19)

Choosing life—*eros* over *thanatos,* peace over war, trust over fear—is not something we can take for granted. Darwin, or some of his followers, painted a picture of life as a struggle for survival. Freud diagnosed the death instinct as one of the two primary drives operative in the human personality. Marx saw history as an inevitable struggle between the classes. Carl Schmitt defined the political as the search for an enemy.[6] Evolutionary psychologists like David Buss tell us that murder is an adaptive strategy for passing on genes to the next generation in a world of reproductive competition.[7] Cognitive psychiatrists such as Aaron T. Beck suggest that hate is the result of projecting onto others the negative aspects of our self-image.[8]

Whatever the explanation, Sir Henry Sumner Maine, the nineteenth-century historian, summed up history when he said, 'War is as old as mankind while peace is a modern invention.'[9] This gives us the first clue to the direction of the journey I want to take in this book, seeking to understand the Jewish story, why it has significance not just for Jews, and how it applies to the threats to Jewish survival today.

The key figure here is the most profound, radical and disturbing philosopher of the past two centuries, Friedrich Nietzsche. Nietzsche was the man who first pronounced the words 'God is dead' and who placed at the centre of his new scheme of values *the will to power.* He was hostile not to Jews but to Judaism, and even more so to Christianity. In 1889, at the age of forty-five, he suffered a mental breakdown from which he never recovered. A year earlier he wrote one of his most impassioned and troubling works, *The Anti-Christ.* In it he said:

> The Jews are the most remarkable nation of world history because, faced with the question of being or not being, they preferred, with a perfectly uncanny conviction, being *at any price* . . . They defined themselves *counter* to all those conditions under which a nation was previously able to live, was *permitted* to live; they made of themselves an antithesis to *natural*

> conditions—they inverted religion, religious worship, morality, history, psychology one after the other in an irreparable way into the *contradiction of their natural values* . . . For precisely this reason the Jews are the most *fateful* nation in world history.[10]

From his perspective Nietzsche was right. Jews opposed all he stood for: nature, pride, animal vitality, the contempt of the strong for the weak, of the intelligent for the foolish and trusting, of the well bred for the masses. He blamed Jews for creating Christianity, and blamed Christianity for emasculating Europe, especially the 'blond beast' of the Aryan race, robbing it of its natural instincts to dominate and control. He called Judaism 'the slave revolt in morals', the revenge of the oppressed against their former oppressors. He saw the Judeo-Christian ethic as a precise inversion of what he believed in, substituting humility for superiority, sympathy for the victim instead of identification with the victor, care for the poor and vulnerable instead of the fellowship of the proud and strong.

Nietzsche would have been horrified by the use the Nazis made of his ideas. But he did identify, earlier and more clear-sightedly than anyone else, the German turn away from reason and enlightenment to the old pagan gods of blood and belonging. He was right. That is the choice: the will to power versus the will to life. Judaism, the religion of the God of life, whose greatest prophet said at the end of his life, 'Now choose life', is a sustained call to the sanctification of life.

There is nothing natural about this at all. The Jewish God is not the god of nature but the God who transcends nature. Nature can seem cruel, remorseless, blind. It breeds birth out of destruction. Stars explode, and planets are created. Life is born and preys on other life. Homo sapiens appears, and by banding together into packs, tribes, clans, cities, states and empires, exercises dominance over others. There is nothing evil about this, and nothing good either. Nature is, to use another of Nietzsche's phrases, 'beyond good and evil'. That is how it is. We can laugh, we can cry, we can develop 'the tragic sense of life', but there is nothing else. All else is fond illusion. We are alone in the universe, and we can either dominate or be dominated. All that exists is the blind, pitiless is-ness of things.

Somehow, through their encounter with the Divine, Jews discovered or were discovered by a different truth, that over and above the 'is' there is an 'ought'. The actual is not inevitable. There can be a different world. Nature is not the final word, for nature itself was created by a being who stands outside it and who, by making us in his image, gave us the power to stand outside it. We are free. We can choose. We are not predestined by chance, fate, the stars, our darker instincts or the human genome. We can opt for freedom over determinism, justice over the power of power; we can stop at the brink of history's endless replays and chart a different course. We cannot defeat death, but we can defeat all those forces that lead human beings to kill other, innocent human beings. We can choose life.

The Call

Long ago, one man and one woman heard a call telling them to leave their land, their birthplace and their father's house and begin a journey. There was nothing conspicuous about them, nothing to suggest that the path on which they were about to embark would eventually change the history of humankind. The man was not a military hero or a miracle worker. He was not a revolutionary or a guru with thousands of followers. He had absolutely nothing in common with the heroes of epic or myth. Yet there can be no doubt that he was the most influential human being who ever lived. Today, 2.2 billion Christians, 1.3 billion Muslims and 13 million Jews—more than half the 6 billion people alive today—claim descent, biological or spiritual, from him. His name was Abraham; the name of the woman, his wife, was Sarah.

What was special, new, about Abraham was not so much the

God he worshipped. According to the Hebrew Bible, Abraham was not the first monotheist. Adam was. What Abraham initiated was the idea of faith as a journey undertaken by a people in search of the Promised Land. It was that journey George Eliot's hero, Daniel Deronda, was about to undertake. It was the journey Martin Luther King Jr. spoke about in his last public address. It was the most daring and controversial of all Jewish undertakings in the modern age, the return to Zion. Yet by one of the ironies of Jewish history, the achievement of that journey has led to a questioning of the very existence of Jews as a single people.

2

Is There Still a Jewish People?

In 1992 a new word appeared in an English dictionary for the first time: *peoplehood.* The spellchecker on the word-processing programme on which I am writing this book has still not come across it: it signals a mistake every time I write the word. According to an article in the Jewish newspaper *Forward,* its appearance may have something to do with Jews.[1] The first uses of the word were either by Jewish writers or by people writing about Jewry. Before 1992 there were peoples, nations, races, ethnic groups, tribes, clans and communities but not *peoplehood.* Why did the word appear in the 1990s, in America, and in a Jewish context?

Words are often born when the phenomenon they name is under threat. The adjective *orthodox* first appeared in a Jewish context in France in the early nineteenth century in the course of the debate about Jewish citizenship in the new nation-state. For the first time in the modern world the traditional terms of Jewish existence were thrown into question. Alternatives were proposed. Some argued that Judaism must change. Those who disagreed were given the label 'orthodox'. Only when something is challenged does it need a name. Until then it is taken for granted, part of the background. So it may have been in the case of Jewish *peoplehood.*

It was at about the same time, in 1990, that a book appeared arguing that the Jewish people was essentially at an end. Written by a historian of Zionism, David Vital, it was called *The Future of the Jews.* In it he argued that nothing now holds Jews together. The definitions of Jewish life are too many. The forms it takes are too diffuse. There is, Vital argued, no substantive common ground between the Jews of Israel and those of the Diaspora.

Their interests are different. So is their sense of Jewishness or Israeliness. 'Where there was once a single, if certainly a scattered and far from monolithic people,' wrote Vital, 'there is now a sort of archipelago of discrete islands composed of rather shaky communities of all qualities, shapes, and sizes.'[2] His conclusion was sombre: 'It is not too much to say that the survival of Jewry as a discrete people, its various branches bound to each other by common ties of culture, responsibility, and loyalty, is entirely in doubt.'

On the face of it, he was right. For centuries, in exile, scattered and dispersed, Jews saw themselves and were seen by others as a single nation. There was no other like it. They lacked all the normal prerequisites of a nation. They had no land. They were not living in the same place. They spoke different languages. They lived within different cultures. There was nothing, apparently, to connect them to one another. But they shared a history, a memory, a faith and a hope. They were God's people whom he had rescued long ago from Egypt. They had made a covenant with him at Sinai. They would worship him and he would protect them. Though they had lost their land, one day they would return. He, through his prophets, had said so. They rehearsed that identity daily through every prayer they said, every text they studied, every command they performed.

There was nothing quite like it anywhere else. The key word of the twenty-first century is 'globalisation'. For most, it is the newest of the new. For Jews it is the oldest of the old. Since the Babylonian exile twenty-six centuries ago, certainly since the Roman era two thousand years ago, Jews lived at great distances from one another, yet they were connected by a thousand gossamer strands of the spirit. They were the world's first and, until recently, its only global people.

That entire configuration changed in the nineteenth century in Europe, where four out of every five Jews lived. The difference was the new nation-state, which demanded a monopoly of people's loyalty. The nation was no longer where you lived. It was who you were. No longer could you be a Jew living in France. You had to be, first and foremost, a 'Frenchman of the Jewish persuasion'. Anything else constituted a dual loyalty and that, in the age of nationalism, was the cardinal sin. But what did that mean in practise? No one was entirely sure. It was a question—*Der Judenfrage,* the 'Jewish question'—that reverberated throughout the nation-states of Europe for the next century and a half, and it placed Jews in an identity crisis that has not been fully resolved to this day.

The result was a fragmentation of Jewish identity the likes of which had not been seen since the last days of the Second Temple. Jews twisted and turned in their attempt to find some mode of existence that would grant them safe space in the modern state which, in the name of tolerance, had developed a more deadly intolerance than any of its medieval predecessors. Modifications made by Reform Jews in Jewish practice and ritual in response to the new scientific way of looking at the world would also to some extent soften the distinctive features of Judaism and show, as far as it could be shown, that Jews were like everyone else.

Meanwhile, Jews in the East were facing a wave of more primitive antisemitism. Pogroms broke out throughout Russia in 1881. In 1882 the notorious May Laws were enacted. Many of those who stayed and many of those who left formulated a variety of secular identities. There were Jewish communists, socialists, culturalists, Yiddishists and campaigners for Jewish autonomy in the Pale of Settlement. There were Zionists of every hue: religious, secular, restorative, revolutionary, Nietzschean, Tolstoyan, socialist, Leninist, mystical or minimalist, to which must be added Theodor Herzl's vision of Israel as the Switzerland of the Middle East.

There was hardly a self-respecting Jewish intellectual in the late nineteenth or early twentieth century who did not have his or her version of utopia, literate, erudite, fastidiously crafted and utterly impracticable, with the sole exception of Zionism itself. The once relatively coherent concept of Jewish identity was shattered into myriad fragments from which it has not recovered to this day. Martin Buber concluded that Jews no longer existed as a people. They were too fragmented. They no longer had a shared set of beliefs. The Enlightenment had undermined classical Jewish self-understanding as a single nation standing before God.[3]

He spoke too soon, for what happened was the Holocaust. Despite all their differences in belief, culture and appearance, Jews seemed to their enemies to be a single entity: a dangerous, subversive race, an alien presence in the lands in which they lived, an international conspiracy, a monster, a parasite, a threat. Jews might be internally hopelessly divided, but to antisemites they were maliciously united. They may have moved in a dozen different directions, chosen a hundred different identities, but if they remained in Europe, they found themselves transported back to a series of extermination camps, united in death if not in life.

It took many years before Jews were able to reflect on the *Shoa* (the Hebrew term for the Holocaust). When they did—after the Eichmann trial in 1961 and the Six Day War in 1967—they began to put into words a profound sense that the Jewish people was a single entity after all. Every Jew in Europe had been under sentence of death by the terms of the Final Solution. After the Holocaust, most Jews felt themselves to be, in George Steiner's phrase, 'a kind of survivor'. They also recognised that whether they lived in Israel or not, it was their city of refuge, the place where they could go in an emergency and where, if nowhere else, they could be safe. So Jews were indeed a single people. 'We are one', as the slogan of Jewish organisations put it at the time.

But by the 1980s, the sense of collective fate, heightened by Holocaust reflection and the traumatic weeks before the Six Day War, had begun to fade. Israel began to face more intractable conflicts. The 1982 Lebanon War was the first in which Jewry was genuinely divided. Israel no longer faced armies but terrorist groups who took refuge among civilian populations. Israel no longer looked like David fighting the Goliath of its neighbouring states. If anything, the roles seemed to be reversed. The divisions within Jewry, between secular and religious, Orthodox and Reform, and in Israel between the Jews from Europe and those from Arab lands, came more to the fore. Neither Jews nor Israel was fighting for survival, and what was left by the retreating tide of fear were all the fragments of Jewish identity, shattered by the whirlwind of nineteenth- and twentieth-century Europe, and seemingly beyond repair.

In 1993, I published my own reflections on Jewish unity-within-diversity and called it, interrogatively, *One People?*[4] Friends in America read it and told me it was already too late. In the United States, Orthodoxy and Reform were too far apart for any conceivable rapprochement. Jews had become, irreparably, two peoples. At about the same time, David Vital had reached the same pessimistic conclusion, basing it in his case on the deep and growing differences between Israel and the Diaspora.

I am not a pessimist. Pessimism in Judaism is usually premature. In chapter 3 we will see how, three thousand years ago, Egyptians and Moabites wrote the obituary of the people called Israel, yet they survived. The same is true about Jewish peoplehood. Jews have often thought of themselves as irreparably divided, yet a sense of kinship remains. But there are good and bad ways of thinking about what makes Jews a people, and the way Jews think today affects what they become tomorrow.

My argument on this subject is the same as on all the others in this book. The definition of Jews as the-people-that-dwells-alone does great harm to Jewish peoplehood. Essentially it defines Jews as victims. It says that Jews are the people who, historically, have been subject to persecution, isolation and alienation. In the nineteenth and twentieth centuries they tried to integrate, assimilate, become like everyone else, but it failed. Inescapably, Jews are different. So, though they share nothing else, they have in common a history of suffering. The music of Jewish life is in the minor key. Jewish literature is an extended book of lamentations. Jews share a fate.

This is the wrong way to think about Jewish peoplehood. Jews are a people of faith, not fate alone. Jews are choosers, not victims; co-authors of their destiny, not swept by the winds of circumstance. Without a positive vision, Jews will indeed cease to be a people. But to begin at the beginning, let us first acknowledge that the fear that Jews might split apart is genuine and justified. It can happen. It happened in the past. There is work to be done if Jews are to stay together in the future.

Three Divisions

Three times in their history Jews have suffered exile: first in the days of the biblical Joseph, a second time with the destruction of the First Temple by the Babylonians, a third with the fall of Jerusalem to the Romans and the later defeat of the Bar Kochba rebellion. Each was a reverberating tragedy.

The first led to slavery in Egypt. To this day, on Passover, Jews annually re-enact that tragedy, tasting the bread of affliction and the bitter herbs of slavery. The Torah commands Jews to remember the exodus all the days of their lives, and in their prayers they do. The second was one of the defining traumas of Judaism, relived each year on the Ninth of Av, the anniversary of the destruction of the Temple, when Jews sit and mourn and read the book of Lamentations as if a close relative had just died. The third led to an exile lasting almost two thousand years, and the longest succession of tragedies experienced by any people in history.

History is complex, but memory is clear. In Jewish memory, all three events have something in common. They were caused by *the failure of Jews to live peaceably together.* In the case of Joseph, the Bible is explicit. Joseph's brothers 'hated him and could not speak a kind word to him' (Gen. 37:4). Their hatred continued to grow as Joseph dreamed dreams of greatness and told his brothers. They resolved to kill him but eventually sold him into slavery. That led eventually to the enslavement of the entire family, by then grown to be a people.

The second was the result of the attempt to unite the people into a single political entity. According to the books of Joshua and Judges, the Israelites for several centuries were a loose confederation of tribes. Eventually, in the days of Samuel, the people requested a king, and the request was granted. The entire project lasted a mere three generations: first Saul, then David, then Solomon. After the death of Solomon, the people came to his son and successor Rehoboam, asking for their tax burden to be lightened. Urged on by his friends, and against the advice of his father's counsellors, Rehoboam refused, and ten of the tribes split off to form a separate kingdom under Jeroboam the Ephraimtie.

It was the beginning of the end. Always a small people surrounded by empires, the Israelites depended on a high level of national unity to survive at all. Split as they were, they became a prime example of Lincoln's adage that a house divided against itself cannot stand. In 722 BCE the northern kingdom fell to the Assyrians. Its population was dispersed, and became known to history as the Ten Lost Tribes. A century and a quarter later, the southern kingdom fell to the Babylonians. Jeremiah repeatedly warned that they had no hope against an enemy of such power, and urged an accommodation. The people refused to listen, and the tragedy Jeremiah had prophesied came about.

The third occasion was, if anything, even worse. The picture we have of the Jewish people in the late Second Temple period is of a hopelessly divided nation, factionalised in every direction. Josephus tells us there were fundamental religious divisions between Pharisees, Sadducees and Essenes. The rabbinic literature tells us that there was a rift among the Pharisees themselves, between the schools of Hillel and Shammai, a division so deep that it threatened to split rabbinic Judaism into 'two Torahs'.[5]

Politically there were divisions between moderates and zealots. The zealots themselves were divided. The more radical, known as the *sicarii,* were among the world's first religious terrorists. It was the worst possible time to mount a rebellion against the disciplined forces of imperial Rome, yet between 66 and 73, that is what happened. Josephus, a military commander in Galilee when the revolt began, could see that it was doomed almost from the outset.

Few narratives are more tragic than the story he tells about the Jews within the besieged Jerusalem. There were moderates headed by Joseph ben Gurion, the former high priest Hanan and Simon ben Gamliel, a descendant of Hillel. There were zealots under the command of John of Gischala, ultra-zealots led by Simon bar Giora, and a third group under Eleazar. This is how Josephus describes the internecine struggle between John and Simon towards the end of the siege:

> To which other parts of the city he [John] turned, he never failed to set fire to the houses that were stocked with grain and supplies of every kind; when he withdrew, Simon advanced and followed his example. It was as if to oblige the Romans they were destroying all that the city had laid up against a siege and hamstringing their own powers. The result at any rate was that all the buildings round the Temple were burnt to the ground, the city became a desolate no man's land where they flung themselves at each other's throats, and almost all the grain—enough to support them through many years of siege—went up in flames. It was hunger that defeated them, a thing that could never have happened if they had not brought it upon themselves.[6]

All Vespasian, and later Titus, had to do was wait while the Jews within slowly destroyed themselves. In an extraordinary outburst, Josephus interrupts his narrative with a lament:

> Unhappy city [Jerusalem]! What have you suffered from the Romans to compare with this? . . . You were no longer the place of God; you could not continue, now that you were the burial place of your own sons and had turned the Temple into a common grave for those who had slain each other.[7]

We have no way of telling how accurate Josephus' account is. Yet the rabbinic literature broadly substantiates his thesis. The sages themselves said that Jerusalem was destroyed because of *sinat chinam,* 'baseless hatred', between Jews.

The most poignant reflection from those times is a statement preserved in the Mishnah, whose full significance is almost invariably lost on readers. Here it is in the version with which most people are familiar:

> Rabbi Chanina, the deputy High Priest, said: Pray for the welfare of the government, for were it not for fear of it, people would swallow one another alive.[8]

This sounds like a simple statement of a Hobbesian political philosophy. We need governments to ensure the rule of law and prevent anarchy. However, early texts have a different reading: 'were it not for fear of it, *we* would have swallowed each other alive'. Rabbi Chanina was deputy high priest. That means that he lived in the days of the Second Temple. The government of which he was speaking was Roman. The Romans were the people who tyrannised Jews, conquered Jerusalem and destroyed the Temple. Yet, says Rabbi Chanina, even being ruled by an enemy can sometimes be preferable to the lawless chaos of a people intent on destroying itself.

Consider the implications of these three stories. Jews have been conquered by some of the greatest empires ever to have appeared on the stage of history, yet each has disappeared, to be remembered today only in museums. The Jewish people outlived them all. They could not be destroyed by others, but three times they almost destroyed themselves. *The only people capable of threatening the future of the Jewish people are the Jewish people.*

Other nations have fought civil wars and undergone revolutions. Yet it would be hard to think of one that has lacerated itself in quite the way the Jewish people have done. Under conditions of independence and sovereignty, Jews have found it hard to live peaceably with other Jews.

Dispersed but United

Yet the paradox is that if we consider the history of Jews in exile, we find an even more remarkable phenomenon in precisely the opposite direction. Jews were dispersed throughout the world, they were not part of the same political jurisdiction, but they continued to see themselves as a single nation, a distinctive and persistent group, often more closely linked to other Jews throughout the world than to the peoples among whom they lived.

They did not share the same culture. While Rashi and the Tosafists were living in Christian France, Maimonides inhabited an Islamic culture, first in Spain, then in Egypt. Nor were their fates the same at any given time. While North European Jewry was suffering massacres during the First Crusade, Spanish Jewry was enjoying its golden age. While the Jews of Spain were experiencing the trauma of expulsion, the Jews of Poland were thriving in a rare moment of tolerance.

They did not use the same language of everyday speech. Ashkenazi Jews spoke Yiddish, Spanish and Portuguese Jews spoke Ladino, and there were as many as twenty-five other vernaculars, among them Judeo-Arabic, Judeo-Slavic, Judeo-Yazdi, Judeo-Shirazi, Judeo-Esfahani and Judeo-Marathi, as well as Yevanic, a form of Judeo-Greek. They did not even, given the fact of conversion, share the same genetic heritage. Nothing united them at all—nothing, that is, that would normally constitute nationhood.

What united them? Rav Saadia Gaon in the tenth century gave the answer: 'Our nation is only a nation in virtue of its religious laws.'[9] Wherever Jews were, they kept the same commandments, studied the same sacred texts, observed the same Sabbaths and fast days, and said essentially the same prayers in the same holy language. They even faced the same spot while doing so: Jerusalem, where the Temple once stood and where the Divine presence was still held to have its earthly habitation. These invisible strands of connection sustained them in a bond of collective belonging that had no parallel among any other national grouping. Some feared this, others respected it, but no one doubted that Jews were different.

Haman said so in the book of Esther: 'There is one people, scattered and divided among the peoples, *whose laws are different from all others*' (Esth. 3:8). So, millennia later, did Jean-Jacques Rousseau, in an unpublished note discovered among his papers after his death:

> But an astonishing and truly unique spectacle is to see an expatriated people, who have had neither place nor land for nearly two thousand years, a people mingled with foreigners, no longer perhaps having a single descendant of the early races, a scattered people, dispersed over the world, enslaved, persecuted, scorned by all nations, nonetheless preserving its characteristics, its laws, its customs, its patriotic love of the early social union, when all ties with it seem broken . . . They mingle with all the nations and never merge with them; they no longer have leaders, and are still a nation; they no longer have a homeland, and are always citizens of it.[10]

That is the paradox. In their own land, the place where every other nation is to some degree united, Jews were split beyond repair. In dispersion, where every other nation has assimilated and disappeared, they remained distinctive and, in essentials at least, united. There is something surpassingly strange about Jewish peoplehood.

Two Covenants

The explanation lies in the fact that Jews and Judaism combine two phenomena that nowhere else coincide. Jews are a *nation*, and Judaism is a *religion*. There are nations that contain many religions. There are religions whose adherents are spread across many nations. What is unique is the way in which Judaism combines both.

Jews, 'the children of Israel', are described in the Bible as both an *am*, a people, and an *edah*, a religiously constituted congregation. They are both an extended family with the same biological ancestor, Jacob/Israel, and a community of faith bounded by the covenant they made with God at Mount Sinai. We catch an intimation of this in the words Ruth spoke to Naomi when she insisted on accompanying her mother-in-law to Israel: 'Where you go I will go, and where you stay I will stay. Your people will be my people and your God my God' (Ruth 1:16). 'Your people will be my people'—that is a bond of nationhood. 'Your God will be my God'—that is the adoption of a religious faith.

The same two dimensions appear in the Talmudic account of the process of conversion:

> Our rabbis taught: If at the present time a person desires to become a proselyte, he is to be addressed as follows: 'What reason do you have for seeking to become a proselyte? Do you not know that Israel at the present time are persecuted, oppressed, despised, harassed and overcome by afflictions?' If he replies: 'I know, and yet am unworthy,' he is to be accepted forthwith . . .
>
> He is also told about the punishment for transgression of the commands, and is addressed thus: 'Know that until now, had you eaten forbidden fat, you would not have been punishable by excision, if you had profaned the Sabbath you would not have been liable to stoning, but now were you to eat forbidden fat or profane the Sabbath you would be liable to these punishments.'[11]

The first conversation is about a people and its circumstances. The prospective convert is asked, 'Do you want to be part of this people and its fate?' The second is about a religion with its prohibitions and punishments. 'Do you want to be part of this faith?' Both are part of Jewish identity.

Hence the paradox. When Israel was a nation in its own land, religious divisions threatened the very integrity of the people. Two or more Judaisms equal two or more Jewish peoples. But the converse also holds. Within a century after the destruction of the Second Temple, Sadducees and Essenes virtually disappeared, leaving rabbinic Judaism, the Judaism of the Pharisees, as the sole survivor. Thus religion was able to unite a people otherwise divided territorially, culturally and in every other way.

To be sure, they were divided along many axes. There were Ashkenazim and Sefardim. There were rationalists and mystics. There were periodic schisms, among them the Karaites in the early Middle Ages, and the followers of various messianic pretenders, most famously Shabbetai Zvi in the seventeenth century. In the eighteenth century, tensions between the Hassidim and their opponents, the Mitnagdim, exploded into mutual recriminations. But what united Jews was Judaism itself, with its own laws and courts, its vastly ramified literature, its schools and houses of study, its fellowships and charitable institutions, and its own microcosmic welfare state. The sages succeeded where the prophets failed, in creating out of the once 'stiff-necked people' a nation often awesomely tenacious in its attachment to Jewish faith.

The combination of religion and nation was restated for a post-Holocaust generation by the Orthodox scholar Rabbi Joseph Soloveitchik. There are, he said, two covenants in Jewish life: *brit goral,* a covenant of fate, and *brit ye'ud,* a covenant of faith or destiny. The *brit goral* was born in the experience of slavery in Egypt. The *brit ye'ud* was formed in the revelation at Sinai.[12]

The *brit goral* expresses the solidarity of a people that has perennially found itself alone in the world. It has four dimensions. First, individual Jews find themselves unable to escape the fate of their people. As Mordecai said to Queen Esther, 'Do not think that because you are in the king's house, you alone of all the Jews will escape.' Second, collective fate leads to collective consciousness. 'When one Jew suffers, all feel pain.' This in turn leads to collective responsibility. 'All Jews are sureties for one another.' And this leads to collective action. Historically, Jews helped one another through acts of charity, welfare and rescue.

What Rabbi Soloveitchik realised was that because of the Holocaust, the covenant of fate had been renewed even if the covenant of faith had not. Jews were united in grief and consciousness of danger. They were united too (he was writing in 1956) in their attachment to Israel. Soloveitchik was clear that fate was only half of Judaism, and faith the more significant half. I want, though, to put it more strongly than he did.

Without the covenant of faith, there is no covenant of fate. Without religion, there is no global nation.[13] The story of Jewish survival-through-catastrophe turned on two critical moments in history, one that led to an institution, the other to an idea. It is not too much to say that between them they saved Jewish peoplehood, and thus the Jewish people. Both were achievements of the spirit, for Jews are a people of the spirit and without that they are not a people at all.

The Synagogue: Virtual Jerusalem

The first took place in Babylon twenty-six centuries ago. It was a crisis the likes of which Jews had not suffered before. The Temple was destroyed. A large part of the people had been taken captive. Their feelings at the time have been preserved indelibly in a famous psalm: 'By the waters of Babylon we sat and wept as we remembered Zion,' they said. 'How can we sing the Lord's song in a strange land?' (Ps. 137:1). Judaism until then had been tied to a land. Losing it, they had lost everything. Or almost everything.

The one thing they had not lost was spelled out in a cryptic verse by the prophet of exile, Ezekiel. 'This is what the Sovereign Lord says: Although I sent them far away among the nations and scattered them among the countries, yet I have been a small sanctuary *[mikdash me'at]* for them in the countries where they have gone' (Ezek. 11:16). The precise meaning of *mikdash me'at* is obscure, but we know what it led to: one of the great religious institutions of all time, the synagogue.

The synagogue was a unique institution. Its origins are lost in the vagaries of time, but it was the first place in history made holy not because it was built on a holy site, or because sacrifices were offered there, but merely because people gathered there to study and pray. Where and when the synagogue as an institution was born is debated by scholars, but it was one of the most revolutionary of all Jewish innovations. It could be built anywhere that Jews gathered to study and pray. It was a reminder of the Temple, a fragment of Jerusalem, a Jewish-home-in-exile. It was, in the language of the Internet, a virtual Jerusalem, a city in cyberspace. Jews no longer physically had a land, but they had one in the mind.[14]

Beneath it all lay the unique theology of the Hebrew Bible. Only a monotheistic people could have invented the synagogue. Other ancient gods were territorial. They were the gods of this land, not that. But the God of Abraham, creator of heaven and earth, was the God of everywhere. Therefore he could be reached anywhere. By the time the Second Temple was destroyed, seven centuries later, the synagogue was a mature institution that, more than any other, ensured the survival of Jews as a distinctive group.

The importance of the synagogue is well known to historians. Less well known is an intellectual drama played out in the first to third centuries in the wake of the Roman conquest. It is then, in the early rabbinic literature, that we begin to hear for the first time a new idea, associated especially with the man regarded as one of the fathers of Jewish mysticism, Rabbi Shimon bar Yohai. Here is one of his parables:

> A man in a boat began to bore a hole under his seat. His fellow passengers protested. 'What concern is it of yours?' he responded. 'I am making a hole under my seat, not yours.' They replied,

> 'That is so, but when the water enters and the boat sinks, we too will drown.'[15]

Jews are all in the same boat. They sail or sink together. Here is another of his sayings:

> 'A [holy] nation'—this teaches that they [the Jewish people] are like one body with one soul [the midrash identifies *goi,* a nation, with the word *geviyah,* a body], and thus it says, 'Who is like your people Israel, a nation one on earth.' When one sins, all are punished . . . When one is injured, all feel the pain.[16]

Jews form a unity. When one suffers, all do. The key principle the sages invoked to express this idea was 'All Israelites are sureties for one another.'[17] There is, between Jews, a bond of collective responsibility. So familiar is this idea that we fail to realise how counter-intuitive it was. Behind it lies a remarkable story, and to understand it we have to pay close attention to a key text.

The Covenant of Collective Responsibility

The book of Leviticus reaches a climax with an account of the blessings and curses attendant on Israel's obedience, or lack of it, to the terms of the covenant. The blessings are relatively brief. The curses are, by contrast, set out at length and with elemental power. They are terrifying. To this day Jews recite them in a low voice, barely above a whisper. This is part of the passage:

> As for those of you who are left, I will make their hearts so fearful in the lands of their enemies that the sound of a wind-blown leaf will put them to flight. They will run as though fleeing from the sword, and they will fall, even though no one is pursuing them. *They will stumble over one another* as though fleeing from the sword, even though no one is pursuing them. So you will not be able to stand before your enemies. (Lev. 26:36–7)

The italicised phrase became the proof-text of the rabbinic doctrine of collective responsibility:

> 'They shall stumble over one another'—one *because* of another. This teaches that all Israel are sureties for one another.[18]

This is the sole source in the rabbinic literature for the principle. It first appears in the *Sifra,* a halakhic midrash of the Mishnaic period, and is quoted several times in the Babylonian Talmud. It is, however, an exceptionally strange text on which to base the idea that all Jews are responsible for one another, for three reasons.

First, the text itself has nothing to do with responsibility. 'Stumbling over one another' is not a description of a nation bound by mutual suretyship. It is an account of panic. In their hurry to escape, people fall over one another. Each is concerned with his own safety, not the common good. Whatever prompted the rabbinic interpretation, it was not the plain sense of the verse.

Second, it is not about the normal life of Israel at all. It is a vision of defeat and despair. The nation is in the process of being crushed by its enemies. The people are fleeing as refugees. Normal life is in ruins. How can a passage that speaks of exile and dislocation serve as the basis of a code of conduct?

Third, *it should not be necessary to search for a proof-text for the idea that the Jewish people are bound by a collective fate.* This is a commonplace of the Bible, and its entire vision of Israel's history is predicated on it. Whenever Moses speaks about the blessings and curses attached to the covenant, he speaks about the nation as a whole, moving seamlessly from singular to plural, the 'you' of individuals to the 'you' of the nation as a whole. One example will stand for many:

> Now, if you will carefully obey My commandments which I command you today . . . then I will provide rain in your land in its proper time . . . and you will eat and be satisfied . . . Beware lest your heart be lured away . . . for you will then

soon perish from the good land which the Lord is giving you. (Deut. 11:13–17)

The governing assumption throughout the Hebrew Bible is that when Israel is rewarded, it is rewarded collectively. When it is punished, it is punished collectively. It experiences fate as a people. Judaism is a collective faith whose central experiences are not private but communal. Jews pray together. They mourn together. On the Day of Atonement they confess together. The idea that 'All Israel are responsible for one another' is presupposed by every syllable of Judaism. No proof-text should be necessary, or if it is, then the sages should have chosen one from the covenant ceremony at Mount Sinai when Israel first became a nation under the sovereignty of God.

The mystery, therefore, is: why, at some stage in the Mishnaic period between the first and third centuries CE, did the rabbis locate the principle of collective responsibility *in one of the curses of Leviticus*? Of all possible sources, it seems the least appropriate. Why did the rabbis not cite any of the other myriad texts that testify to this idea? Why choose instead a verse which speaks about Israel in exile in the land of their enemies? Only when we sense the full incongruity of the rabbis' choice of text will we have an intimation of the depth of crisis into which Jewish life was plunged in the first century CE with the destruction of the Second Temple.

It is easy to think of collective responsibility as a distinctively religious idea, and an unusual one. It is far from obvious that if you sin, I should bear part of the blame. It is your sin, not mine; your responsibility, not mine. Each of us is surely separately accountable for our own lives and no one else's. In fact, though, the idea is neither strange nor difficult to understand. To be the citizen of a state, or a resident in a neighbourhood, is to be involved in collective fate of some kind. If my neighbours let their properties deteriorate, the value of my house declines. If our fellow citizens allow moral standards to disintegrate, the resulting lawlessness affects us all. What happens to me is only partly determined by what I do. It is also determined by what others do. With or against our will, we are affected by those around us.

Inevitably, then, we are caught up in a wider framework of responsibility. However, this requires one of two conditions: physical proximity or an overarching political structure. Physical proximity is what binds us together as neighbours. A political structure is what binds us together as fellow citizens. That is why, during virtually the whole period covered by the Hebrew Bible, collective Jewish responsibility was self-evident and taken for granted. During that period, the Israelites were a people living together in a bounded physical space, and a political entity under the leadership of judges or kings. The Israelites were geographically concentrated and politically defined. They were neighbours and fellow citizens.

The destruction of the Second Temple, the loss of political autonomy under the Romans and the gradual dispersion of Jews to other lands therefore constituted an immense and potentially terminal crisis for Israel's existence as a nation. Suddenly the possibility became real that the Jewish people might no longer be a people. It had lost its political structures, and it was no longer geographically concentrated. This had happened before, during the Babylonian exile, but that lasted briefly enough for Jews not to lose hope of return.

The sheer scale of the defeat following the destruction of the Second Temple and the later Bar Kochba rebellion made it clear that this time exile and the loss of power would be prolonged. The prospect for the future of the Jewish people was, by any realistic standards, dim. How could Jews sustain their collective identity—the bond of shared belonging and responsibility—if they were neither neighbours nor fellow citizens? In what sense were Jews still a nation?

Only against this background can we appreciate the full pathos of the rabbis' search for a proof-text. The question they faced was not 'Where do we find in the Bible the concept that all Israel are responsible for one another?' The whole Pentateuch presupposes this concept. But that is because it speaks of Israel as a nation of neighbours and fellow citizens who live and act together and whose actions self-evidently affect one another. The question that faced the sages was 'Where do we find that this principle still applies *even when the Jewish people is exiled, dispersed and shorn of power,* when it is no longer bound together by geographical proximity or membership in the same body politic?'

There are, in fact, only two passages in the Pentateuch that speak about such an eventuality, namely the two passages of curses which envision Israel defeated and scattered in the land of their enemies.[19] That is why the sages chose the text 'They will stumble over one another', understanding it to mean, 'They will stumble *because* of one another's sins.' For it was this text, referring to a time when Jews were in exile, that hinted at the profound spiritual truth that even though Jews were shattered politically and scattered geographically, they were still a nation. Even at such a time they are bound by a covenant of mutual responsibility. Jewish fate and destiny are indivisible.

That is how, from the epicentre of tragedy, the sages rescued a vestige of hope. The covenant of Sinai was still in force. The Jewish people were still bound by its terms. They were therefore still a nation—constituted by the responsibility they had undertaken together, first at Sinai, then on the banks of the Jordan at the end of Moses' life, then again in the last days of Joshua, and subsequently during the period of Israel's kings and in the days of Ezra. Bound to God, they were bound to one another. No other nation had ever constituted itself in such a way. Lacking all the normal prerequisites of nationhood—territory, proximity, sovereignty—Jews remained *even in exile* a people, held together solely by the bond of mutual responsibility.

It was in the midst of this crisis that Shimon bar Yohai began his teachings about the mystical unity of the Jewish people: 'They are like a single body and a single soul. If one is injured, they all feel the pain.' Divided geographically and politically, they are united spiritually. It is not too much to say that this affirmation saved the Jewish people. Without it, Jews in exile might have gone their separate ways as individuals, and there would be no Jewish people today.

The covenant of fate existed only because Jews were bound by a covenant of faith. That is the essential point. In Israel, Jews were a nation in the normal sense, bound together because they lived in the same land, under the same government. Shared fate, under such circumstances, requires no special faith, no theology, no leap of the imagination. Outside Israel, however, *only* the covenant of faith sustained a covenant of fate. And only such faith will, in the long run, keep Jews together in a bond of mutual responsibility. Only this will sustain the attachment of Diaspora Jews to Israel.

That explains a phenomenon that, when I first encountered it, disturbed me deeply. My late father used to believe that Jews instinctively recognise one another; so did almost everyone of his generation. Yet when I walk in the street in London, wearing a Jewish headcovering and looking unmistakably Jewish, and I pass secular Israelis, there is no sign of recognition whatsoever. Why should there be? They are Israeli; I am British. If all there is to identity is secular nationality, then there is nothing in common between us at all.

Fate or Faith?

Arthur Koestler, the author and intellectual, was a supporter of Zionism, spent time in the 1920s in a kibbutz, and was there to witness Israel's war of independence. Afterwards he returned to Britain, where he spent the rest of his life. In 1949 he published his account of the birth of Israel, *Promise and Fulfilment.* His view was that with the creation of the state, Jews everywhere now faced a choice. Either they could live in Israel and be a member of a normal nation state or they could live in the

Diaspora, assimilate and cease to be Jews. There was no third alternative. 'The mission of the wandering Jew is completed.'[20] Essentially, that is the view of a whole range of Jews, in Israel and outside. Many Israelis believe in *shelilat ha-golah*, the view that Jewish life is impossible anywhere but in Israel. Some religious Jews believe that Israel, a secular state, has nothing to do with Judaism.

My own view, as I explain elsewhere in the book, is that Israel and Judaism are essentially connected, not at the level of politics or interests, or any other secular category, but at the deepest level of Jewish identity. Israel is the only place in the world where Jews can create a society, and that is a religious task even though Israel is a secular state. But Judaism is also a religion that, as first Ezekiel then the sages taught, can be practised anywhere, centred on the synagogue as an institution and on collective Jewish responsibility as an idea. Judaism is both fate and faith, and it is impossible to separate the two.

In Israel, Jewish life is a community of fate. There Jews, from the most secular to the most pious, suffer equally from war and terror, and benefit equally from prosperity and peace. Judaism, in Israel, is a presence you breathe, not just a religion you practise. In Israel as nowhere else, Jewishness is part of the public domain, in the language, the landscape, the calendar. There you can stand amid the ruins and relics of towns that were living communities in the time of the Bible and feel the full, astonishing sweep of time across which the Jewish people wrestled with its fate as Jacob once wrestled with the angel. And there you become conscious, in the faces you see and the accents you hear, of the astonishing diversity of Jews from every country and culture, brought together in the great ingathering as once, in Ezekiel's vision, the dismembered fragments of a broken people joined together and came to life again. That is why, for Diaspora Jews, spending time in Israel is an essential and transformative experience of Jewish peoplehood, and why Birthright, the American programme aimed at sending all young Jews to Israel, is so successful.

At the same time, it is equally important that young Israelis spend time in the Jewish communities of the Diaspora. There they discover what it is to live Judaism as a covenant of faith, something many of them have never fully experienced before. One Israeli ambassador to Britain, a secular Jew, realised that if he wanted to get to know the community he would have to attend synagogue (British Jewry, far more than American Jewry, is synagogue-based). One Friday night he visited the synagogue where I was praying, and spent the service reading through the prayers in English translation. At the end he came over to me and said, 'Those prayers—you know, I've never really read them before. *They're good, aren't they!*' He had to read them in English before he could appreciate them in Hebrew, his native language. When his term of duty was at an end, he came to see me to thank our community for helping him rediscover his Judaism.

The Jewish people exists in all its bewildering complexity because it is both a religion and a nation, a faith and a fate. Remove either element and it will fall apart. That is what is wrong in focusing exclusively on fate—antisemitism, the Holocaust, the people that dwells alone. For it is faith that keeps bringing us back to the idea that Jews are a people: it was as a people that our ancestors left Egypt, as a people that they made a covenant with God in the desert, as a people that they took up the challenge of life in the Holy Land, and as a people that they understood their destiny. Jewish life is quintessentially communal, a matter of believing *and* belonging. Maimonides rules: 'one who separates himself from the community, even if he commits no sin but merely holds himself aloof from the congregation of Israel . . . and shows himself indifferent to their distress' has no share in the world to come.[21]

Judaism is not a sect of the like-minded. The Jewish people is not a self-selecting community of saints. It is not, in other words, like most communities of faith. Jewish identity, with the exception of conversion, is something into which we are born, not something we choose. This mix of fate and faith, nationhood and religion, means that from the very beginning, Jews have had to live with the tension of these two very different ideas, and it is that tension that has made Jews creative, unpredictable, diverse, conflicted, yet somehow more than the sum of their parts.

There were times—between the first and nineteenth centuries—when the primary bond between Jews was faith. There were others—during the Holocaust—when it was fate. It is that double bond that has held Jews together. When one failed, the other came to the fore. Call it chance, or the cunning of history, or an invisible hand, or Divine providence, but the old polarities—fate and faith, *goral* and *ye'ud*—remain, dividing Jews and uniting them in a way that is sometimes exasperating but often inspiring. A people Jews were. A people they still are. But if they are to survive as a people, they will have to solve another and yet more fundamental problem: the challenge of Jewish continuity.

3

Jewish Continuity and How to Achieve It

In the Cairo museum stands a giant slab of black granite known as the Merneptah stele. Originally installed by Pharaoh Amenhotep III in his temple in western Thebes, it was removed by a later ruler of Egypt, Merneptah, who reigned in the thirteenth century BCE. Inscribed with hieroglyphics, it contains a record of Merneptah's military victories. Its interest might have been confined to students of ancient civilisations, were it not for the fact that it contains the first reference outside the Bible to the people of Israel. It lists the various powers crushed by Merneptah and his army. It concludes:

> All lands together, they are pacified;
> Everyone who was restless, he has been bound
> By the King of upper and lower Egypt.

Among those who were 'restless' were a small people otherwise unmentioned in the early Egyptian texts. Merneptah or his chroniclers believed that they were now a mere footnote to history. They had not merely been defeated, they had been obliterated. This is what the stele says:

> Israel is laid waste, his seed is no more.

The first reference to Israel outside the Bible is an obituary.

So is the second. This appears on a basalt slab dating from the ninth century BCE. It stands today in the Louvre. Known as the Mesha stele, it records the triumphs of Mesha, king of Moab. The king thanks his deity Chemosh for handing victory to the Moabites in their wars, and continues, 'As for Omri, king of Israel, he humbled Moab for many years, for Chemosh was angry with his land. And his son followed him and he also said, "I will humble Moab." In my time he spoke thus, but I have triumphed over him and over his house, while Israel *has perished forever.*'

The Jewish people has read its obituary many times, yet until now it survived. But in 1991 a piece of research, the 1990 National Jewish Population Survey, showed that this survival is, for large sections of the Jewish world, wholly in doubt. It showed that among American Jews marrying between 1985 and 1990, 57 per cent were outmarriages: Jews marrying non-Jews. Of these only a handful, 5 per cent, were marriages in which the non-Jewish partner converted to Judaism. The report sent shockwaves through the community, but almost twenty years later the trend continues unabated. Statisticians eventually challenged the 57 per cent figure. It was, they argued, based on faulty methodology, and they revised it downward to 43 per cent. But the rate continued to rise, reaching 47 per cent in the 2000 survey even on the new system of measurement. One in two young Jews is deciding not to marry another Jew, build a Jewish home, have Jewish children and continue the Jewish story. Outside orthodoxy, the one group that is growing, Jewish life in America is slowly dying out.[1]

Not only in America: something similar is happening in almost every Jewish community in the Diaspora. In most, the outmarriage rate has also reached one in two, or will in the foreseeable future. In small communities such as those in Scandinavia, it has reached four in five. In fact, the situation is worse than it seems, because outmarriage is not the only factor in the demographic decline. Jews are also marrying late, or not marrying at all, and if they marry, they are not having large families.

The transformation happened in the space of a mere two generations. In the first two decades of the twentieth century, American Jewish outmarriage rates were low: about 2 per cent. Throughout the 1950s it was 6 per cent. In the early 1960s it rose to 17.4 per cent. By the late 1960s it stood at 31.7 per cent. Between

1960 and 1985, in other words, the outmarriage rate had risen by almost 1,000 per cent. Something failed in American Jewish life.

It led to a spate of books with titles like *Vanishing Diaspora, The Vanishing American Jew* and my own *Will We Have Jewish Grandchildren?*[2] In 2006 a national British newspaper carried an article headed, 'Is this the last generation of British Jews?'[3] The significance of this is immense. The Jewish capacity to survive, its identity intact, was legendary and evoked awe in many non-Jewish writers, among them Blaise Pascal, Jean-Jacques Rousseau, Leo Tolstoy and Mark Twain. Despite millennia of persecution, Jews stayed Jews.

In all those centuries, there was one question they never asked: 'Will the Jewish people continue?' They knew it would. Moses had said so. So had Jeremiah. So God himself had promised. What is happening today is the greatest collective exit from the Jewish people since the Assyrians conquered the northern kingdom of Israel in the eighth century BCE. They deported its population, which gradually merged into the surrounding peoples, becoming known to history as the Ten Lost Tribes. The people with a legendary ability to survive every catastrophe are beginning to lose the art of survival. The irony is intense. Jews today are not generally persecuted. They have civil rights and equality, they have reached the heights in almost every sphere of human achievement, and Judaism itself is respected. We are, in other words, living through one of the more counter-intuitive phenomena of Jewish history. *When it was hard to be a Jew, people stayed Jewish. When it became easy to be a Jew, people stopped being Jewish.* Globally, this is the major Jewish problem of our time. Can anything be done about it?

Creating Continuity

It can, and I take as an example British Jewry. When I became Chief Rabbi in 1991, I knew this was the major challenge. I had read the American research, and for two years I read everything I could about Jewish demography, sociology and history, and about identity maintenance among minorities other than Jews. In 1993 I launched the organisation Jewish Continuity, dedicated to promoting everything that strengthened Jewish identity, from schools to the arts and Jewish culture generally. I wrote a series of pamphlets, to make the leaders and funders of the community aware of the problem, its dimensions, and the solution as I saw it. We then set out to create an awareness of the crisis. We took out a series of full-page advertisements in the Jewish press. The first and most effective showed a group of young Jews walking across a floor and then falling into an abyss. The headline read, 'Anglo-Jewry has been losing ten Jews a day, every day, for forty years.'

It worked. Fifteen years later, Anglo-Jewry had built more Jewish day schools than at any previous time in its history. It had moved from being a community in which only a quarter of children attended full-time Jewish education, to one in which more than 60 per cent do so. For three and a half centuries, people had complained that British Jewry had too few Jewish schools. Now they complain it has too many.

There has been an explosion of educational and cultural activities as well. Jewish Book Week has grown to the point that some 8,000 take part in its activities. There have been Jewish arts, music and film festivals and a new Jewish cultural centre. Adult educational activities take place everywhere, especially in synagogues, in a way unknown a generation ago. Limmud, Anglo-Jewry's most remarkable creation, is a winter learning retreat that attracts 2,500 participants taking 600 different courses. There was nothing like it anywhere else in the Jewish world, and it has now been exported to 46 other centres outside Britain, from Los Angeles to Cape Town, Russia to Israel.

In 1989 Daniel Elazar, then the greatest scholar of contemporary Jewish life, wrote about the British Jewish community:

> Its pre-eminence in world Jewish affairs has almost disappeared and its cultural creativity has been stilled . . . Jewish education is limited and not many young people study in Jewish schools . . . Jewish cultural life is even more limited . . . Adult education is minimal . . . By and large, the powers-that-be in British Jewry are content with the status quo and do not seek change. At most they bemoan the decline of British Jewry but, like their British peers, do little to try to alter their state.[4]

Today in all of these fields British Jewry is among the leaders. Recall that in 2006 a national British newspaper asked, 'Is this the last generation of British Jews?' On 21 May 2008 the BBC website carried an item headed 'Jewish population on the increase', continuing, 'The UK's Jewish population is growing for the first time since World War II.'[5] The situation can be changed.

I do not wish to give the impression that British Jewry is unique. Other communities have addressed the challenge. One of the most astonishing phenomena in the past twenty years has been the renaissance of Jewish life in Central and Eastern Europe, where it was almost extinguished by the double impact of the Holocaust and Soviet communism. Today there are Jewish day schools in Moscow, new Jewish community centres in Poland, restored synagogues in Hungary and a rabbinical seminary in Berlin. German Jewry is today the fastest-growing Jewish community in the world.

French Jewry, too, despite the reappearance of antisemitism, has seen a resurgence, with more Jewish day schools than ever before and a profusion of kosher restaurants. Commonwealth Jewry, with major centres in Australia, Canada and South Africa, remains strong, with a higher proportion of young Jews attending Jewish day schools than anywhere else in the Diaspora, and with a strong commitment to Israel.

American Jewry, the largest centre of Jews outside Israel, was the first to monitor and respond to the alarming rise in outmarriage and send warning signals throughout the system. The result has been a significant rise in Jewish day schools, adult education and other continuity programmes, among them the Taglit-Birthright scheme bringing young American Jews on trips to Israel. In my travels around the Jewish world I do not see inevitable decline.

Jews have a way of defying gloomy predictions. Leopold Zunz, the early-nineteenth-century scholar, maintained that for the first time Jewish culture could be studied scientifically because it was dead, a museum exhibit. Hebrew was in terminal decline. No one wrote it anymore, and within a few generations almost no one would be left who could read it. On meeting the Hebrew poet A. D. Gordon, he is said to have asked, 'Tell me, when did you live?' In 1965 a Harvard population study predicted that by 2067 there would be no more than 10,000 Jews left in America. So systemic have been the prophesies of doom that the historian Simon Dubnow called Jews the 'ever-dying people'. Every time a eulogy was being pronounced over Jewish life, however, a rebirth was taking place beneath the radar of perception.

Jews have survived catastrophe after catastrophe, in a way unparalleled by any other culture. In each case they did more than survive. Every tragedy in Jewish history was followed by a new wave of creativity. The destruction of the First Temple led to the renewal of the Torah in the life of the nation, exemplified by the work of Ezra and Nehemiah. The destruction of the Second Temple led to the great works of the oral tradition, Midrash, Mishnah and the two Talmuds. The massacres of Jewish communities in northern Europe during the First Crusade led to the emergence of Hasidei Ashkenaz, the German-Jewish pietists.

The medieval encounter with Christianity led to a renewal of Bible commentary. The meeting with Islam inspired a renaissance of Jewish philosophy. The Spanish Expulsion was followed by the mystical revival in Safed in the sixteenth century. The greatest catastrophe of all led to the greatest rebirth: a mere three years after standing eyeball to eyeball with the angel of death at Auschwitz, Bergen-Belsen and Treblinka, the Jewish people responded by their greatest collective affirmation of life in two thousand years, with the proclamation of the state of Israel.

The history of Judaism is a sustained defiance of entropy, the law that states that all systems lose energy over time. Judaism, as Freud noted in *Moses and Monotheism,* did not have a single definitive era, one figure and one age regarded as the first and last word of its message. Moses was followed by successive generations of prophets. The prophets themselves were succeeded by scribes and sages, and they by codifiers and commentators, poets and mystics. Judaism has consistently found unpredictable ways of renewing itself. Nor do Jews give way to defeat or despair. They are the people of hope.

The Chinese ideogram for *crisis* also means 'opportunity'. Perhaps that is why Chinese civilisation has survived for so long. Hebrew, however, is more hopeful still. The word for crisis, *mashber,* also means a 'childbirth chair'. The Jewish reflex is to see difficult times as birth pains. Something new is being born.

Much has been written about the challenge of Jewish continuity and the programmes designed to reverse it. I want to do something else, to examine the deep factors that created the crisis. As we will see, they are part of the unresolved question of Jewish identity that lies beneath every other issue we consider in this book, from antisemitism to Israel and the place of Jews and Judaism in the world. They are part, in other words, of the wider tension between the universal and the particular, and the self-definition of Jews as the people that dwells alone.

Ambivalence

The single most profound remark about Jewish identity was made by Marx: not Karl but Groucho. In his letter of resignation from the Friars Club in Beverly Hills, Los Angeles, he wrote, 'I do not want to belong to any club that will accept people like me as a member.' Mordecai Kaplan said something similar in the opening sentence of his 1934 classic, *Judaism as a Civilization:*

'Before the beginning of the nineteenth century all Jews regarded Judaism as a privilege; since then most Jews have come to regard it as a burden.'

We are dealing with one of the classic examples of an *injured identity.* It is there in sentence after sentence of Jewish self-definition. Heinrich Heine said, 'Judaism is not a religion: it is a misfortune.' The English-Jewish writer Frederic Raphael said, 'I feel myself alien from everyone; that is my kind of Jewishness.' Arthur Koestler said, 'Self-hatred is the Jew's patriotism.' Sidney Morganbesser, professor of philosophy at Columbia, said that for the modern Jew, *incognito ergo sum.* Jews became, in the modern age, secular Marranos (secret Jews), Jewish in private, non-Jewish in public. A profound ambivalence entered Jewish life.

We can freeze-frame this process at the very beginning by looking at the life of the man who became known as the first 'Enlightenment Jew', Moses Mendelssohn (1729–86).[6] Mendelssohn, born in Dessau, son of an impecunious scribe, was almost entirely self-taught, acquiring a facility in English, French and Latin through which he was able to read and master the philosophical classics of Western civilisation. In 1763 he won the philosophy prize of the Berlin Academy, beating Immanuel Kant, perhaps the greatest philosopher since Aristotle. His literary work won him renown and he was hailed as 'the German Socrates'. He became friendly with Gotthold Lessing, who made him the model of the eponymous hero of his play *Nathan the Wise.* No Jew since the golden age of Spanish Jewry in the tenth to twelfth centuries had won such public admiration.

To many of his Christian contemporaries, however, the idea of an 'enlightened Jew' was a contradiction in terms. One of them, Kaspar Lavater, publicly challenged Mendelssohn to do 'what wisdom, the love of truth and honesty must bid him': to renounce his faith and become a Christian. Realising the immense difficulty Jews would face in gaining acceptance, Mendelssohn devoted the rest of his life to showing the compatibility of Judaism with the most advanced ideas of the time. He produced a translation of and commentary to the Pentateuch, and in 1783 published his masterpiece, *Jerusalem*, an argument for liberalism and freedom of conscience that Kant described as 'irrefutable'.

Behind the public mask of the brilliant, urbane intellectual, though, Mendelssohn was a profound pessimist about the ability of Europe, Germany in particular, to make space for Jews. In 1780, taking a walk in Berlin one summer evening with his wife and children, he was attacked by a gang of youths yelling 'Jews, Jews' and throwing stones. His children turned to him and said, 'What have we done to them, Papa? . . . They are always chasing after us in the streets, cursing us—*Juden, Juden*. Is just being a Jew enough reason for those people to hate us?'[7]

It was a defining moment. In one of his last letters he wrote, 'The prejudices against my nation are too deeply embedded to be easily uprooted.' He had already written to his doctor that though he and other Jews had hoped that enlightenment would banish prejudice, 'we can see, from the other side of the horizon, the night with all of its ghosts and demons is already falling. More frightening than anything is that evil is so active and potent. Delusion and fanaticism are acting while reason contents itself with talk.'

Fear entered his soul. Towards the end of *Jerusalem*, that defence of the right to be different, he wrote these words to his fellow Jews:

> Adapt yourselves to the morals and the constitution of the land to which you have been removed, but hold fast to the religion of your fathers too. Bear both burdens as well as you can. It is true that, on the one hand, the burden of civil life is made heavier for you on account of the religion to which you remain faithful, and, on the other hand, the climate and the times make the observance of your religious laws in some respects more irksome than they are. Nevertheless, persevere; remain unflinchingly at the post which Providence has assigned to you, and

> endure everything that happens to you as your lawgiver foretold long ago.[8]

'Burden', 'irksome', 'persevere'—these are not words of confidence and conviction, still less of pride. Unsurprisingly, four of his six children converted to Christianity and within three generations none of his descendants were still Jews.

Ambivalence can never be the basis of an enduring identity. Sooner or later, children or grandchildren will resolve it by walking away. We cannot understand the failure of Jewish identity in our time without taking into account this long and painful history. What is happening in America today had, after all, already happened in pre-war Europe. By 1929, three Jews in ten were marrying out in Berlin and Bohemia. In 1927 the intermarriage rate in Trieste was 56.1 per cent. In pre-war Vienna, thousands of Jews every year declared themselves *Konfessionloss,* 'of no religion'. In 1927, in France, Edmund Fleg published a book titled *Why I Am a Jew,* in which he asked of the next generation, 'Will there still be Jews?'

Even in America it had happened to earlier waves of Jewish immigration, first the Spanish and Portuguese Jews who came in the seventeenth and eighteenth centuries, then the German Jews who came in the nineteenth, both of which had assimilated and largely disappeared. The statistical rise noted since the 1960s is simply the most recent iteration of the process as it has affected the single largest group of American-Jewish immigrants, those who came from Eastern Europe between 1880 and the start of the First World War. The Jews who came earlier outmarried earlier. And the ambivalence has continued in our time.

Two of the most influential accounts of post-Holocaust Jewish life perfectly, even frighteningly, exemplify it. One was written by a non-Jew, Jean-Paul Sartre, in *Sur le Question Juif,* published a year after the war, in 1946. In it he argued that Jews did not create antisemitism: antisemitism created Jews. The only thing Jews had in common, he wrote, was that they were hated.

Therefore they must remain Jews in order to defy the antisemite.[9] The other was the distinguished Holocaust theologian Emil Fackenheim, who became famous for the formulation of Jewish existence he made in the 1960s. He called it 'the 614th commandment': Jews must stay Jewish so as not to grant Hitler a posthumous victory.[10]

Never has identity of any kind, let alone that of a people as ancient as the Jews, been given so utterly negative a definition. Essentially it says, 'I am hated, therefore I am.' There is no sane way out of this cul-de-sac. For more than three thousand years, Jews had defined themselves as a people loved by God. This preserved their self-respect during the ages of persecution. They might be seen by others as a pariah people, but they never internalised that image. They were chosen, different, holy; God's children, bearers of his covenant, his witnesses in an often godless world.

At some stage Jews stopped defining themselves by the reflection they saw in the eyes of God and started defining themselves by the reflection they saw in the eyes of their Gentile neighbours. That was when they discovered that they were not loved; they were resented, envied, distrusted, looked down upon. The generation that came of age in the 1980s was not faced with Gentile disdain, but it was obsessed by the Holocaust. American Jews dedicated themselves to building Holocaust memorials, funding Holocaust programmes at universities, writing books about it, organising Holocaust seminars, and taking as their credo 'Never Again'.

The generation of American Jews raised on a diet of Holocaust education is deciding, at the rate of one in two, not to hand on Jewish identity to their children. For the most obvious reason: if people died in the Holocaust because their grandparents were Jewish, the best way of ensuring that your grandchildren will not die is to stop being Jewish. No one knowingly and willingly passes on misfortune to their children. Even the pioneer of Holocaust history, Lucy Dawidowicz, expressed her concern, towards the end of her life, that the community was focusing too much on that event. Children will grow up, she said, knowing about the Greeks and how they lived, the Romans and how they lived, the Jews and how they died. It was a disastrous turn in Jewish history, done for the highest possible motives but profoundly misconceived.

If Jews and Judaism are to continue, the ambivalence many still feel about a faith and fate associated with suffering and persecution will have to be resolved. Jews will have to learn to walk tall; to recover the self-confidence, born of faith, that sustained Jews in the past; to remember that Judaism is about sanctifying life, not just commemorating death. Otherwise they will not want their children to belong to a club that will accept them as members. Ambivalence will be the death of Jewish identity.

Ethnicity

There is, of course, an alternative: to see Jewish identity not in terms of faith, a way of life, a vocation, but simply as an ethnicity. In the diverse, multicultural, liberal democracies of the West, ethnicity has become an acceptable mode of being different. Each year on Holocaust Memorial Day I make a point of visiting non-Jewish schools to tell the story of man's inhumanity to man. Each time I discover a school population of between thirty and fifty different ethnic groups, so diverse is Britain's population today. Everyone is ethnic nowadays.

In 2000 a British Jewish research institute came up with precisely this proposal: that Jews in Britain be defined as an ethnic group and no longer as a religious community. It took a non-Jewish journalist, Andrew Marr, to state the obvious: 'All this is shallow water,' he wrote, 'and the further in you wade, the shallower it gets.' There is nothing challenging in ethnicity. It embodies no ideals, no aspirations, no purpose or vocation.

Ethnicity is where we came from, not where we are going to. It involves culture and cuisine, a set of memories meaningful to parents but ever less so to their children, and beyond that, nothing. In any case, there *is* no Jewish ethnicity: there are ethnicities in the plural. That is what makes Sefardi Jews different from their Ashkenazi cousins, and Sefardi Jews from North Africa and the Middle East different from those whose families originally came from Spain and Portugal.

Besides which, Jewish ethnicity is not even Jewish. It is a lingering trace of what Jews absorbed from the circumambient non-Jewish culture: Polish dress, Russian music, North African food, the Spanish-Jewish dialect known as Ladino and a lexicon of local and essentially alien superstitions. It is a collection of borrowings thought of as Jewish because their origins have been forgotten. If Jews had been no more than an ethnicity, they would have died out long ago, along with the Canaanites, Perizzites and Jebusites, known only to students of antiquity and having left no mark on the civilisation of the West. Here is Andrew Marr again, in the same article:

> The Jews have always had stories for the rest of us. They have had their Bible, one of the great imaginative works of the human spirit. They have been victim of the worst modernity can do, a mirror for Western madness. Above all they have had the story of their cultural and genetic survival from the Roman Empire to the 2000s, weaving and thriving amid uncomprehending, hostile European tribes.
>
> This story, their post-Bible, their epic of bodies, not words, involved an intense competitive hardening of generations which threw up, in the end, a blaze of individual geniuses in Europe and America. Outside painting, Morris dancing and rap music, it's hard to think of many areas of Western endeavour where Jews haven't been disproportionately successful. For non-Jews, who don't believe in a people being chosen by God, the lesson is that generations of people living on their wits and hard work, outside the more comfortable mainstream certainties, will seed Einsteins and Wittgensteins, Trotskys and Seiffs. Culture

> matters . . . The Jews really have been different; they have enriched the world and challenged it.[11]

Judaism is not an ethnicity and Jews are not an ethnic group. Go to the Western Wall in Jerusalem and you will see Jews of every colour and culture under the sun, the Beta Israel from Ethiopia, the Bene Israel from India, Bukharan Jews from central Asia, Iraqi, Berber, Egyptian, Kurdish and Libyan Jews, the Temanim from Yemen, alongside American Jews from Russia, South African Jews from Lithuania, and British Jews from German-speaking Poland. Their food, music, dress, customs and conventions are all different. Jewishness is not an ethnicity but a living lexicon of ethnicities.

The late Arthur Koestler believed that most Jews today are not ethnically Jewish at all but are descendants of the semi-nomadic Turkic people from the Caucasus, the Khazars, who converted to Judaism in the seventh to tenth centuries.[12] The latest theory in this tangled story, advanced by Tsvi Misinai, a retired Israeli computer expert, is that the Palestinians are ethnically Jewish. They are descendants of Jews who remained in the land when, under Roman rule, most Jews went into exile in Babylon and elsewhere. The Jews who left continued to practise Judaism. Those who stayed became first Christian, then Muslim.[13] It is a theory once held by none other than David Ben-Gurion. So the Palestinians at war with Israel may be Jewish, while the Jews may not be genetically Jewish at all. Ethnicity tells us too much and too little about what it is to be a Jew.

Besides which, it does not last. If Jews are merely an ethnic group, they will experience the fate of all such groups, which is that they disappear over time. Like the grandchildren of Irish, Polish, German and Norwegian immigrants to America, they merge into the melting pot. Ethnicity lasts for three generations, for as long as children can remember immigrant grandparents and their distinctive ways. Then it begins to fade, for there is no reason for it not to.

Culture and Command

If Jewishness is not an ethnicity, then perhaps it is a culture or, as Mordecai Kaplan proposed, a civilisation. After all, Jews or the children of Jews produced many of the icons of Western culture: Spinoza, Marx, Freud, Einstein and their contemporary counterparts. But what is Jewish culture? If Spinoza, Marx, *et al.* are the benchmark, then what they seem to have in common is a pronounced antagonism to Judaism. And if a commitment to social justice, voting Democrat in American elections, enjoying Woody Allen's humour, peppering your speech with Yiddishisms and believing with religious fervour in the separation of church and state are benchmarks of Jewish culture, then you do not need to be Jewish to share it. Non-Jews also do these things.

One of the most insightful comments on Jewish continuity was offered by Professor Ruth Wisse of Harvard University. She was speaking about Jewish culture generally, and about Yiddish literature (her field) in particular. She noted that the shapers of that literature believed that their work would sustain the Jewish identity of their children. But it did not. There are, she said, more than a million Yiddish books lining the shelves of the National Yiddish Book Center at Amherst, but not even half that amount of people in the world who can still read them. She then said:

> Modern culture rejects pledges of allegiance, daily prayer. Yet this is what the process of meaningful transmission finally comes down to. A single Yiddish poem, even a single word—God, Israel—repeated once a day, because one feels directed to do so, can help guarantee the survival of a people. Contrarily, all the world's great books can be discounted as yesterday's junk so long as one does not consider oneself bound by duty to inscribe them on the minds of one's children and one's children's children.[14]

'Inscribe them on the minds of one's children' is, of course, a reference to the *Shema,* the most sacred Jewish prayer ('You shall teach these things repeatedly to your children . . .' [Deut. 6:7]). 'Consider oneself bound by duty' is a secular translation of the word *mitzvah,* which means 'commandment'. The question Wisse is posing is this: is Jewish continuity truly possible without *mitzvah,* that is, a sense of being bound by the covenant the Israelites made in the days of Moses with the invisible God who had brought them out of slavery to the Promised Land?

Much investment has been made in Jewish culture as part of the effort of Jewish continuity. That was part of our programme in Jewish Continuity. I value Jewish culture, *but not because it will guarantee that Jews will have Jewish grandchildren.* It will not. At stake here is what philosophers call a category mistake. Culture is the expression of a group's creativity, but it does not bind future generations, because it does not bind at all. As long as we are watching a play, or reading a book, or listening to music, we enter the imaginative world of the artist and are moved, inspired, transported. But once the play is over, the book is finished, the music has reached its closing chord, the work makes no further demands of us. Culture inspires, but it does not command. In Wisse's words, it involves no 'pledges of allegiance'.

I love Greek philosophy, the French impressionists, Italian design and the serene beauty of a Japanese garden, but that does not make me Greek, French, Italian or Japanese. You do not have to be Jewish to enjoy Jewish humour, klezmer music or chicken soup with noodles. Culture involves no act of commitment. That is why people have always been able to immerse themselves in the cultures of many lands, languages and creeds. Culture excludes nothing. One school of painting does not compete with another. Novels do not negate the short story, or symphonies the pop song. The existence of French does not refute the existence of Italian.

Identity is different. It involves duty, commitment, loyalty, fidelity. It comes wrapped up with a sense of obligation. Identity is the point at which 'I am' shades into 'I must'—because these are my people and this is my heritage. Identity involves responsibility. There were Jews, among them the writer Ahad Haam and the poet Hayim Nahman Bialik, who believed that religion could be translated into the language of culture, but it cannot. Something is lost in translation. To paraphrase Ruth Wisse: no continuity without command.

Reducing Dissonance

So, if Jewish identity is not about antisemitism or ethnicity or culture, if it is what it always was, a religious identity, then surely, to guarantee continuity, Judaism must be made more 'user-friendly' and 'relevant', less out of step with the norms and forms of contemporary society. There were many people who believed this, and their intentions were honourable. Jewish faith, they argued, could be modified to accord better with the scientific mindset. Jewish prayers could be rewritten to be more in keeping with modern sensibilities. The demands of Jewish law could be softened, amended. The world had changed. Why not Judaism?

They had a point. Judaism—tradition in an untraditional age—is hard to translate into the language of modernity. The idea of *halakhah,* Jewish law, is incompatible with contemporary belief in personal autonomy as the highest good. Jewish ethics, with its emphasis on the sanctity of marriage, is out of keeping with today's sexual freedoms. Judaism is about community, not about the 'sovereign self'. It is about keeping faith with the past in an age that prioritizes the present. Surely—so the argument went—the sacrifices Judasim demands of its followers are just too great for it to survive. It must be adapted to be more consonant with the tenor of the times.

All this sounds eminently reasonable. The only problem is that the reality is quite different. Consider the three pilgrimage festivals, Passover (Pesach), Pentecost (Shavuot) and Tabernacles

(Sukkot). Which is most widely observed? The answer given by all audiences I have asked has been: first Passover, then Tabernacles, then Pentecost.

Then consider which is the most demanding. First is Passover, which involves lengthy, even exhausting, preparations. The house must be thoroughly cleaned. The kitchen and utensils must be koshered. All bread and leavened products must be removed. Many families have special Passover crockery and cutlery. The arrangements are exacting and time-consuming. The second most strenuous is Tabernacles. This involves constructing a *sukkah,* a hut or shed with leaves for a roof, in which one eats for the seven (or, outside Israel, eight) days of the festival. It also involves purchasing the 'four kinds'—a palm branch *(lulav),* a citron *(etrog),* and willow and myrtle leaves used in the festival services. The least demanding is Pentecost, which has few special demands other than an all-night study session *(tikkun),* itself a post-Talmudic custom. The more demanding the festival, the more it is observed.

This is manifestly the case when it comes to the most exacting day of all, Yom Kippur, the Day of Atonement, in which Jews spend an entire day in the synagogue, fasting, praying and repenting. On the thesis that the easier a ritual, the more widely it is observed, one would expect the synagogue to be empty on this day. In fact, it is more crowded than on any other day of the year.

If all this is correct, it explains why, for two centuries, Jews have pursued policies that seemed to make sense but were destined to yield a result precisely the reverse of that expected.[15] The less demanding the religion, the less it will be observed. The explanation lies in Leon Festinger's famous discovery known as 'cognitive dissonance'. One corollary of this theory is that *we value most what costs us the most.*[16] The more demanding the task, the greater commitment it evokes. That can be seen to be true today, not only within Judaism but in all the world's faiths. We value most that for which we make sacrifices.

Judaism survived two thousand years of exile, not because it was user-friendly but because it was difficult, sometimes heartbreakingly so. It is normally assumed that Jews made sacrifices for their faith because they valued it. The opposite may also be true: Jews valued their faith because they made sacrifices for it. In 2008 two Christian American teenagers published a book that became a best-seller. It had one of the most unexpected titles I have seen in recent years. It was called *Do Hard Things,* and was subtitled *A Teenage Rebellion Against Low Expectations.*[17] Judaism, with its 613 commands and its vast literature that requires years of study to master, is about doing hard things. That was why, throughout the ages, Jews valued it and sought to hand it on to their children. They knew there were easier options, and they declined them. When people abandoned the strictures and structure of *halakha,* they found that their children abandoned Judaism.

Make It Possible for Jews to Give

There is a fascinating verse in Exodus: 'When you take a census [literally, "when you lift the head"] of the Israelites to determine their number, each one is to give to the Lord an atonement offering for his life when they are counted, *so that they will not be stricken by plague* when they are counted' (Exod. 30:12). Evidently, it is dangerous to count Jews. Why?

I once offered the following explanation. Nations normally take a census to estimate their strength: military (the number of people who can be conscripted into an army), economic (the number from whom taxes can be raised) or simply demographic (the numerical growth or decline of the nation). The assumption behind every census is that there is strength in numbers. The more numerous a people, the stronger it is.

That is why it is dangerous to count Jews. Jews are a tiny people. The late Milton Himmelfarb once wrote that the total population of Jews throughout the world is smaller than a small statistical error in the Chinese census. Jews constitute one-fifth of a per cent of the population of the world: by any normal standards, too small to be significant. Nor is this something new.

In one of his concluding addresses in Deuteronomy, Moses said, 'The Lord did not set his affection on you and choose you because you were more numerous than other peoples, *for you are the fewest of all peoples*' (Deut. 7:7). The danger in counting Jews is that if they believed, for a moment, that there is strength in numbers, they would long ago have given way to despair.

How, then, do you estimate the strength of the Jewish people? To this the Hebrew Bible gives an answer of surpassing beauty. *Ask Jews to give, and then count their contributions.* Numerically, Jewry is small, but in terms of its contributions to civilisation, it is vast. Somehow this small people produced an unceasing flow of patriarchs, priests, poets and prophets, masters of *halakhah* and *aggadah* (Jewish law and teachings), codifiers and commentators, philosophers and mystics, sages and saints. It was not once that the Jewish imagination caught fire but in century after century, sometimes under the worst persecution known to any nation on earth.

If you want to know the strength of the Jewish people, ask them to give, and then count the contributions. To win the Jewish battle, the battle of the spirit, the victory of heart, mind and soul, you do not need numbers. You need dedication, commitment, study, prayer, vision, courage, ideals and hope. You need to offer people tough challenges through which to grow. I learned this when I was a child.

My late father came to Britain with his family when he was six years old. They were poor, and he had to leave school at the age of fourteen. He had little formal education, either secular or Jewish. When I became Chief Rabbi, people used to ask him, 'Mr Sacks, what did you do to make your son a Jewish leader?' He always answered, 'It was his mother.' He was right: it was. But it was him as well, and I knew the explanation.

When I was four or five years old, I used to ask him questions on our way back from the synagogue. Why do we do this? Why do we say that? He always answered the same way, and I never forgot his answer: 'Jonathan, I did not have an education, so I cannot give you the answers. But one day you will have the education I did not have, and then you will teach me the answers.' If you want your child to become a leader, that is how it is done. He gave me the greatest privilege. He allowed me, encouraged me, to become his teacher. He challenged me to do hard things. That is a habit Jews must recover.

Faith

Judaism is not an ethnicity, a culture, a set of folkways, a defiance of antisemitism or political correctness plus a *yarmulkah* (cap) and Jewish jokes. It is a faith, and the people who are in a state of denial about this are Jews. It was as a faith that Jews were born as a people, and it is as a faith that Jews will survive as a people. Leave faith out of the Jewish equation and what is left is a body without a soul.

Judaism is a faith, and for the first time in history we have a chance to share that faith with others on equal terms, as Christians strive to rediscover the Jewish roots of their own faith, as moderate Muslims seek to understand how religion is compatible with democratic freedoms, and as Hindus and Sikhs turn to Jews for guidance in the delicate art of integration without assimilation, preserving religious identity while playing a part in the wider society and the human project as a whole.

When it comes to the future, we see as through a glass, darkly. Yet this I know, that Judaism made great demands on its followers and in doing so made them great. Jews never had demographic strength, yet person for person they made astonishing contributions, some spiritual, some secular, to civilisation. It would be the irony of ironies if, at the very time when Jews and Judaism stand as equals on the stage of history, they lost the vocation that called them into being as a nation.

There is more to Judaism than ethnicity and the fear of antisemitism. There is more to the state of Israel than a liberal democracy like any other except for the fact that it is situated in a part of the world hostile to both liberalism and democracy. Judaism is larger than Jews have sometimes allowed it to seem.

In calling Judaism a faith, I do not mean to exclude secular Judaisms or interpretations of faith other than my own. In the widest sense, Judaism is the ongoing conversation of the Jewish people with itself, with heaven and with the world. It is a conversation scored for many voices, often in the argumentative mode. But it is an unusual faith, and with this we approach a cluster of issues at the heart of the troubled, sometimes tragic, fate of Jews in the modern world.

By 'faith' we often mean a set of doctrines or dogmas that, if true, apply everywhere to everyone. That is certainly true of Christianity and Islam, but it is not true of Judaism. Judaism is the faith of a particular people who prided themselves on their distinctiveness. Why do Jews associate faith with being different? Why do they resist assimilation into the dominant culture? Why, for that matter, do they not seek to convert the world? Long ago I realised that the problem of Jewish continuity was intimately bound up with the difficulty of making sense in the modern world of this ancient, strange idea of a people called on to be different; and to it I now turn.

4

The Other: Judaism, Christianity and Islam

On 25 January 1904, Theodor Herzl, leader of the Zionist movement, met Pope Pius X. It was a significant moment, part of Herzl's programme to meet world leaders to gain support for a Jewish state. Forty-three at the time, he was already exhausted by his frenetic efforts to gain a place of safety for Jews against the virulent antisemitism he had witnessed in Paris during the Dreyfus trial. In seven years he had worn himself out. The meeting at the Vatican would be his last. He died six months later.

It was a bitterly disappointing encounter. The Pope told him, 'We are unable to favour this movement. We cannot prevent the Jews from going to Jerusalem—but we could never sanction it . . . As the head of the Church, I cannot answer you otherwise. The Jews have not recognised our Lord, therefore we cannot recognise the Jewish people. Jerusalem cannot be placed in Jewish hands.'

'What if Jews do not go into Jerusalem, but only to the other parts of the land?' Herzl asked the Pope.

'We cannot be in favour of it,' the Pope replied. Only if Jews were prepared to convert to Catholicism could he support them. 'And so,' he continued, 'if you come to Palestine and settle your people there, we shall have churches and priests ready to baptise all of you.' Only in 1993 did the Vatican formally recognise the state of Israel.

Jews have long had difficulty finding the space to be: to have their integrity, their right to live on their own terms, recognised by others. In extremis, this becomes (not in the case of Pope Pius X, but in others) the phenomenon known as antisemitism, the subject of the next chapter. In this chapter I want to look at something prior and more fundamental, which is nonetheless essential if we are to understand the roots of antisemitism. There are many theories as to the roots of prejudice and hate. It comes, say some, from the tribal instinct that makes us fear the one-not-like-us. It comes, say others, from splitting and projection. We detach the parts of ourselves we do not like and attribute them to someone else. Some, like Amy Chua, argue that hate is the resentment a larger group feels towards any conspicuously successful minority in its midst.[1] René Girard argues that it arises from internal tensions within a group that can only be resolved by identifying and killing a scapegoat.[2]

Such theories fail to answer the question: Why the Jews? On these accounts, hatred could attach to anyone given the appropriate conditions. Hate *has* attached to many groups in the course of history, but none with the persistence of hatred of the Jews for two thousand years. Besides which, there were great civilisations in which Jews lived (albeit not in large numbers), notably India and China, that did not give rise to antisemitism at all. Why not? Surely Indians and Chinese have the same psychology as everyone else, the same tensions, the same resentments. Overwhelmingly, antisemitism has arisen in societies that either practised or were influenced by Christianity and Islam.

No sooner have we noted this than it becomes obvious why. Christianity and Islam trace their descent to Abraham, and their religious origins to God's covenant with him. But so do Jews. And Judaism, the religion of biblical Israel, has existed twice as long as Christianity, three times as long as Islam. So Christianity and Islam faced a theological problem: what about the Jews? Somehow it had to be argued that two thousand years ago in the case of Christianity, or in the seventh century for Islam, something changed. The Abrahamic covenant was no longer with the Jewish people.

In the case of Christianity, it was argued, from Paul and the Church Fathers onward, that since Jews had rejected the Christian messiah, God had rejected them. He had made a new covenant and chosen a 'new Israel'. Islam put it differently. Abraham was a Muslim. The religion he taught was a preparation for Islam. In any case, the succession did not pass through Isaac as the Bible taught, but through Ishmael. Hence the difference in the sacred scriptures of these two faiths. Christianity included the Hebrew Bible but reordered its books to tell a story that culminated in the New Testament. Islam did not include the Hebrew Bible, since it claimed that Jews—in the account of the binding of Isaac, for example—had falsified events.

Generically, theologies of this kind are called supersessionist, meaning that they argue that the old has been superseded, displaced or replaced, by the new.[3] The result was to deny legitimacy to Jews because they deny legitimacy to Judaism. It might have been valid once, but no longer. Hence the difficult situation of Jews in Christian or Islamic cultures. By definition, they were less than fully human. Since they had rejected the dominant faith, God had rejected them, and they bore the stigma of that rejection.

This had political consequences. In the map of reality constructed by these faiths, they lacked conceptual space. They had no natural home. According to Augustine, Jews were the embodiment of Cain, condemned to be 'a restless wanderer on earth' (Gen. 4:12). In Islam, Jews, like Christians, were at best *dhimmi,* subject peoples under Islamic rule. In both faiths Jews had been disinherited. The promise of the land that God had, seven times, given to Abraham was null and void—in a word, superseded. That is what the Pope was trying to explain to Herzl. Only if you convert do you have a right to live in the Holy Land.

It is important to say that not all Christian theologies are alike, nor were all Christians opposed to the founding of the state of Israel. Far from it. As we saw in the first chapter, there were Christians, among them George Eliot and Lord Shaftesbury, who actively supported it even before the word *Zionism* was coined. Neither Christianity nor Islam had anything to do with the racial antisemitism that led to the Holocaust. To the contrary, Christians were committed to Jewish survival. Islamic countries gave refuge to Jews fleeing Christian persecution, most notably the Ottoman Empire in the wake of the Spanish Expulsion. Both faiths recognised some form of kinship with the Jews, and both at times protected Jews from persecution.

My argument in this chapter is not about antisemitism as such, but about the phenomenon that led to the parting of the ways between Judaism on the one hand and Christianity and Islam on the other. Christianity and Islam are *universal* monotheisms. Judaism is a *particularistic* monotheism. It does not claim to be the sole path to salvation. The righteous of all nations, taught the rabbis, have a share in the world to come. You do not have to be Jewish to be good, wise or beloved of God. That is what God taught the prophet Jonah when he expressed dismay that God had forgiven Israel's enemies, the Assyrians of Nineveh.

The God of Israel is the God of everyone, but the religion of Israel is not the religion of everyone. Even at the end of days, the prophets did not foresee that the nations of the world would embrace the religion of Israel with its complex code of commands. They would recognise God. They would come to Jerusalem to pray. They would beat their swords into ploughshares and wage war no more. But they would not become Jewish. Judaism is not a conversionary faith.

Why not? That is the question. Christianity and Islam borrowed much from Judaism, but not this. On the face of it, their approach is more logical. If God is the God of everyone in general, why did he make a covenant with this people—Jacob's children—in particular? A universal God must surely lead to a universal truth, a universal faith. Why does Judaism embody the tension between the universal and the particular, embracing both, denying neither? We will not understand Judaism or the modern state of Israel until we find an answer to this question, and to locate it we must turn to the Hebrew Bible itself.

From All People to One People

In essence the Hebrew Bible is the story of a single people, the children of Israel, later called the Jews, and their relationship with God. Yet *the Bible does not begin with this people.* It begins instead with a series of archetypes of humanity as a whole: Adam and Eve, Cain and Abel, Noah and the Flood, Babel and its builders.

Not until chapter 12 do Abraham and Sarah appear on the scene, and from then on the entire narrative shifts its focus, from humanity as a whole to one man, one woman and their children. They become an extended family, then a collection of tribes, then a nation and eventually a kingdom. In some obscure yet unmistakable way—this is the Hebrew Bible's fundamental theme—they were to become the carriers of a universal message. For the God they believed in was not a tribal deity, a God of this people and not that, this land and not that. He is the God of all, creator of heaven and earth, who in love set his image on all humanity.

The people he chose to carry this message, on the testimony of the Hebrew Bible itself, were not an obvious choice. They were not large: 'The Lord did not give you his love and choose you because you were more numerous than other peoples, for you were the fewest of all peoples' (Deut. 7:7). Nor were they especially pious: 'It is not because of your righteousness or the uprightness of your heart' (Deut. 9:5). The impression we gain of the Israelites throughout is of a fractious, often wayward group, a 'stiff-necked people'.

Yet Moses and the prophets were convinced that the message they carried was not for their people alone. It had a universal significance. Moses said that the laws the Israelites had been commanded 'will show your wisdom and understanding to the nations, who will hear about all these decrees and say, "Surely this great nation is a wise and understanding people" ' (Deut. 4:6). Isaiah famously spoke about Israel being a light for the nations, a covenant of the peoples. Zechariah foresaw a time when 'Ten men from all languages and nations will take firm hold of one Jew by the hem of his robe and say, "Let us go with you, because we have heard that God is with you"' (Zech. 8:23).

The idea is present in the first words God spoke to Abraham: 'Through you all the families of the earth shall be blessed'—a sentiment that appears no less than five times in the book of Genesis. Israel's message is a universal one. Why then *one* people, not *all* peoples? Why this land, not all lands? Why were Jews not commanded to take their message everywhere and convert everyone to the one true faith?

Anti-imperialism

I spent years wrestling with this problem, for it seemed to me to lie at the very heart of the tragic encounter between Jews and others, at least since the birth of Christianity and possibly even before.[4] I found myself returning time and again to those early chapters of the book of Genesis, paying special attention to the order of the narrative.

Universalism in the Hebrew Bible is set at the beginning and end of time. The beginning is the first eleven chapters of Genesis. The end is the prophetic vision of peace and harmony, 'when God will be king over all the earth, on that day he will be one and his name one'. In the meantime, in historical time, life under God is marked by particularity: the multiplicity of languages, cultures, natures and civilisations. That is the Jewish narrative. Why?

Clearly the answer lies in the story of the Tower of Babel, the prelude to the choice of Abraham and the point at which humanity is divided into different language groups. Babel is the turning point from the universal to the particular. It is here that the Bible is setting forth a fundamental proposition, but what is it? What was wrong with the project of Babel?

The great nineteenth-century commentator Rabbi Naftali Zvi

Yehudah Berlin gave a fascinating answer.[5] The story of Babel begins with the words 'Now the whole world had one language and a common speech.' Why the apparent repetition? Berlin suggests that the phrase 'a common speech' means 'they all had the same opinions', they were of a like mind. There was nothing dangerous in this initially. They all wanted to build a city and a tower. The danger lay in the future. Having built cosmopolis, a total and totalising man-made environment, the risk was that they would impose a man-made uniformity on all who lived there. There would be no freedom of speech, no dignity of dissent. Any disagreement would be held to endanger the necessary unity of the *polis,* the city-state. Berlin, who taught in the yeshiva (college) of Volozhyn in Belarus, died in 1893, before the Russian Revolution, but in retrospect his words were prophetic. Babel was, he implied, the first totalitarianism.

The story of Babel is, of course, set against the historical backdrop of the Babylonian ziggurats, man-made artificial mountains where, it was believed, heaven and earth touched. This is the area from which Abraham's family came and which they were commanded to leave. The biblical critique of Babylon becomes clearer in light of the book of Exodus, set centuries later, this time in Egypt. What was common to these two ancient civilisations, the Mesopotamian city-states and Egypt of the Pharaohs, was their monumental architecture—in both cases, physical symbols of concentrated power. The ziggurats, pyramids and temples of the ancient world were built at the cost of turning most of their population into slaves.

We begin to see an immense idea slowly taking shape. Judaism was born in two journeys, Abraham's from Mesopotamia, Moses' and the Israelites' from Egypt. What is unusual about both journeys is their direction. At most times, in most places, migration is from poor countries to rich ones, from weak nations to strong ones. The two founding Jewish journeys were in the opposite direction, from advanced urban civilisations to a land of small towns, nomadic shepherds and agricultural settlements. This remains the utopian prophetic dream. Micah envisions a future in which 'Every man will sit under his own vine and under his own fig tree, and no one will make them afraid' (Mic. 4:4).

Judaism is a critique of empire and the rule of the strong.[6] In the first chapter of Genesis we are told that every human being is in the image and likeness of God. This is not an abstract metaphysical proposition. It is a political statement of potentially explosive force. The kings and pharaohs of the ancient world were seen as gods, the children of the gods, or the sole intermediary of the gods. They presided over hierarchical societies in which there was an absolute, ontological difference between rulers and ruled.

By stating that not just the king but everyone is in the image of God, the Bible was opposing the entire political universe of the ancient world. Every individual is sacrosanct. Every life is sacred. The human person as such has inalienable dignity. Here is the birth of the biblical revolution, which did not materialise in the West until the seventeenth century with the articulation of the concept of human rights, meaning the rights we bear simply because we are human. Babel is the symbol of the sacrifice of the individual to the state. Abraham, by contrast, is to become the symbol of all individuals in search of worth as individuals. The Hebrew Bible is a sustained protest against empire, hierarchy, ruling elites and the enslavement of the masses. But what has this to do with particularity?

A Mishnah in the tractate of Sanhedrin makes the famous statement—included in Steven Spielberg's film about the Holocaust, *Schindler's List*—that 'One life is like a universe. Save a life and you save a universe; destroy a life and you destroy a universe.'[7] It goes on to say, 'When a human being makes many coins in the same mint, they all come out the same. God makes everyone in the same image—His image—and they all come out different.' In this teaching, I eventually realised, the rabbis had decoded the story of Babel and the biblical narrative as a whole.

The fundamental difference between human sovereignty and

divine sovereignty—the rule of humankind and the rule of God—is that *humans impose uniformity; God makes space for difference.* It is the nature of totalitarianisms like Nazi Germany and the Soviet Union to allow only one image—the Aryan race, the proletariat—to prevail. All those who fail to fit that image forfeit their rights and, often, their lives. The Tower of Babel and Egypt of the Pharaohs are symbols of the negation of the principles in which Judaism vests its faith: the dignity of the individual, the sanctity of life, the rule of justice over the powerful and powerless alike, the compassionate society and law-governed liberty.

Its key is diversity. *We are all in God's image, and we are all different.* Another great nineteenth-century thinker, Rabbi Samson Raphael Hirsch, saw this idea already foreshadowed in the symbol of the covenant God made with humanity after the Flood, namely the rainbow.[8] Hirsch suggests that it represents the white light of God's radiance refracted into the infinite shadings of the spectrum. For Hirsch and Berlin, the division of humanity into many languages and cultures is the necessary precondition of human freedom and dignity until the end of days.

The Counter-Platonic Narrative

Berlin's critique of Babel is almost identical with Aristotle's critique of Plato's *Republic,* restated in modern times by Karl Popper in *The Open Society and Its Enemies.*[9] In the civic ethic of ancient Greece, the highest value was the *polis,* to whose ends all social institutions were subservient and in whose service lay the path to honour and glory. In Greece, as in Babel and ancient Egypt, the people existed to serve the state; the state did not exist to serve the people. That is directly contrary to Judaism, which emphasises the primacy of the personal over the political.

That led to the next insight. For Plato, in *The Republic,* truth lies in universals, not particulars. Plato's famous image of the world of the senses as shadows on the walls of a cave was his way of saying that truth exists not in particular things—this tree, that flower—but in the 'form', the concept, the universal archetype of things. Hence the Western narrative, embedded so deep in our consciousness that we hardly realise it is there, that the direction of knowledge, wisdom and civilisation is from the particular to the universal. We begin as children relating to our parents. Our world gradually expands to include friends, neighbours, town, nation and ultimately humanity as a whole. The movement from lower to higher forms of life and understanding is from local to global, parochial to cosmopolitan, concrete instances to conceptual generalisations. That is the Platonic narrative.

The Torah tells the opposite narrative. It moves from the universal to the particular, from all humanity to one man, Abraham, and one woman, Sarah. God's first covenant, with Noah after the Flood, is universal. It applies everywhere, to everyone. God's second covenant, with Abraham, then with his descendants at Mount Sinai, is particular. Universality is where we begin, not where we end. Judaism is the West's greatest counter-Platonic narrative.

So we have in Genesis 9–12 three sequential developments. First, God makes a covenant with all humanity, based on the sanctity of human life (chapter 9). Then God divides humanity into a multiplicity of languages and cultures (chapter 11). Then God addresses one man, Abraham, calling on him to become 'the father of many nations' through whom 'all the families on earth will be blessed'.

The result is a combination, unique to the Hebrew Bible, of universality and particularity. The human condition is universal, but the expressions of that condition are particular. Each nation, each language, each culture has its distinctive character. One nation, that of Abraham and his descendants, is charged with the duty of embodying in its history and laws the sovereignty of God. As this idea became gradually clearer, I found myself putting it in the form of the following proposition: God took one man, then one people, and summoned it to be different *to teach all humanity the dignity of difference.*[10]

The result was that Jews and Judaism have stood from that day to this as the perennial challenge to imperialism, totalitarianism and fundamentalism, which I define as *the attempt to impose a single truth on a plural world*. Universalism is the creed of empires.

Throughout history, nations and powers have sought to establish dominance by conversion or conquest. That does violence to the human condition as conceived by the Torah. The human condition is indeed universal—we are each in the image of God and we each share in the covenant with God. But we are all different, and that difference is sacrosanct. It is what makes us unique, irreplaceable, and thus possessed of inalienable dignity. No one has the right to rule over us except one we have chosen ourselves. No one has the right to attempt to obliterate another culture. Our diversity meets in God's unity. The supreme truth to which the Torah gives witness is that one who is not in my image—whose creed, culture or colour is not like mine—is nonetheless in God's image. That is the principle of the dignity of difference.

The Unique and the Universal

From this, one consequence follows. If the God of Israel is the God of all humanity, but the religion of Israel is not the religion of all humanity, then you do not have to be a member of the religion of Israel to be in the image of God, or blessed by God. You do not have to be Jewish to pray to God and be answered by God. At the heart of the biblical view of humanity is a rejection of the principle that *extra ecclesiam non est salus*—there is no salvation outside the church, or, in other words, there is only one gate to God's presence.

That is what, in fact, we find. The God who appears to Abraham also appears to Melchizedek, king of Shalem, described in the Torah as 'a priest of the most high God' though not party to the Abrahamic covenant. He appears to Abimelech, king of the

Philistines, and to Laban, Jacob's high-handed father-in-law. Even an Egyptian Pharaoh can relate to the divine. After Joseph has interpreted his dreams, Pharaoh says, 'Can we find anyone like this man, one in whom is the spirit of God?'

The Hebrew Bible seems to delight in this discovery of godliness outside the Abrahamic covenant. It is none other than the daughter of the Pharaoh who enslaved the Jewish people who rescues Moses, gives him his name and adopts him, saving his life. It is Zipporah, Moses' Midianite wife, who in an obscure passage saves his life by circumcising their son.

The most perfect human being in the Bible is Job, yet Job is not Jewish. He is everyman. The book of Job—the last book in the Hebrew Bible in which God speaks—brings closure to the human narrative. Job is the antitype of Adam. Adam, given everything, sins. Job, losing everything, stays loyal to God. So when, in the early centuries CE, the sages said that the righteous of every nation have a share in the world to come, they were doing no more than making explicit a view implicit in the Torah throughout, that Israel has no monopoly on virtue or wisdom or grace.

Only the combination of a particular faith and a universal God can yield this conclusion. If God is everywhere, and has set his image on everyone, then God exists outside the Abrahamic covenant as well as within. That is the only form of theology that can yield the God-given integrity of otherness, the dignity of the stranger. The alternatives are tribalism—many nations, many gods—or universalism—one God, one faith, and only one gate to salvation.

The Voice of the Other

At the heart of Judaism is the belief in the reality of otherness. God is not humankind. Humankind is not God. God creates otherness in love, as we, when we become parents, create otherness in love. Hate is the inability to accept the other. Cain could not live with the otherness of Abel, and he killed him. The builders of Babel could not live with the politics of otherness—they insisted on 'one language and a common speech', rejecting the dignity of dissent. The Egyptians could not live with the otherness of the Hebrews, so they enslaved them. Germany could not live with the otherness of the Jews, and so it set about murdering them. *Judaism is the voice of the other throughout history.* The whole of Judaism is about making space for the other, about God making space for us, us making space for God, and about human beings making space for one another.

That is why the way a culture treats its Jews is the best indicator of its humanity or lack of it, not because Jews are special but because they are other. The Greeks scorned the Jews because they were not Greeks. The Romans despised the Jews because they were not Romans. Christians condemned Jews because they did not become Christians. Muslims looked down on Jews because they did not embrace Islam. The Germans resented Jews because they were not Aryans.

Jews refused to do one thing: disappear. With astonishing tenacity, for the most part they neither converted to the dominant faith nor assimilated to the dominant culture. Jews were not the only people to suffer, nor is there anything special, ennobling or elevating in suffering. Jews did, however, insist, often with great courage, on the right to be other. For without an other there is no self. Without the space to be different there is no love. Without the right to stay true to your faith there is no freedom. The desire to remake humanity in your image—the imperial instinct throughout the ages—is a betrayal of God. For God sets his image on all humankind to teach us that one who is not in our image is still in God's image.

So, time and again, the Torah commands us to love the stranger, the embodiment of otherness:

> Do not oppress a stranger; you yourselves know what it feels like to be a stranger, for you were strangers in Egypt. (Exod. 23:9)

> When a stranger lives with you in your land, do not mistreat him. The stranger living with you must be treated as one of your native-born. Love him as yourself, for you were strangers in Egypt. I am the Lord your God. (Lev. 19:33–4)

> For the Lord your God is God of gods and Lord of lords, the great God, mighty and awesome, who shows no partiality and accepts no bribes. He defends the cause of the fatherless and the widow, and loves the stranger, giving him food and clothing. So you must love the stranger, for you yourselves were strangers in Egypt. (Deut. 10:17–19)

God is the voice of the other within the self, that tells us that neither we, nor our desires, nor the group to which we belong is the measure of all things. There is a higher court than the bar of human reason; there is a higher imperative than the law of the land; there is a force greater than that of human might; there are larger considerations than human interests and larger perspectives than the here and now. God is the absolutely other and the otherly absolute, without knowledge of whom people have destroyed one another in the past and may destroy life on earth in the future.

God loves particulars. He is not Plato's god, who lives in a remote heaven amid the conceptual forms of things-in-general. He is the God who made the universe with its hundred billion galaxies, each with a hundred billion stars; the God who made the three million different species of life thus far known to us; who made the human person, each of whom is different from the others; who created diversity and asked us to celebrate it, honouring the individual above the collective, the person above the state, the nation above the empire, the particular, not just the universal.

So God tells Abraham to leave his land, birthplace and father's house, the roots of tribalism, of blood and belonging. He makes his children experience the dark side of empire, discovering and never forgetting what it feels like to be enslaved by the ruling power. The people of the covenant are born as a people through the experience of being strangers in a strange land, and are then commanded (thirty-six times, as the rabbis noted) to love the stranger. Jews became the archetypal strangers; and only those who can make space for strangers can make space for the God of the Hebrew Bible.

This, for me, was the only form of theology that made sense of the otherwise paradoxical insistence in Judaism on the unique and the universal, the covenant with Abraham and the prior covenant with Noah. No other religion, certainly not the two other Abrahamic monotheisms, saw things this way. Then I understood the troubled relationship between Judaism and the world.

Jews became the target of empires because Judaism is a protest against empires. Whether in ancient times, in the Middle Ages, or most recently within the Soviet Union, Jews remained different, neither assimilating to the dominant culture nor converting to the majority faith. Jews became the target of tribalism—the combination of nation and race—whose most fearful modern incarnation was Aryan supremacy and the Third Reich, because Jews are not a tribe and the God of Israel is not a tribal God. Hitler, in a strange but significant phrase, called conscience 'a Jewish invention'.

Even contemporary anti-Zionism is part of this pattern. The irony of the contemporary claim that the modern state of Israel is an imperialist power (part of the 'Zionist-Crusader alliance' or the 'globalising West', depending on the critic) is that since the days of Joshua more than three thousand years ago, only under Jewish rule has Israel been an independent nation, not part of an empire. The land has been ruled by the Assyrians, the Babylonians, the Persians, the Alexandrians, the Ptolemies, the Seleucids, the Romans, the Byzantines, the Umayyads, the Abbasids, the Fatimids, the Seljuks, the Crusaders, the Ayyubids, the Mamluks, the Ottomans and the British mandatory power, but only under Jewish rule was it a self-governing nation, and it continues to be a major obstacle to the restoration of the Caliphate, the imperial dream shared by Al Qaeda, Hamas and Hezbollah.

If so, then Judaism does indeed contain a message for humanity as a whole. It tells us that each nation, each culture, each faith (within the parameters of the covenant with Noah), has its own integrity, that we are wrong to seek to impose our culture or religion on others, that there is a global covenant of human solidarity, while at the same time we are called on to respect cultural and religious difference. The test of any human collectivity is whether or not it respects the stranger, the outsider, especially those without power.

Seen in this light, the moral failure of modern Europe becomes clear. The universalism of the Enlightenment in the eighteenth century was not neutral: it was a secularisation of the earlier universalism of Christianity and Islam. That is why Immanuel Kant, the greatest universalist since Plato, could argue for what he called 'perpetual peace' while at the same time holding antisemitic attitudes and calling for the 'euthanasia' of Judaism. Universalism cannot tolerate the otherness of the other. It is the imperialism of the rationalistic mind.

The Enlightenment was bound to fail, as it did, giving rise in the nineteenth century to an equally dangerous form of tribalism, the romantic nationalism of blood and belonging, which produced in the twentieth century two world wars, costing tens of millions of lives. We face in the twenty-first century new forms of imperialist universalism, aptly described by Benjamin Barber as 'Jihad versus MacWorld', and by Samuel Huntington as the clash of civilisations. Simultaneously, we are living through the resurgence of a new tribalism, sometimes called 'multiculturalism', that argues that nothing transcends our particularity. There is no truth; there are only truths. The nation state is giving way to a cacophony of conflicting ethnic and religious ghettoes with no overarching conception of the common good.

It seems as if humanity is constantly threatened by the pendulum swing between the unique and the universal, neither of which, in and of itself, does justice to the human condition. We are constituted by both our commonalities and our differences. To put it simply: *If we were completely different, we could not communicate, and if we were completely the same, we would have nothing to say.* Judaism is the most sustained attempt known to me to do justice to both, seeing both as essential to the human condition under the sovereignty of God.

The otherness of God is the ultimate expression of the otherness of the other, and the love of God is, or should be, the ultimate grounding of love of the other. That is where some of the greatest civilisations known to history failed. They regarded the other as less than fully human, and so they became, themselves, less than fully human. It happened in ancient Greece; it happened again in twentieth-century Europe. Those who have faith only in the-truth-that-is-universal have more faith than is safe for the future of humanity.

Judaism is a faith that did not take as its mission the conversion of the world. It calls on us to love others for their own sake, in the integrity of their otherness. Judaism teaches that God grants a place in heaven to those whose religion is not the same as ours. He asks us to be true to our faith while being a blessing to others regardless of their faith. God tells us never to forget what it feels like to be a slave, to be poor, to be homeless, to eat the bread of affliction. The greatest of his commands, the simplest yet the hardest, is this: love the stranger. In an age of clashing civilisations, that is a vital insight.

Until we make theological space for the other, people will continue to hate in the name of the God of love, practise cruelty in the name of the God of compassion, wage war in the name of the God of peace, and murder in the name of the God of life. That is the greatest theological challenge of the twenty-first century. It is a challenge for Jews, Christians and Muslims alike, and its epicentre today is in the same, tiny, fateful land to which God summoned Abraham four thousand years ago.

Peace will come to the Holy Land only when Jews, Christians

and Muslims make space for one another. Politically, this is called the 'two-state solution', that has been on the table since the United Nations vote on 29 November 1947. The broad parameters of that solution have never been in doubt, whatever the arguments about details. What I have sought to show in this chapter is that geographical space depends on political space, which depends in turn on theological space. Jews, Christians and Muslims all speak of peace. They love peace, they pursue peace, their God is the God of peace. Yet each has waged sometimes brutal war in the name of God. Peace means making space for the other. That is the religious imperative of Abraham's God.

One Night in Auschwitz

I began this chapter with a painful account of how Christian and Islamic theologies denied sacred space for Jews to be Jews. But that is not how the story ends. In November 2008, two days after the seventieth anniversary of Kristallnacht, the Archbishop of Canterbury and I led a mission of leaders of all the faiths to Auschwitz: not just Jews and Christians but also Muslims, Hindus, Sikhs, Buddhists, Jains, Zoroastrians and Bahai. It was a moment of intense theological resonance. Faiths that had been estranged for millennia had come together in friendship and respect, and had opened their arms to the other in an embrace of human solidarity.

As we stood together in Auschwitz-Birkenau that chill November night, at the end of the railway lines that carried more than a million victims to be gassed, burned and turned to ash, lighting candles and saying prayers together, we knew to the core of our being where hate, unchecked, can lead. We cannot change the past, but by remembering the past we can change the future. And though we cannot bring the dead back to life, we can help ensure that they did not die in vain. We must fight hate, whoever is the hater and whoever the hated: for the sake of the victims, for the sake of our children and for the sake of God, whose image we bear.

5

Antisemitism: The Fourth Mutation

Late January 2009: antisemitic attacks in Britain reach their highest point since record-keeping began. In five weeks in London alone, 220 antisemitic incidents are recorded by the police. There is an arson attack on a synagogue. Jewish buildings are daubed with antisemitic graffiti. Jews are attacked in the street. In north-west London a Jewish driver is pulled from his car and assaulted by three men. Anti-Israel demonstrators shout 'Kill the Jews', 'Be afraid, Jews', 'Heil Hitler' and 'Jews to the gas'. Worshippers on their way to the synagogue at which I pray are shouted at by a passer-by with the words, 'Hitler should have finished the job.'

Something similar is happening throughout the world. During the same period there are attacks on Jews, synagogues and Jewish buildings in France, Germany, Belgium and Scandinavia. In Toulouse, on 5 January, a car containing firebombs is rammed into the front gate of the synagogue and explodes. On 11 January a Chabad centre in the northern Paris suburb of Saint-Denis is hit by nine Molotov cocktails and set on fire. Jews are stabbed in the street. In Europe as a whole, antisemitic incidents are up 300 per cent over the previous year. In Caracas, Venezuela, a synagogue is vandalised. Fifteen armed men break into Caracas's Sephardic synagogue at night, hold the guard at gunpoint, wreak havoc on the building and damage Torah scrolls. Before leaving, they scrawl 'Death to the Jews' and 'We don't want Jews here' on the synagogue walls.

Much of this activity was, of course, related to events in Israel, specifically the Gaza campaign conducted at the same time. But these attacks were on Jews, not Israelis; on synagogues and Jewish schools, not buildings connected with the state of Israel.

Nor was the rhetoric the usual language associated with political protest. Millions of people throughout the world took to the streets between 2002 and 2007 in protest against the war in Iraq. People carried banners saying 'Stop the War', 'War Is Not the Answer', 'Troops Out', and 'Not In My Name'.

In 2009, in New York's Times Square, protesters against the war in Gaza carried placards written in a different kind of language altogether: 'Israel, the Fourth Reich', 'Stop Israel's Holocaust' and 'Stop the Nazi Genocide in Gaza'. In Chicago they read 'Palestinian Holocaust in Gaza Now'. In a Los Angeles demonstration, the Star of David in an Israeli flag was replaced by a swastika, and underneath was written, 'Upgrade to Holocaust Version 2.0'. At one rally in Washington, protesters carried an effigy of the Israeli prime minister wearing a swastika armband and holding a dead baby.

Nor was this language confined to street activists. A British Member of Parliament compared Israel's actions to those of the Nazis. Venezuelan President Hugo Chavez asked on television, 'Don't Jews repudiate the Holocaust? And this is precisely what we're witnessing.' A Catholic cardinal was reported by the *New York Times* as saying that Gaza increasingly 'resembled a big concentration camp'. A Norwegian diplomat based in Saudi Arabia sent out an e-mail: 'The grand-children of Holocaust survivors from World War II are doing to the Palestinians exactly what was done to them by Nazi Germany.'

It is not my concern to discuss the politics of Israel or the rightness or wrongness of its military campaigns. This chapter is about antisemitism, not Israel. Yet the return of antisemitism, especially to Europe, home of the Holocaust, is deeply shocking. Rebecca West once said that Jews, who had seen the greatest of evils, have 'an unsurprisable soul'. When antisemitism reappeared in the twenty-first century in Britain, once the most tolerant of nations, I discovered I had a surprisable soul.

From Never Again to Ever Again?

It is with deep reluctance that I write about antisemitism. I never experienced it as a child. When we came to the passage in the Haggadah (the retelling of the Passover story) that says, 'It was not one [Pharaoh] alone who stood against us to destroy us, but in every generation they stand against us and try to destroy us,' I felt a wry detachment. That was then, not now; my parents' world, not mine. My father spent his early childhood in Kielce in Poland. Only after his death did I read about the chilling event that took place there: a pogrom on 4 July 1946, a full year after the war had ended and the facts of the Holocaust had become known. A Jewish communal building was surrounded. Jews were shot, stoned to death, or killed with axes. Some were murdered in their homes, others in the streets. Forty-two Jews were killed that day. A hundred thousand Jews fled Poland.

My father knew about antisemitism but rarely spoke about it, and when he did, it was often in the form of a joke. 'Antisemitic traffic lights', he would say when they turned red as he approached. He did not want his children burdened with the knowledge. For him, too, antisemitism was sometime else, somewhere else.

So when, in 2002, I began to alert our community and the British public to the phenomenon of the return of antisemitism, it was against inclination and experience. Yet it was real, dangerous and consequential. The evidence was too blatant to be ignored. The emergence of a virulent new strain of antisemitism, after sixty years of Holocaust education, interfaith dialogue and anti-racist legislation, is a major historical event. Far-sighted historians like Bernard Lewis and Robert Wistrich had been sounding the warning since the 1980s.[1] Already in the 1990s, Harvard literary scholar Ruth Wisse argued that antisemitism was the most successful ideology of the twentieth century. German fascism, she said, came and went. Soviet communism came and went. Antisemitism came and stayed.[2]

A mere two years earlier, on 27 January 2000, I had been present when twenty European heads of state met in Stockholm to commit themselves to an ongoing programme of Holocaust remembrance and anti-racist education. Yet despite that, the hate had returned. 'Never again' had become 'Ever again'.

It is wrong to exaggerate. We are not now where Jews were in the 1930s. Nor are Jews today what their ancestors were: defenceless, powerless and without a collective home. The state of Israel has transformed the situation for Jews everywhere. What is necessary now is simply to understand the situation and sound a warning. That is what Moses Hess did in 1862, Judah Leib Pinsker in 1882 and Theodor Herzl in 1896—seventy-one, fifty-one and thirty-seven years respectively before Hitler's rise to power. To understand is to begin to know how to respond, with open eyes and without fear.

A Mutating Virus

What is antisemitism? It is less a doctrine or set of beliefs than a series of contradictions. In the past Jews were hated because they were rich and because they were poor, because they were capitalists and because they were communists, because they kept to themselves and because they infiltrated everywhere, because they held tenaciously to a superstitious faith and because they were rootless cosmopolitans who believed nothing.

The best way to understand antisemitism is to see it as a virus. Viruses attack the human body, but the body itself has an immensely sophisticated defence, the human immune system. How, then, do viruses survive and flourish? By mutating. Antisemitism mutates, and in so doing defeats the immune systems set up by cultures to protect themselves against hatred. There have been three such mutations in the past two thousand years, and we are living through the fourth.

Some trace the origins of antisemitism to the Hellenistic Age, but this is, I believe, a conceptual confusion. The Greek and Latin writers of antiquity were often hostile to Jews, accusing them of clannishness, strange customs and superstitions. Horace condemned them for trying to make converts. Apion criticised them for failing to worship the same gods as the Alexandrians. Seneca held that they rested on the seventh day because they were lazy. The worst of the pre-Christian polemicists was the Egyptian priest Manetho (third century BCE), who described the Hebrews as a race of lepers who had been thrown out of Egypt.

Many of these calumnies survived to be taken up and adapted in later centuries. That has been the fate of anti-Jewish myths: they may be dormant, but they never die. Yet it would be wrong to describe reactions to Jews in antiquity as a form of antisemitism, for two reasons. First, the Hellenistic writers were not universally hostile. There is evidence to suggest that Alexander the Great thought highly of them and rewarded them for their loyalty. Aristotle spoke well of them, as did his successor Theophrastus.

Second, and more significantly, it was part of a larger phenomenon. The Greeks did not like foreigners. They considered them barbarous, uncivilised. Using an onomatopoeia, a word that sounded like the bleating of sheep, they called them barbarians. In this they attached no special significance to Jews. They felt the same way about many of their neighbours. This, then, was not antisemitism: it was the more general phenomenon of xenophobia, hatred of the foreigner, the alien.

The First Mutation

That changed with the birth of Christianity, or at least with its earliest texts. Christianity was an offshoot of Judaism. Its founder and focus was a Jew. As would happen later with Islam, the adherents of the new religion believed that as a development of Judaism, incorporating many of its teachings, Jews would recognise the new dispensation as their own. It did not happen on either occasion. This lack of recognition became a source of hatred. Among the early Christians a series of beliefs slowly took shape that would poison relationships for centuries to come: Jews failed to recognise their own messiah. Worse: Jews were complicit in the death of the messiah. With gathering momentum, already evident in the later gospels, a note of hostility to Jews begins to pervade the emerging literature of the new faith.

Over the next few centuries, beginning with marginal figures like Marcion, and spreading to more central ones like Chrysostom and Jerome, a new genre of works began to appear, known as the *Adversos Judeos* ('Against the Jews') literature, dedicated to demonstrating the blindness and recalcitrance of the Jews. The French historian Jules Isaac gave this the name of 'the teachings of contempt'. Jews were blind, they were slaves, they were Cain, murderers condemned to wander through the world.[3]

A series of disdainful oppositions was formulated: the Old Testament God of vengeance against the New Testament God of mercy (despite the fact that they were, in Christian belief, the same God); the religion of law against the religion of love; the old, rejected Israel against the new people of the covenant. Not all, but some Christians took the fateful step of defining their faith in opposition to a living people, whom they could not but see as the embodiment of all they rejected. Some of these oppositions remain in place today.[4] This was no longer generalised xenophobia. It was precisely targeted against Jews: it was Judeophobia. That was the first mutation.

The Second Mutation

The second can be dated roughly to 1096, when the first Crusaders paused on their way to the Holy Land to massacre Jewish communities in northern France and Germany, in Worms, Speyer and Mainz. Jews were no longer merely the people who rejected Christianity. They began to be seen as a demonic force, responsible for all the evils of a troubled age. They were accused of desecrating the host, poisoning wells, engaging in ritual murder and spreading the plague. They were no longer people: they were an active force of evil, children of the devil, offspring of Satan, agents of the Antichrist.[5] It was the beginning of what one historian has called 'a persecuting society'.[6] In the years following the Black Death alone (1347–50), some two hundred Jewish communities were destroyed. Jews were expelled from Brittany in 1239–40, from Anjou and Maine in 1289, from England in 1290, from France at various periods from 1182 to 1394, and from regions of Germany throughout the fifteenth century.

In Spain, where they had experienced a rare Golden Age, an onslaught took place in 1391, during which synagogues and homes were burned, businesses looted and many Jews murdered. From then on, Spanish Jews faced increasing hostility until their expulsion in 1492. Nor did the tragedy end there. Still to come were Luther's tirade against Jews ('their synagogues should be set on fire . . . their homes should likewise be broken down and destroyed . . . they should be deprived of their prayerbooks and Talmuds'), the invention of the ghetto (Rome 1555, by edict of Pope Paul IV) and the Chmielnicki pogroms (1648–58) during which as many as a hundred thousand Jews died. The experience of Jews in Christian Europe is one of the tragedies of humankind. That was the second mutation: demonic anti-Judaism.

The Third Mutation

The third was born at the very height of enlightened Europe in the nineteenth century. The promise of the Enlightenment was an age of reason, rid once and for all of the prejudices of the past. Rationality would replace revelation; science would displace superstition. There would be a new age of toleration, in which the hatreds of the past would be consigned to history. As the French Revolutionary Declaration put it: all men are born and remain free and equal in rights.

The question was, did this include the Jews? In a speech to the French Revolutionary assembly, the Count of Clermont Tonerre made a famous statement: 'To the Jews as individuals, everything; to the Jews as a nation, nothing.' He added that if the Jews insisted on behaving as a people apart, then they would have 'no choice but to expel them'.

Against both prediction and promise, the prejudices of the past lived on. Clearly, though, the old rationale for Judeophobia could no longer be sustained. It was religious in origin and logic, and religion no longer had a vote in the secular nation-states of Europe, or in its secularised culture. A new explanation was needed for the old and persisting hatred.

In 1879 a German journalist, Wilhelm Marr, gave it a local habitation and a name. He called it antisemitism. The fact that a new name was needed signals the change from the past. No longer could a rationale for prejudice be based on the sacred texts of Christianity. It was therefore relocated from religion to race. Jews were hated not because of their beliefs but because of their ethnicity. They were an alien race, polluting the bloodstream of Europe. Thus racial antisemitism was born: the third mutation.

The simplest reflection is sufficient to see why this hatred was deadlier than any in the past. You can change your faith; you cannot change your race. While Christians could work for the conversion of the Jews, racial antisemites could work only for their elimination. The logic of genocide was implicit in the third mutation from the beginning. There is, said Raul Hilberg, a straight line from 'You no longer have a right to live among us as Jews' to 'You no longer have a right to live among us' to 'You no longer have a right to live'.[7]

It is important to make clear that the new antisemitism was not the product of sensationalist journalists, mass movements and demagogues alone. It came from the finest minds of Europe. Immanuel Kant spoke of Jews as 'the vampires of society' and called for the 'euthanasia' of Judaism. Fichte argued against giving civil rights to Jews and said that the only cure was to 'cut off their heads'. Hegel took Judaism as his model of a slave morality.

Schopenhauer spoke of Jews as 'no better than cattle'. Nietzsche blamed Judaism for the 'falsification' of values. The great logician Gottlob Frege wrote in 1924 that he regarded it as a 'misfortune that there are so many Jews in Germany'. Martin Heidegger, the greatest German philosopher of the twentieth century, was an early member of the Nazi party who never subsequently apologised for his admiration of Hitler or his betrayal of Jewish colleagues.[8]

By the time the movement had run its course, more than half the Jews of Europe had been murdered, shot, gassed, burned and turned to ash, and there was silence where once European Jewry had lived.

The Fourth Mutation

The new antisemitism is different. It is no longer directed against Jews as individuals. It is primarily directed against Jews as a nation with their own state in their own land. It is a mutant form of anti-Zionism.

It consists of the following three elements. First, Jews are not entitled to a nation-state of their own, a denial, in other words, of the right of Israel to exist. The irony of this development was succinctly stated by Amos Oz. In the 1930s, he said, antisemites carried banners saying: Jews to Palestine. Now the banners read: Jews out of Palestine. He continued, 'They don't want us to be there. They don't want us to be here. They don't want us to be.' This is not yet antisemitism. It is anti-Zionism.

The second set of beliefs is that the existence of Israel is not merely an aberration. It is responsible for all the evils of the world, from a lack of peace in the Middle East to avian flu, the destruction of the space shuttle *Columbia,* the Danish cartoons blaspheming the prophet Mohammed, the Pope's criticism of Islam, even the 2004 South-east Asian tsunami. All these have been called Zionist plots. In significant parts of the world, Israel has become the demonic force once attributed to Jews in the worst days of the Christian Middle Ages. Jews and their state are a conspiracy against humanity.

The third proposition—the bridge from anti-Zionism to antisemitism—is that all Jews are Zionists; therefore all Jews are responsible for the sufferings caused by Israel; therefore all Jews are legitimate targets of attack. When the Jewish community centre in Argentina is bombed, when synagogues in Paris, Antwerp, Djerba and Istanbul are attacked, when Jewish cemeteries are desecrated and Jews are physically attacked in the streets, these are not Israeli targets but Jewish ones.

Often the argument is heard that what Jews take as antisemitism is in fact no more than criticism of the state of Israel. I know of no significant figure who takes this view. Criticism of a state and its policies are part of the text and texture of public life. Often the sharpest criticism of Israel's policies comes from within, from its writers and intellectuals, academics and journalists. That is what makes Israel the free society it is. Israel is not perfect. No nation or government is. Therefore criticism of it is legitimate. If justified, it should be heeded; if unjustified, it should be argued against. Antisemitism is not part of the normal cut-and-thrust of political debate or the clash of national interests.

A set of criteria distinguishing antisemitism from criticism of Israel was set out by the European Monitoring Centre on Racism and Xenophobia (now the European Union Agency for Fundamental Rights). It includes the following: denying the Jewish people their right to self-determination, e.g., by claiming that the existence of a State of Israel is a racist endeavour, applying double standards by requiring of it a behaviour not expected or demanded of any other democratic nation, using the symbols and images associated with classic antisemitism (e.g., claims of Jews killing Jesus or blood libel) to characterise Israel or Israelis, drawing comparisons of contemporary Israeli policy to that of the Nazis, or holding Jews collectively responsible for actions of the state of Israel.[9] Such claims have become standard fare in Arab and (some) Western media and on websites.[10]

Legitimating Hate: Human Rights and Wrongs

The new antisemitism is clearly continuous with the old. It has recycled all the old myths, from the Blood Libel to The Protocols of the Elders of Zion. Yet it is different. It is not Christian anti-Judaism, nor is it the racial antisemitism of Nazi Germany. It is, as I have already said, focused not on Jews as individuals but on Jews as a nation in their land. It is to that extent political, with an admixture of religion. Three other features differentiate it from earlier strains.

The first is its legitimation. Hatred of the other, the outsider, the one not like us, may be endemic to the human psyche; it may be genetically hardwired into our brains from the days in which our ancestors were hunter-gatherers who needed to be alert to the danger of other tribes. But since the axial age and the dawn of a sense of human solidarity, prejudice has stood in need of justification. Homo sapiens have developed a strong set of defences against brute xenophobia. 'Love your neighbour as yourself,' taught Leviticus. The New Testament took this teaching and made it a centre point of its faith. Treat human beings not as means but as ends, said Immanuel Kant. Hate, therefore, is anything but self-justifying. It cannot be publicly aired without some form of justification. And since it is the lowest form of evil, it stands in need of legitimation from the highest source of authority available within the culture at the time.

In the early Christian centuries, and even more so in the high Middle Ages, the supreme source of authority was religion. Accordingly, we find hostility to Jews in those ages legitimated by religion itself, from the Gospels to the church fathers to the dualistic and demonising literature of the Middle Ages.

That justification was not available in the nineteenth century. There were still religious antisemites, but religion was no longer the supreme source of authority in post-Enlightenment European culture. That place was now occupied by science. Accordingly, anti-Jewish sentiment now found its validation in the form of two pseudo-sciences. The first was the so-called 'scientific study of race', drawing support from anthropology to philosophers of racial difference, such as Herder. Different races had different civilisational attributes and these could be traced by physical markers, such as the colour of a person's skin or shape of the nose.

The other pseudo-science was the curious hybrid of biology and sociology known as social Darwinism. This argued that the evolution of society followed the same laws as the evolution of species. Nature is a battleground in which the ruthless survive and the weak perish. So is human history. The strong prevail; the weak die and disappear. There is nothing moral or immoral about this process. It is simply how things are. Hitler was a great admirer of Darwin, who, it must be said, would have been horrified at this perversion of his ideas.

So racial antisemitism was validated by science and found some of its most enthusiastic supporters among academics, medical scientists, doctors, lawyers and judges. Today, though, science no longer carries the pristine aura it once had. Once thought to carry the promise of unprecedented progress, it is now seen as giving us the power to destroy life on earth. Science has lost its aura as the undisputed benchmark of morality.

What has emerged in its place, in part because of the Holocaust, is the arena known as 'human rights'. Enshrined as the response of the world to the evils of the Holocaust, it emerged as the new standard-bearer of humanity, enshrined in such doctrines as the United Nations Declaration of Human Rights, 1948, and its multiple offspring such as the 1950 European Convention and the 2000 Charter of Fundamental Rights of the European Union.

Inevitably, therefore, the new antisemitism is cast in terms of human rights, and one of the arenas of its promulgation has become the United Nations itself. At the 2001 United Nations Conference Against Antisemitism at Durban, Israel (and by implication the Jewish people as a whole) was accused, especially in the parallel sessions involving human rights NGOs, of the five cardinal sins of the post-Holocaust world: racism, apartheid, ethnic cleansing, crimes against humanity and attempted genocide.

This is the answer to the question that must bemuse Jews and others in the twenty-first century. How did the virus of antisemitism so easily penetrate the most sophisticated immune system ever developed by a set of cultures to ensure that the Holocaust should never happen again? It happened in precisely the way viruses defeat the immune system. They do so by posing not as enemies but as friends; not as intruders against the human body but as part of the body itself.

The new antisemitism emerged by a strategy of devastating simplicity and effectiveness. It goes as follows. Antisemitism is evil. The Holocaust is the worst crime of human being against human being. Any civilised human being must be against it in all its manifestations, whoever its perpetrator and whoever its victim. Israel behaves towards the Palestinians as the Nazis behaved towards Jews. It is practising slow genocide against its neighbours. If, therefore, you oppose antisemitism—which, as a civilised human being, you must—you must therefore oppose the state of Israel and all those who support it, who happen to be Jews. Rarely was an immune system so easily penetrated.

Information Technology and the Transmission of Hate

The second difference between the new antisemitism and the old is that it is communicated by the new global technologies, especially satellite television and the Internet. Changes in information technology are the most profound of all carriers of cultural change. In the phrase of Walter J. Ong, they 'restructure consciousness'.[11] Benedict Anderson, in his *Imagined Communities,* argued that the nation-state was made possible by one specific form of communication, the newspaper.[12] I have argued, in *The Home We Build Together,* that the Internet may spell the death of the nation-state and the emergence of new political structures whose shape we cannot yet predict.[13]

Racial antisemitism was a by-product of the nation-state. It emerged at the same time and for the same reason. The nation-state, as conceived in Germany and France, tended to abolish all intermediary structures between the individual and the state. That was one of the differences between those countries and Britain and America. For the latter, civil society—the arena of communities, charities and voluntary associations—was seen as a virtue. For Rousseau and Hegel, it was seen as a vice. Nothing should intervene between the citizen and the state. Jews maintained their identity within civil society-type structures: congregations, fellowships, philanthropies and so on. In Britain and America this was seen as contributing to good citizenship, but in France and Germany it was viewed as a form of separatism and disloyalty. Hence in those countries, but not in Britain and America, antisemitism became part of the mainstream of political debate.

Today the nation-state hardly exists, in Europe at any rate. The ideas of a single culture, or of government as the embodiment of national identity, have long been swept away by the tide of multiculturalism. Today, anyone can choose his or her culture or lifestyle, and be connected with others across the globe through the various media of the Internet. The result is that antisemitism is no longer the product of national cultures, as it was in the 1930s. It is highly targeted to individuals without even their next-door neighbours knowing about it. One of the aftershocks of the 7 July 2005 terrorist attacks on London was the discovery that the suicide bombers were British citizens who had grown up and been educated locally. They were well known to, and well liked by, their neighbours and work colleagues. Their hostility to the West and their training in terror came from religious colleges in Pakistan. There was almost nothing local about it at all.

The new antisemitism can therefore exist in cultures that are not in any way antisemitic and may even be models of tolerance.

It is visible globally but not locally. Two groups are aware of it: the perpetrators and the victims—in other words, antisemites and Jews. The general public is wholly or largely unaware, and is bemused when Jews complain about it. 'Britain an antisemitic country? Of course not.' And they are right: Britain is *not* an antisemitic country. Occasionally certain facts come to light, such as during the trial of the radical cleric Abu Hamza in January 2006, who preached that Jews are guilty of 'treachery, blasphemy and filth' and that it was for this reason that 'Hitler was sent into the world'. But this is seen as an exception, an aberration.

It is exceptionally difficult to fight hatred spread by satellite television and the Internet. It is difficult even to give the general public a sense of its prevalence. It is one of the many contemporary phenomena, including terror, for which we have not yet evolved adequate defences. They are global problems for which we lack global mechanisms and institutions, and they will remain a danger for many years to come.

The Change Within Islam

The third difference is that the epicentre of the old antisemitism was in Christian Europe. Today it is to be found in the extremist versions, often called Islamicist, of the cultures of Islam. Here an important point must be made. There is a tendency in some circles to accuse Islam of systemic antisemitism. That is not the case. Antisemitism is not intrinsic to Islam as it once was to Christianity. Its appearance in Islam since the nineteenth century comes from without, not within. Its roots lie elsewhere.

As a whole, Jews fared better during the Middle Ages under Muslim than under Christian rule. What they experienced was not tolerance in the modern sense, but it would be anachronistic to have expected it. The modern doctrine of toleration, like that of human rights, was born in the seventeenth century and existed almost nowhere beforehand. To be sure, the early Muslims, like the early Christians, expected Jews to embrace the new faith, which claimed to include and supersede earlier revelations. When this did not happen, reprisals were sometimes harsh.

Islam began with a massacre of Jews in Medina, and incorporated anti-Jewish sentiments into its sacred texts. There were times, especially in its early period of expansion, when relative tolerance prevailed, within limits. Jews were given *dhimmi* status as second-class citizens, which meant that they had to pay special taxes and wear distinctive clothing. They were banned from government service and from building new houses of worship, and were subject to periodic public humiliations. At times, extreme Islamic sects made life intolerable. In 1066 the community of Granada was attacked and three thousand Jews were killed. In 1090 the community was assaulted again by an Islamic sect known as the Almoravids, and during the next century it suffered an onslaught from a new group, the Almohads.[14]

However, there was a fundamental difference between Christianity and Islam. Islam, in the view of its followers, absorbed Judaism; it did not predicate itself on its superseding Judaism. Muslim attitudes to Jews were based more on contempt than hate and, as Bernard Lewis points out, contempt is less dangerous than hate.[15] Jews were seen as cowardly and unmilitary, not dangerous and fearful. There was no counterpart within classical Islam to the antisemitism of medieval Christianity that saw Jews as a cosmic embodiment of evil.

The myths that dominate contemporary Islamist antisemitism have no provenance within the sacred texts and historic teachings of Islam. To the contrary, they are recognisably non-Islamic. Two dominate antisemitic discourse today: the Blood Libel and The Protocols of the Elders of Zion. The Blood Libel is one of the strangest phenomena in European history.[16] It originated in Norwich in 1144, where a child named William was discovered stabbed to death. A rumour circulated that Jews were responsible. No one took it seriously at the time, but it became a cause célèbre five years later when an account appeared, written by a monk, Thomas of Monmouth. It was an absurd fantasy: if anything is abhorrent to Jews, it is blood, and child sacrifice. The Blood Libel was officially condemned by several popes—among them Innocent IV, Gregory X, Martin V, Paul III and Nicholas V—as well as by Emperor Frederick II. That did not stop the accusation from spreading throughout Europe. There were more than 150 recorded cases, many leading to massacres of the local Jewish population.

The Blood Libel makes sense only to those who believe in transubstantiation. It is unintelligible within the language of Judaism and Islam, both of which reject the doctrine. Nonetheless, it was introduced to the Middle East in the early nineteenth century by Christians, making its appearance in Aleppo (1811, 1853), Beirut (1824), Antioch (1826), Hamma (1829), Tripoli (1834), Dayr al-Qamar (1847), Damanhur (1877) and Damascus (most famously in 1840, but also in 1848 and 1890). In 1983 the Syrian Defence Minister Mustapha Tlas wrote a book, *The Matzo of Zion,* to prove that the libel was true ('The Jew can kill you and take your blood in order to make his Zionist bread'), and in 1991 the Syrian delegate to the United Nations Human Rights Commission urged its members to read the book, the better to understand 'Zionist racism'. It remains a best-seller.

The Protocols of the Elders of Zion—exposed as a forgery by *The Times* in 1921—was concocted by Russian antisemites in the Parisian office of the Tsarist secret police at the end of the nineteenth century.[17] The authors drew on various fictions and conspiracy theories, none of which was originally about Jews. Despite its exposure as a forgery, it sold widely, first in Russia, then in Nazi Germany, and from there it spread to the Middle East. In 2002 a forty-one-part television dramatisation of the Protocols, *Horseman Without a Horse,* was shown on Egyptian television during Ramadan.[18] In 2003 a similar series, *Al-Shatat (Diaspora),* was shown on Syrian television.[19] In November 2003 a copy of the Protocols was displayed, next to a Torah, in the new library in Alexandria, Egypt, as part of an exhibition of 'holy books for the monotheistic religions', and was withdrawn only after protest by UNESCO. The Director of Manuscripts, Dr Youssef Ziedan, explained his decision to include it because 'although it is not a monotheistic holy book, it has become a holy book for the Jews, their primary law, their way of life'. These fantasies have no historic basis in Islam.

Islam is closer to Judaism than any other faith in its austere monotheism, its reverence for texts and education, its emphasis on social justice and respect for law. During the Middle Ages, Islam preserved the wisdom of ancient Greece, bringing Europe new techniques of mathematics as well as such giants of philosophy as al-Fārābī, Avicenna and Averroës and the path-breaking historian Ibn Khaldun. Maimonides, the greatest medieval Jewish sage, was deeply influenced by Islamic thought, as was his son Abraham by Sufi mysticism. From the eighth century onwards, Baghdad and Basra became world centres of commerce, encouraging trust and trade between distant lands. The Hanafite school of Islamic jurisprudence pioneered the development of business contracts. For several centuries, the Umayyads created in al-Andalus one of the most tolerant of all regimes in the Middle Ages, beautifully evoked by María Rosa Menocal in her *The Ornament of the World*.[20] It is therefore deeply tragic that Western antisemitism has penetrated some sections of this ancient faith.

Against Internalisation

What, therefore, should be our response? First, Jews must fight antisemitism but never internalise it. That is easier said than done. If you are hated, it is natural to believe that you are hateful, that the defect lies in you. It rarely does. Hate exists in the mind of the hater, not in the person of the hated.

The idea that Jews drink blood made sense to Christians who believe in transubstantiation; it makes no sense at all to Jews, to whom blood is forbidden and abhorrent. The idea that Jews have a secret conspiracy to rule the world makes sense to people in the service of Tsarist Russia; it makes none at all to Judaism, the one major monotheism never to have given rise to an empire or the desire for one. Jews have faults, and Judaism is a religion of self-criticism and repentance, but those faults have nothing to do with those of which they are accused by their enemies. Antisemitism tells us about antisemites, not Jews.

Internalised, antisemitism gives rise to either self-righteousness or self-hatred, neither of which is a constructive attitude. Jews are the *objects* of antisemitism, not its *cause*. There has been an almost endless set of speculations about what the cause of antisemitism actually is. Some have seen it in psychological terms: displaced fear, externalisation of inner conflict, projected guilt, the creation of a scapegoat. Others have given it a sociopolitical explanation: Jews were a group who could conveniently be blamed for economic resentments, social unrest, class conflict or destabilising change. Yet others view it through the prism of culture and identity: Jews were the stereotyped outsiders against whom a group could define itself. Yet others, noting the concentration of antisemitism among the very faiths—Christianity and Islam—that trace their descent to Abraham and Judaism, favour a Freudian explanation in terms of the myth of Oedipus: we seek to kill those who gave us birth. It would be strange indeed if so complex a phenomenon did not give rise to multiple explanations.

But the roots of antisemitism belong within the mind of the antisemite, not among Jews. The response must be to fight it, but never to internalise it or accept it on its own terms. Racial antisemitism eventually cost the lives of six million Jews. But it left another, less visible scar. One of the mistakes made by good, honourable and reflective Jews was to believe that since Jews were hated because they were different, they should try as far as possible *not* to be different.

So, some converted. Others assimilated. Yet others reformulated Judaism to eliminate as far as possible all that made Jews and Judaism distinctive. When these things failed—as they did, not only in nineteenth-century Germany and Austria but also in fifteenth-century Spain—some internalised the failure. Thus was born the tortured psychology known as Jewish self-hatred: the result of Jews ceasing to define themselves as a nation loved by God and instead seeing themselves as the people hated by Gentiles. It was a tragic error. Antisemitism is not caused by Jews; they are merely its targets. There can be antisemitism in countries where there are no Jews at all. Hatred is something that can happen to us, but it is not who we are. It can never be the basis of an identity.

One episode, told by a rabbinical colleague, has long lingered in my mind. It took place in Russia in the early 1990s, following the collapse of communism. For the first time in seventy years, Jews were free to live openly as Jews, but at the same time antisemitic attitudes, long suppressed, also came to the surface. A British rabbi had gone there to help with the reconstruction of Jewish life, and was one day visited by a young lady in distress. 'All my life,' she said, 'I hid the fact that I was a Jew and no one ever commented on my Jewishness. Now, though, when I walk past, my neighbours mutter *Zhid* [Jew]. What shall I do?'

The rabbi replied, 'If you had not told me you were Jewish, I would never have known. But with my hat and beard, no one could miss the fact that I am a Jew. Yet, in all the months I have been here, no one has shouted *Zhid* at me. Why do you think that is?'

The girl was silent for a moment and then said, 'Because they know that if they shout *Zhid* at me, I will take it as an insult, but if they shout *Zhid* at you, you will take it as a compliment.' That is a deep insight. Beyond eternal vigilance, the best way for Jews to combat antisemitism is to wear their identity with pride.

Winning Allies, Standing Together

The second point follows from the first. Jews cannot fight antisemitism alone. The victim cannot cure the crime. The hated cannot cure the hate. It would be the greatest possible mistake for Jews to believe that they can fight it alone. The only people who can successfully combat antisemitism are those active in the cultures that harbour it.

When, in the spring of 2002, antisemitism began to rise alarmingly and Jewish students were being intimidated on campus, I brought together the leadership of the Union of Jewish Students and told them, 'You will face difficult months ahead. I promise you that in your fight, you will not be alone. We will be with you, giving you all the support you need. And now I want you to do the most unexpected thing. I want you to lead the fight against Islamophobia.' Thus was born the Coexist Foundation, a group of Jews and Muslims fighting antisemitism and Islamophobia together.

Interfaith co-operation is vital. I work closely with the leadership of all faiths in Britain: Anglican, Catholic, the Orthodox Church, Baptists, Methodists and Evangelicals, Muslims, Hindus, Sikhs, Buddhists, Jains, Zoroastrians and Bahai. So does the Board of Deputies, the lay representative body of Anglo-Jewry. In November 2008 the Archbishop of Canterbury and I led a mission of leaders of all these faiths to Auschwitz. One of our aims is to fight antisemitism, but we must recognise that Jews are not the only people who face prejudice and hate. So do the other groups, and we must stand with them if we are to expect them to stand with us. We share a covenant of fate and human solidarity.

Most important, we have taken our concerns to the government and Members of Parliament. It was Parliamentarians who set up their own Committee of Inquiry into antisemitism in 2005. Their report was published in 2006. An All-Party Parliamentary Committee was established to monitor all forms of antisemitism. The government set up an interdepartmental committee to liaise with the Jewish community and take the requisite action. The leaders of all parties in Britain have made a public stand against antisemitism. The Prime Minister, Gordon Brown, provided government funding to ensure that every senior school in Britain is able to send teachers and pupils to Auschwitz to learn about the Holocaust. In 2007, I took our concerns to the Presidents of the European Commission and the European Parliament.

One of the sharpest insights into antisemitism was given by Hannah Arendt in *The Origins of Totalitarianism*. She argued that it is not when Jews are strong that they are attacked but precisely when they are weak.[21] When Jews did hold significant economic power in Europe, antisemitism did not thrive. (By the time Hitler came to power, she notes, German banks had passed out of Jewish ownership, and German Jewry was declining so rapidly that demographers predicted its disappearance in a few decades.) The point is subtle and difficult to grasp at first, because for antisemitism to sound plausible, it must be possible to make people believe that Jews are powerful. Otherwise, how could they credibly be portrayed as a threat? That is the whole point of The Protocols of the Elders of Zion. At the same time, it must *in fact* be the case that Jews are powerless, for if they were not, they would not be attacked. It is this strange, convoluted thought—the claim that Jews control everything, together with the knowledge that actually they control very little—that is at the heart of all antisemitic conspiracy theories.

Jews *are* relatively powerless. They are a tiny people, less than a fifth of one per cent of the population of the world. They have never had either the power or influence myths like The Protocols have attributed to them. For Jews to stand alone is a strategy that invites danger. We must stand together with other victims of hate, and that means active engagement with other faith communities and ethnic groups, and with society as a whole.

In Defence of Difference

The third point follows from the root cause of antisemitism, spelled out by the world's first recorded antisemite, Haman, when he said to King Ahasuerus, 'There is a certain people dispersed and scattered among the peoples in all the provinces of your kingdom *whose customs are different* from those of all other people.' Antisemitism is the paradigm case of dislike of the unlike, the fear of the stranger, the outsider, the one not like us. It is the hatred of difference.

Throughout history, Jews have borne the burden of difference. Whether in Christian Europe or the Muslim Middle East, they were the quintessential Other. *That is Judaism's great contribution to humanity:* to show that one can be other and still human, still a loyal and active citizen, still make contributions to every field of human endeavour, still be loved by God and held precious in his sight.

That is our argument to humanity: antisemitism—the hatred of difference—is an assault not on Jews only but on the human condition as such. Life is sacred because each person—even genetically identical twins—is different, therefore irreplaceable and non-substitutable. Every language, culture and civilisation (within the terms of the universal moral code) has its own integrity and because each is different, each adds something unique to the collective heritage of humankind. Cultural diversity is as essential to our social ecology as biodiversity is to our natural ecology.

Antisemitism begins with Jews, but it never ends with them. A world without room for Jews is one that has no room for difference, and a world that lacks space for difference lacks space for humanity itself. The only adequate response to the fear and hatred of difference is to honour the dignity of difference. That is the Jewish message to the world, and if Jews are true to it they will discover that though they have enemies, they also have friends. But it is antisemitism, more than anything else, that has led to the syndrome I mentioned in chapter 1, of Jews defining themselves as 'the people that dwells alone'.

6

A People That Dwells Alone?

There are moments when a vague intuition suddenly resolves itself into a life-changing insight. It happened to me in May 2001. The date was Shavuot (Pentecost), the place, Jerusalem. We were having lunch with a former leader of Diaspora Jewry who, together with his wife, had made *aliyah* (immigration to Israel). Also at the table were a senior Israeli diplomat and Professor Irwin Cotler, an inveterate campaigner against the new antisemitism. Cotler, a professor of international law at McGill University and a former president of the Canadian Jewish Congress, became a member of the Canadian parliament and subsequently its justice minister.

The conversation turned to the forthcoming United Nations Conference Against Racism at Durban, later to become notorious as the launchpad of a new and serious assault against the legitimacy of the state of Israel. Israel was accused of racism, apartheid and attempted genocide. There was an attempt to downgrade the Holocaust by spelling it with a lowercase 'h' and seeing it as just one of many such incidents. Kofi Annan once called the notorious 'Zionism is racism' resolution the United Nation's lowest ebb,[1] but Durban may have been worse. The atmosphere, according to the testimony of Jews present, was poisonous and intimidating, reminiscent of Germany in the 1930s. Less than a week later, 9/11 took place, and the world changed. All this, on that Shavuot, lay months in the future.

When Cotler raised the subject, I was interested, because I had been involved in an attempt to rescue the hijacked conference agenda.[2] Cotler's point was born out of his own long experience in the field. Israel, he told us, had mechanisms for dealing with other governments but none, or at least too few, for dealing with NGOs. This was serious because Israel underestimated the influence of such groups on public opinion around the world, and especially on the United Nations itself. Since the mid-1970s there had been a systematic and largely successful attempt to enlist NGOs, especially those involved in human rights, to the Palestinian cause. The result was that the Palestinian narrative was the frame through which such groups saw the conflict. Israel was underrepresented, even excluded, from their deliberations. Among the opinion shapers of the new global organisations, Israel was dangerously isolated.

It was then that the diplomat, a religious man, spoke, probably intending no more than to dispel some of the gloom that the conversation had generated. 'It was ever thus,' he said, and quoted the famous lines of the prophet Balaam:

> *Hein am levadad yishkon*
> *Uvagoyim lo yitchashav*
> It is a people that dwells alone,
> Not reckoned among the nations. (Num. 23:9)

It was, he said, Israel's destiny to find itself alone.[3] It was an honourable remark, but at that point I experienced what can only be described as an explosion of light in the mind. 'What makes you so sure that Balaam meant those words as a blessing?' I asked. 'Might it not have been that he intended them as a curse?'

Consider, I said, the incidence of the word *badad*, 'alone', in the Hebrew Bible. It is used about a leper: 'He shall live alone *[badad]*; his dwelling place shall be outside the camp' (Lev. 13:46). It was used by Isaiah: 'The fortified city stands desolate *[badad]*, an abandoned settlement, forsaken like the desert' (Isa. 27:10). Most famously, it occurs in the first line of the book of Lamentations: 'How solitary *[badad]* sits the city once full of people.'

Badad always has a negative connotation except when used

of God, who, in monotheism, is necessarily alone. The phrase 'a people that dwells alone' is like Max Weber's description of Jews as a 'pariah people'. The first time the words 'not good' appear in the Torah, a similar term is used: 'It is *not good* for man to be alone *[levad]*.' Loneliness, isolation, exclusion—these are not blessings in Judaism. The first article I ever published was a critique of Rabbi Joseph Soloveitchik's essay 'The Lonely Man of Faith'. In Judaism, I argued, faith is not lonely. It is the redemption of solitude, not its celebration.[4]

Consider, I continued, who said the words, 'It is a people that dwells alone.' It was the pagan prophet Balaam, who, according to the Pentateuch, was an enemy of the Israelites. It was he who, having failed to curse the people, advised the Moabites and Midianites to use another strategy that proved more effective (Num. 31:16). The Talmud says, 'Better the curses with which Ahijah the Shilonite cursed Israel than the blessings with which Balaam blessed them.'[5] It also says that *all Balaam's blessings eventually turned into curses,* with one exception: 'How goodly are your tents, Jacob, and your dwelling places, Israel.'[6] The sages believed that though Balaam had blessed the people, he had done so in deliberately ambiguous terms, so that the blessing would become a curse.

I realised I had delivered an outburst, but I felt driven to continue. There is the psychological phenomenon, I said, of the self-fulfilling prophecy. There is a mass of scientific evidence that people adjust their behaviour to the image they carry of themselves. Pupils told they are gifted do well in exams; those who are made to believe they are failures tend to fail. Perception affects performance. The Torah itself gives an example of this. Ten of the spies sent by Moses to spy out the land return and say: we cannot conquer it; the cities are fortified; the people are giants. They added, 'We were like grasshoppers in our eyes, and *so we were in their eyes*' (Num. 13:33). The spies succeeded in demoralising the people, and the result was that their entire generation, other than the two dissenting spies, Joshua and Caleb, was condemned to die in the desert. If you believe you will be defeated, you will be.

That, I concluded, was the perennial Jewish danger. If you define yourself as the people that dwells alone, that will be your fate. You will convince yourself that you have no friends; you are isolated; no one understands you; the world hates you. Your efforts at self-explanation will be half-hearted. Your expectations of winning allies will be low. You will not invest as much effort as others do, to make your case in the audience chamber of the world. For inwardly you are convinced that all efforts will fail. You will have decided that this is the Jewish fate that nothing can change. It was ever thus and always will be.

Jews have enemies, I said, my passion spent, but we also have friends, and if we worked harder at it we would have more.

The Fateful Split: Universalism Versus Particularism

The story I have to tell here is fundamental to understanding contemporary Jewry and why, I believe, it has lost touch with its story and the classic terms of Jewish self-definition. It is a tragic story, of hope unfulfilled, a dream turned into nightmare, a tale of three great betrayals. It began with the French Revolution.

Until the nineteenth century, in most places at most times Jews interacted primarily with one another. They had their own language, their own culture, their own schools, courts and communal sanctions. Within limits, they had autonomy. They were not part of a national culture, because there was no national culture for them to be part of. Besides which, they had few civil rights. They could not attend universities, enter the professions, or become part of the legislature. Even in Britain, one of the most tolerant of modern nations, Jews were not able to sit in the House of Commons as Jews (that is, without taking a Christian oath) until 1858, more than two hundred years after their return under Oliver Cromwell in 1656.

The birth of the nation state changed that situation fundamentally and radically.[7] For the first time, Jews had to ask themselves, 'Who are we? Are we first and foremost Jews who happen to be in France or Germany or England, or are we French, German or English citizens who happen to be Jewish by religious persuasion?' The secularity of nineteenth-century Europe was not neutral. It was based on an essentially Protestant notion that the place of religion is confined to private life—the home and house of worship. Judaism, with its code of conduct governing the whole of life, could not be translated into this language. Hitherto, Jews had defined themselves primarily in terms of their relationship with God. Now, for the first time, they had to define themselves in terms of their relationship with other people: their neighbours and fellow citizens. Were they the same, or were they different?

The result was a fateful split between Jewish universalists and particularists. The universalists embraced the modern world with a passion that was often little less than messianic. At last, a social order was in the making that would end the terrible isolation of the Jews. Any price was worth paying, even if the cost was—as it inevitably was—the compromise of Jewish singularity, the very thing that through the ages had made Jews, Jews. The particularists, often though not always Orthodox Jews, took the opposite view, that Jewish identity was worth saving even if that meant declining the 'brutal bargain' of the modern world.

The current isolationism of Jews, the fearful sense that they are forever destined to be 'the people that dwells alone', is the result of the failure of three great universalist dreams: European emancipation, Russian communism and secular Zionism. The first was destroyed in the Holocaust, the second in the Stalinist purges, and the third is happening today in the form of European anti-Zionism. These were not minor tragedies but major ones, with massive physical costs and traumatic psychological consequences. The result is an inward turn in Jewish life in Israel and most parts of the Diaspora. It is, I believe, a very dangerous development indeed.

If that is the choice—universalism or particularism, *either* engaging with the world at the cost of Jewish identity *or* holding fast to Jewish identity at the cost of disengaging from the world—then Jews would have to make it, one way or another. That is what Jews are doing throughout the world. In the Diaspora, one young Jew in two is marrying out or disaffiliating in some other way. In Israel, many no longer believe in the Jewish identity of the state. The first is individual, the second, collective assimilation. Others are opting for self-imposed segregation. More are going exclusively to rabbinical colleges and avoiding university, and disengaging with the wider culture. They will survive as Jews, but they will be deeply isolated.

My argument is that this is not the choice. Judaism is *both* particularist *and* universalist. Abraham lived apart from his neighbours, but he fought for them, prayed for them, and engaged with them. Moses and the prophets saw Judaism as unique *and* as having a message for all humankind. The split between particularism and universalism, the dissociation of sensibilities in the mind of the modern Jew, is nothing less than a breakdown of traditional identity at the very time that the Jewish future, and the world, need Jews to be both. That is the central argument of this book.

The result has been, since the millennium, a series of dysfunctional responses on behalf of the Jewish people. Two things have happened. Often Jews, and Israelis, have not effectively made their case in the court of world opinion. This is surprising. In the past, Jews lost many things—their property, their homes, their freedoms, sometimes their lives—but one thing they did not lose: an argument. They were the world's great debaters; their culture encouraged it. Yet in the twenty-first century, on many key issues, they *have* lost the argument. Encountering this time after time, I was forced to conclude that Jews had, perhaps unconsciously, internalised the conviction: 'We have no friends but ourselves. The world failed us in the past, and it will fail us again when we need it most.' Jews today tend to protest in shrill terms, without subtlety or nuance, without taking account of the arguments on the other side, failing to notice that the terms in which they construct the argument speak to other Jews, not non-Jews. They fail to follow the first rule of communication: *first seek to understand, and only then seek to be understood.* Having failed to persuade the general public, they conclude: 'We told you so. The world hates us. We are alone.'

Second, Jews have failed in their efforts to create Jewish continuity. A people that dwells alone is a people that most people will not wish to be part of. Who, given the choice, would seek to be a pariah? Who, in all responsibility, would wish to confer on his or her children the fate of being a victim? In pre-modern times, when leaving Judaism meant in effect embracing another faith, Jews had the necessary survival instincts. Conversion was an act of disloyalty against one's people and their past, and few were willing to embrace it. But once the secular society appeared, one could cease to be Jewish without necessarily becoming anything else. Spinoza was the first; many followed; today, in most Diaspora communities, a majority does so. One could have predicted that the only sector of the Jewish people who would thrive under this environment would be those who happily embraced the fate of dwelling alone, that is, segregationist orthodoxy. That is in fact what has happened.

The Universalist Dream

The late Shlomo Carlebach, folk singer extraordinaire, spent much of his life visiting campuses. Towards the end of his life he made a revealing comment: 'I ask students what they are. If someone says, "I'm a Catholic," I know that's a Catholic. If they say, "I'm a Protestant," I know that's a Protestant. If they say, "I'm just a human being," I know that's a Jew.' This is more than just an anecdote. It is a vestige of one of the most tragic episodes in Jewish history: the universalist dream.

It is hard for us in retrospect fully to understand the depth of Jewish belief in the nineteenth century that the messianic age was about to arrive, not in Jerusalem but in Europe, and not in the form of the restoration of the Davidic monarchy but in that of the French Revolution. The Enlightenment promised a new age of science in place of dogma, reason in place of revelation, and a new political order in which, in the words of the French Declaration of the Rights of Man and the Citizen, 'All men are born, and remain, free and equal in rights.'

Wordsworth wrote of that moment,

> Bliss was it in that dawn to be alive
> But to be young was very heaven.

Many Jews invested a similar passion in the new age. They carried with them the memories of centuries of persecution, most recently and vividly the Chmielnicki massacres, of ghettoes, expulsions and pogroms. In Frankfurt, Jews were still confined to the ghetto.[8] Throughout the Middle Ages, there had been a string of false messiahs. The culmination came in the worldwide movement around Shabbetai Zvi in 1665–66. When that ended in savage disappointment—in captivity he converted to Islam—the shockwaves reverberated for generations.

Something had been shaken loose in that upheaval. Jews were restless for redemption. They had experienced exile for too long. Many of them could no longer put their faith in religious redemption. So when a new prospect opened up, of a secular society in which they might have equal rights as citizens, this could not but break the dam of centuries of pent-up expectation and hope. Jews became among the most passionate devotees of the Enlightenment and the prospect it offered of Jewish emancipation. In the words of J. L. Talmon, Jews 'looked upon the French revolution as a date comparable to the exodus from Egypt, and to the issuing of the law from Mount Sinai'.[9] The early Jewish revolutionaries, he writes, dreamed of 'a new religion, a religion of mankind'.[10]

One of the driving ideas of the Enlightenment was universalism. Its aspiration was to seek truth divorced from dogma, which had given rise to the wars of religion that had raged since the Crusades, and in more recent times the Reformation. Its master disciplines were philosophy and science. Science is universal. Its laws, if true, are so everywhere and at every time. Reason, too, is universal. Logic knows no boundaries. If something is logically true, it is true in all possible worlds. Immanuel Kant argued that the same applies to ethics. To behave morally means to act in accordance with a law you would be willing to prescribe for all humankind. Anything less than universal is ipso facto less than moral. That, in effect, condemned Judaism, the very model of a particularist faith.

Yet many Jews embraced the new order, even though it meant relinquishing, downplaying, or reforming their religion. How could they not? For the first time it offered them equality, civil rights and the prospect of societies without discrimination. The dream of reason had among its first and greatest a dvocates a Jew who eventually broke with Judaism, Spinoza. But the same rationalism could be found in other Jewish thinkers from Moses Mendelssohn to Hermann Cohen to Henri Bergson.

There is a universalist dimension to Judaism. It is part of the messianic vision, when 'The Lord will be king over all the earth; on that day he will be one and his name one' (Zech. 14:9). It is present in Jewish ethics, in the commands to love the neighbour and the stranger. It is evident in Isaiah's statement of the role of Israel, to be 'a light to the nations'. These became key texts for the Jewish universalists. Even discounting this, the very secularity of the new nation-states allowed Jews to leave Judaism without embracing either Christianity or Islam. For the first time, society seemed to offer neutral space, an alternative to divisive religious identities.

Messianic universalism took three different forms within European Jewry: Reform Judaism, Marxist socialism and secular Zionism.

The Reform of Judaism

Historically, the first to arise was Reform Judaism, intelligible only against the background of Germany and its deep opposition to the emancipation of the Jews. How, the opponents asked, could Jews become Germans? They could not be loyal citizens of the state, because they dreamed of one day returning to Zion. They could not acquire German culture, *Bildung* and *Sittlichkeit*, because they held to an anachronistic and superstitious faith. They could not fully participate in society, because they kept to a code of law which set them apart in terms of what they ate, what days they kept holy and so on. Judaism was a code of difference in an age in which all citizens were supposed to be the same.

The first Reform place of worship was the Temple opened in Hamburg in 1817. Jews had never before called a synagogue a Temple. The Hamburg reformers gave it this name as a political act: they wanted to show that they no longer sought to return to Jerusalem. A Temple could be built in Hamburg as well. Its leaders assiduously set out to show that none of the features of Judaism that Germans held objectionable were essential. Judaism could be rewritten to exclude them all: the use of the Hebrew language for prayer, the dietary laws and all other socially divisive rituals. Even the Sabbath could be moved to Sunday.

The messianic dimension of Reform was evident to all. By 1843, the *Frankfurter Journal* could write:

> A new Jewish sect has been founded here . . . The supporters—and they already amount to a considerable number—do not adhere to any Jewish-Talmudic ceremony of law; do not look upon circumcision—either as a religiously or as a civilly obliging act; and believe that the Messiah has come in the form of the German Fatherland.[11]

The messianic hope had been translated from the return to Zion into social integration into the new nation-states of Europe. Reform utopianism reached a high point in the declaration of American Reform Jews, the 'Pittsburgh Platform' of 1885:

> We recognize, in the modern era of universal culture of heart and intellect, the approaching of the realization of Israel's great Messianic hope for the establishment of the kingdom of truth, justice, and peace among all men. We consider ourselves no longer a nation, but a religious community, and therefore expect neither a return to Palestine, nor a sacrificial worship under the sons of Aaron, nor the restoration of any of the laws concerning the Jewish state.[12]

However, already in 1862, Moses Hess could write, in his *Rome and Jerusalem,* that it was all in vain. 'Because of the Jew hatred which surrounds him, the German Jew is only too eager to cast aside everything Jewish and to deny his race.' But it was a futile endeavour. Even baptism was not enough to save Jews from 'the nightmare of German Jew-hatred'. Jews believed that Germans hated Judaism, but their real hate was directed at Jews. They objected not to what Jews did but to what they were. As Hess put it, they hated not Jewish practices but 'Jewish noses', not their religion but their race.[13] You can reform a religion; you cannot change your race. He was prophetic. The dream of emancipation died in the Holocaust.

Communism

The second form of Jewish universalism was communism, whose prophet, Karl Marx, was descended from a line of rabbis but whose father had him converted to Christianity when he was six years old. Marx had no residual sympathy for Judaism. His 1843 essay 'On the Jewish Question' drew heavily on the antisemitic theories of Bruno Bauer. Jews epitomised the capitalist order he sought to overthrow.[14] There were many Jews drawn to the revolutionary cause, and they too were attracted to its messianic universalism, which led them to oppose not only Judaism but also Zionism and Jewish socialism (Bundism), which they saw as particularistic and parochial.

'What significance can the interests of a handful of Jews have,' wrote the Jewish revolutionary Pavel Axelrod, when compared to the liberation of the working classes as a whole? Yet he received a rude awakening when the 1881 pogroms revealed a deep streak of antisemitism among the Russian working classes. At that point Axelrod drafted a pamphlet, giving expression to the trauma he felt. Jewish socialists, he wrote, had persuaded themselves that 'there really was no such thing as a Jewish people, that Jews were merely a group of Russian subjects who would later become a group of Russian citizens'. The events of 1881 revealed that in fact most Russians regarded the Jews as a separate nation, as 'Yids harmful to Russia whom Russia should get rid of by any and all means'. He added, 'The Jewish social revolutionaries understood now that they were wrong in forsaking the Jewish masses in the name of cosmopolitanism.' The pamphlet was never published.[15]

Axelrod was a relative rarity. Many leading Jewish communists never realised their mistake until it was too late. Rosa Luxemburg resolutely refused to identify as a Jew. To followers of Marx, she wrote, 'The Jewish question as such does not exist.' When a Jew wrote to her claiming her attention for the atrocities being committed against her people, she wrote back, 'Why do you come with your special Jewish sorrows?' She felt, she said, every people's pain, none more than others. 'I cannot find a special corner in my heart for the ghetto.' Eventually she was murdered.[16]

Leon Trotsky, born Lev Davidovich Bronstein, was similarly indifferent to Jews and Judaism, though he harboured a virulent hatred of Herzl and the Zionist movement. In 1940 he was murdered by a Stalinist agent, his skull split by an ice axe. First Lenin, then Stalin, took his reprisals against the Jews. Only Stalin's sudden death halted the famous 'Doctors' Plot' show trial, widely believed to have been planned as the first act of a drama that would involve the mass deportation of Jews to Siberia, and Russia's own version of the 'Final Solution'.

Secular Zionism

Secular Zionism, of which Moses Hess was the first prophet, was born in the failure of religious reform. Jews had done everything possible to make themselves part of Europe and it had achieved nothing. Theodor Herzl realised this in a moment of life-changing lucidity when he saw the crowds in Paris after the verdict of the Dreyfus trial, shouting, '*Mort aux Juifs.*' Though at the time he knew nothing of the work of Hess, he arrived swiftly at the same conclusion. There was no place for Jews in the nation-states of Europe. Their only hope was to have a nation-state of their own.

For many of the original Zionists, the movement offered the prospect of normalising the Jews, so that they could become 'just human beings'. One of their slogans was *Kechol hagoyim,* 'like all the nations'. Jakob Klatzkin, a radical, wrote that 'Herzl appeared among us not from the national consciousness of a Jew, but from a universal human consciousness. Not the Jew but the man in him brought him back to his people.'[17]

A. D. Gordon, Zionism's secular prophet, said, 'Our revolution is the revolution of the man in the Jew.'[18] Amnon Rubinstein writes that 'within the Zionism there grew a non-Jewish, even anti-Jewish sentiment, stunning in its strengths and in its longings for the pagan and the Gentile'.[19] In 'The Sermon', the famous short story written by Hayim Hazaz, the hero says, 'Zionism and Judaism are not at all the same, but two things quite different from each other, and maybe two things directly opposite to each other! At any rate, far from the same. When a man can no longer be a Jew, he becomes a Zionist.'[20]

In *Galut,* exile, Jews were helpless, powerless, forced to demean themselves constantly, to beg for rights, dependent at every stage on the goodwill of others. There was no chance for Jewish culture to grow, for Jews to express the healthy normality that was, certainly before two world wars, associated with military prowess and national pride. In Israel, Jews would cease to be Jews. They would become—the preferred term of many secular Zionists—Hebrews. Some even suggested that they be called Canaanites.

Central to most streams of Zionism was *shelilat hagolah*, rejection of the Diaspora and everything associated with it. For years after the Holocaust, Israelis did not speak about it, for shame that the Jews of Europe had in their eyes gone like sheep to the slaughter. The only event they were prepared to incorporate into their collective memory was the Warsaw ghetto uprising, the turning point in history when Jews fought back. Israel, for the secularists, would give Jews a normal place among the nations. It would end antisemitism, itself the product of Jewish homelessness. That was Hess's and Herzl's deepest dream.

Three Betrayals

The fact that Israel lies at the heart of the new antisemitism is, for the universalists, the third betrayal. It began with the 1975 United Nations resolution equating Zionism with racism, and has continued unabated ever since. NGOs, the media of Europe and many of its academics turned against Israel at the very time when it had made its most strenuous efforts at peace. It spent seven years negotiating with the PLO (Palestine Liberation Organisation), with which, as a terrorist organisation, it had previously refused to meet. It offered the Palestinians their own state, something the Jordanians and Egyptians had notoriously failed to do. Israel's isolation in the international arena could not but be seen by many as a reprise of the antisemitism of old, this time on a national rather than an individual level. Israel had become 'the Jew among the nations', the pariah state.

I have drawn this thumbnail sketch of modern Jewish history because it is impossible to understand the contemporary power of the phrase 'a people that dwells alone' without it. This is not the classic language of Jewish self-understanding.[21] Jews were chosen by God to be a holy people, not a hated one. The day would come, said Moses, when 'All the peoples on earth will see that you are called by the name of the Lord, and they will be in awe of you' (Deut. 28:10). If Jews suffer exile, it is because of their sins, said the prophets, not because of metaphysical destiny or inexorable fate.

Singular, distinctive, unique, the Jewish people believed themselves to be, as did the Greeks and Romans in antiquity and the English, French, Italians, Germans and Americans in the nineteenth century. But Jews did not believe themselves to be friendless and isolated, for the simplest of reasons. Until the nineteenth century they never defined themselves in terms of what other people thought of them. They defined themselves by their relationship with God. The irony is that though it is often religious Jews who use the phrase 'a people that dwells alone', they invest it with a meaning that could arise only once Jewish identity had been secularised.

It is impossible to comprehend the inward turn of the Jewish people in recent years without recognising the profound sense of betrayal that stands close to the heart of many Jews' understanding of their relationship with the world. Three times, Jews dreamed the universalist dream that they would inhabit a world of equality and dignity, free of the religious prejudice of the Middle Ages, and three times the dream became a nightmare.

European nationalism did not deliver its promises. The Enlightenment failed to enlighten. Emancipation failed to emancipate. The Holocaust took place on European soil with the tacit acquiescence, sometimes the active participation, of its leading minds, its philosophers, scientists, doctors, judges and academics. Half the participants of the 1942 Wannsee Conference that planned the Final Solution, the murder of all of Europe's 11 million Jews, carried the title Doctor.[22] Communism, too, turned against the Jews. Even the birth of the state of Israel failed to dissipate prejudice. The old myths, from the Blood Libel to The Protocols of the Elders of Zion, resurfaced, this time directed against the Jewish state. Whichever way they turned, Jews found themselves trapped in a fate they thought they had escaped. They tried everything; everything failed. Modern Jewish history has had the character of a Greek tragedy, and it has happened to a people whose culture is based on the principled rejection of tragedy.

The God of One People or of All?

I have told a story of the inner divide within the Jewish people that opened up in the nineteenth century, between the universalists who sought to save the world at the cost of Jewish singularity and the particularists—mainly the separatist Orthodox—who, to save their Jewish singularity, turned their backs on the world. The result was that Jews were fatally weakened at the time when they needed the greatest strength.

At first, the universalists seemed to be on the winning side, but after the threefold betrayal—the Holocaust, the Stalinist purges and the new anti-Zionism—it is hardly surprising that an era of Jewish particularism has emerged. Jews, at least those intent on staying Jewish and raising their children as Jews, have turned inwards. They are profoundly disillusioned. Who would not be? There could be no contrast greater than that between European Enlightenment on the one hand and Marxism on the other, yet both turned on the Jews who had been among their most passionate devotees. The savage condemnation of Israel by Western intellectual elites and their alliance with totalitarian religious extremism—the *trahison des clercs* ('the betrayal of the intellectuals') of our time—have merely added to their disenchantment. Jews have learned not to trust the world, not to hope, not to expect anything but isolation. 'Jews can rely only on other Jews. We are the hated people, the people that dwells alone.'

Understandable though this reaction is, it is deeply dangerous.

If Jews distrust the world, they will not seek to understand it and learn how to make their case and win allies in the world. They will see antisemitism where other factors are at work. They will lend Jewish identity a negativity that will encourage many young Jews to leave rather than stay. They will fall into the trap of moral solipsism, of talking to themselves in terms only intelligible to themselves. The phrase 'a people that dwells alone' will become a self-fulfilling prophecy that will not augur well for the future of Jews, Judaism or Israel. Those who believe that they are destined to be surrounded by enemies will lack the will and conviction to try to make friends.

It is also misconceived. Jews are not destined to be outcasts, pariahs, friendless in the world. With the birth of the state of Israel, Jews are now part of the world, and they have a vital message to impart, a healing presence to enact. They have earned the right and acquired the duty of speaking to the world, engaging with the world, and to do so as Jews, in the particularity of their faith and the universality of their God.

The universalist dream may have died, but it was the wrong dream to begin with. The view that says Jews are like everyone else, only more so, is vapid; it is also self-deceptive. If Jews are not accepted in their difference, they will not be accepted at all; and if they are not accepted at all, then neither will other minorities be accepted. Antisemitism is never ultimately about Jews. It is about a profound human failure to accept the fact that we are diverse and must create space for diversity if we are to preserve our humanity. Whatever their disguise, their rhetoric, their façade of concern, their intellectual legerdemain, antisemites are enemies of freedom.

Equally unsustainable is the strategy that turns radically inwards, substituting the ghetto of the mind for the ghetto in the street. Some—segregationist orthodoxy—will do this, and it is an honourable vocation. Essentially it has re-created in our time what the priesthood was in biblical times, a segregated elite who minister in the temple of the Lord. But it is always an elitist strategy, with all the virtues and dangers of an elitist culture. When it becomes the general response—the world is not with us or for us; we are destined to dwell apart—Jews will indeed find themselves alone.

The inward-looking strategy made sense for two thousand years, when Jews were dispersed across the globe, everywhere a minority, without rights and without a voice in the public domain. It makes no sense now, in the diverse, multifaith and multicultural liberal democracies of the West. For perhaps the first time in history the Jewish voice is respected. It is turned to for wisdom. If Jews fail to make their voice heard, there will not be silence. The space will be filled by other voices not always sympathetic to Jews and Judaism. Jews were called on to be a blessing to the world. They cannot do that if they are disengaged from the world. The place where that engagement is most important is Israel, the land where Judaism was born.

7

Israel, Gateway of Hope

In 1871, my great-grandfather, Rabbi Arye Leib Frumkin, left his home in Kelm, Lithuania, to go and live in Israel, following his father, who had done so some twenty years earlier. One of his first acts was to begin writing a book, *The History of the Sages of Jerusalem,* a chronicle of the continuous Jewish presence in Jerusalem since Nachmanides arrived there in 1265 and began reconstructing the community that had been devastated during the Crusades.

In 1881, pogroms broke out in more than a hundred towns in Russia. In 1882, the notorious antisemitic May Laws were enacted, sending millions of Jews into flight to the West. Something happened to him as a result of these experiences. Evidently he realised that *aliyah,* going to live in Israel, was no longer a matter of a pilgrimage of the few but a vital necessity for the many. He moved to one of the first agricultural settlements in the new Yishuv. It had been settled some three or four years earlier, but the original farmers had contracted malaria and left. Some were now prepared to go back to work the land but not to live there. It was, they believed, simply too much of a hazard to health.

He led the return and built the first house there. When the settlers began to succeed in taming the land, they were attacked by local Arabs, and in 1894 he decided that it was simply too dangerous to stay, and he moved to London. Eventually he returned and was buried there. On his gravestone it records that he had built the first house.

What fascinates me is the name the settlers gave to the village. I do not know why they decided on this particular name, but I have a guess. It was set in the Yarkon Valley, and when they discovered that it was a malarial swamp, it appeared to them as a valley of trouble. But they knew the Hebrew Bible, and they recalled a verse from the prophet Hosea in which God promised to turn the 'valley of trouble' into a 'gateway of hope' (Hos. 2:15). That is the name they gave the village, today the sixth largest town in Israel: Petach Tikva, the gateway of hope.

I tell this story because opposition to Israel is at the epicentre of the new antisemitism, the spread of which, as I explained in chapter 5, is one of the most significant events of my lifetime. Antisemitism is never harmless. In the past, it has always been a prelude to tragedy. The new antisemitism, born within living memory of the Holocaust, almost defies belief. That Israel finds its very right to exist called into question cannot be passed over in silence. A narrative is taking shape and a climate of opinion is being formed that are dangerous in the extreme, and must be challenged.

It is often said that Israel was created, at the expense of the local population, to make amends for the Holocaust. Europe committed the crime; the Palestinians were forced to pay the price. That is untrue. As my great-grandfather's story makes clear, the return to Zion was being thought about and acted on long before the Holocaust. The Jewish attachment to Israel goes back before the Balfour Declaration in 1917, ratified in 1922 by the League of Nations; before 1890, when the word *Zionism* was coined; before 1862, when Moses Hess wrote the first great document of secular Zionism, *Rome and Jerusalem*.

It goes back to the first recorded syllables of Jewish time, some four thousand years ago, when God told Abraham to leave his land, his birthplace and his father's house and travel to 'the land which I will show you'. Seven times God promised the land to Abraham, once to Isaac and three times to Jacob. The book of Genesis ends with Joseph telling his brothers, 'God will surely come to your aid and take you up out of this land to the land he promised on oath to Abraham, Isaac and Jacob.' Exodus opens with God summoning Moses to lead the Israelites to the 'land flowing with milk and honey'. The whole of the Pentateuch—in a sense the whole of Jewish history—is about the long, arduous journey to Israel, the Promised Land.

The Jewish connection with the land goes back for twice as long as the history of Christianity, three times that of Islam. Jews are the West's oldest nation, and from the beginning Israel was its birthplace, its homeland, its heritage. Benjamin Disraeli, who despite the fact that he had been baptised as a Christian retained enormous pride in his Jewish ancestry, said in reply to an insult by the Irish Catholic Daniel O'Connell, 'Yes, I am a Jew, and when the ancestors of the right honourable gentleman were brutal savages in an unknown island, mine were priests in the temple of Solomon.' Disraeli was in fact a proto-Zionist, and wrote two of the first Zionist novels, *Alroy* and *Tancred*.

Why a Land?

At the heart of Judaism is a mystery, or more precisely a proposition that successive generations have found it hard to understand. Why Israel? Why does the Hebrew Bible so resolutely and unerringly focus on this place, what Spinoza called a mere 'strip of territory'?[1] The God of Abraham is the God of the whole world, a God unbounded by space. Why, then, does he choose any particular space, let alone one so small and apparently unprepossessing?

'Why Israel?' is not unrelated to the more commonly asked question, 'Why the Jews?' The answer lies in the duality that defines Jewish faith and constitutes one of its most important contributions to civilisation. Judaism, as I explained in chapters 4 and 6, embodies and exemplifies the necessary tension between the universal and the unique, between everywhere in general and somewhere in particular.

If there were only universals, the world would consist of empires, each claiming the totality of truth and each demonstrating that truth by attempting to conquer or convert everyone else. When, in 1532, Pizarro and his Spanish troops massacred the Incas, seized their land and took their vast treasures of gold, he told Atahualpa, ruler of the Incas:

> We come to conquer this land . . . that all may come to a knowledge of God and of his Holy Catholic Faith; and by reason of our good mission, God, the creator of heaven and earth and of all things in them, permits this, in order that you may know him and come out from the bestial and diabolical life that you lead . . . When you have seen the errors in which you live, you will understand the good that we have done you by coming to your land . . . Our Lord permitted that your pride should be brought low and that no Indian should be able to offend a Christian.[2]

If there is only one truth, and you have it, then others do not. They live in error, and to save them from that error you can claim religious justification for conquering, converting or even killing them. That has been the source of many crimes and much imperialism in the past and present, and that is why Judaism is a protest against empires.

If, on the other hand, there are only particulars—only a multiplicity of cultures and ethnicities with no universal moral principles to bind them—then the natural state of the world is a ceaseless proliferation of warring tribes. That is where we are today, in a morally relativist world with ethnic conflicts, violence and terror scarring the face of many parts of the globe.

The Abrahamic covenant as understood by Judaism is a principled way of avoiding these two scenarios. Jews belonged somewhere, not everywhere. Yet the God they worshipped was the God of everywhere, not just somewhere. So Jews were commanded to be neither an empire nor a tribe, harbouring neither universal aspirations nor tribal belligerence. Theirs was to be a small land but a significant one, for it was there, and there alone, that they were to live their destiny.

That destiny was to create a society that would honour the proposition that we are all created in the image and likeness of God. It would be a place in which the freedom of some would not lead to the enslavement of others. It would be the opposite of Egypt, whose bread of affliction and bitter herbs of slavery they were to eat every year on the festival of Passover to remind them of what they were to avoid.

It would be the only nation in the world whose sovereign was God himself, and whose constitution—the Torah—was his word. Philo, in first-century Alexandria, struggled to explain this to an audience that was either Greek or Roman, and to do so he had to invent a word: *theocracy,* literally 'rule by God'. But since theocracy has come to mean rule by clerics, the better word is *nomocracy,* 'the rule of divinely ordained laws'.

Judaism is the code of a self-governing society. We tend to forget this, since Jews have lived in dispersion for two thousand years, without the sovereign power to govern themselves, and because modern Israel is a secular state. Judaism is a religion of redemption rather than salvation. It is about the shared spaces of our collective lives, not an interior drama of the soul, though Judaism, in the books of Psalms and Job, knows this as well.

The Jewish God is the God of love: you shall love the Lord your God with all your heart, all your soul and all your might; you shall love your neighbour as yourself; and you shall love the stranger. But because Judaism is also the code of a society, it is also about the social virtues: righteousness *(tzedek/tzedakah),* justice *(mishpat),* loving-kindness *(chessed)* and compassion *(rachamim).* These structure the template of biblical law, which covers all aspects of the life of society, its economy, its welfare systems, its education, family life, employer–employee relations, the protection of the environment and so on.

The broad principles driving this elaborate structure, traditionally enumerated as 613 commands, are clear. No one should be left in dire poverty. No one should lack access to justice and the courts. No family should be without its share of the land.

One day in seven, everyone should be free. One year in seven, all debts should be cancelled. One year in fifty, all land that had been sold was to revert to its original owners. It was the nearest thing the ancient world had ever seen to an egalitarian society.

None of this was possible without a land. The sages said, 'Whoever lives outside Israel is as if he had no God.'[3] Nachmanides in the thirteenth century said that 'the main purpose of all the commands is for those who live in the land of the Lord'.[4] These are mystical sentiments, but we can translate them into secular terms. Judaism is the constitution of a self-governing nation, the architectonics of a society dedicated to the service of God in freedom and dignity. Without a land and state, Judaism is a shadow of itself. In exile, God might still live in the hearts of Jews but not in the public square, in the justice of the courts, the morality of the economy and the humanitarianism of everyday life.

Jews have lived in almost every country under the sun. *In four thousand years, only in Israel have they been a free, self-governing people.*[5] Only in Israel are they able, if they so choose, to construct an agriculture, a medical system, an economic infrastructure in the spirit of the Torah and its concern for freedom, justice and the sanctity of life. Only in Israel can Jews today speak the Hebrew of the Bible as the language of everyday speech. Only there can they live Jewish time within a calendar structured according to the rhythms of the Jewish year. Only in Israel can Jews live Judaism in anything other than an edited edition. In Israel, and only there, Jews can walk where the prophets walked, climb the mountains Abraham climbed, lift their eyes to the hills that David saw, and continue the story their ancestors began.

That, not antisemitism, is why my great-grandfather travelled there to be part of the great rebuilding, and why George Eliot saw the return of Jews to Zion as the rebirth of this ancient people who had taught the world so much.

Why This *Land?*

Why there? The Bible doesn't say. We can only speculate. But implicit in the biblical narrative is an answer: Israel is a place from which it is impossible to build an empire. The geography is wrong. The Judean hills in one direction, the Sinai desert in the other, block easy access to the surrounding lands. The coastal plain is narrow and, in ancient times, open to easy attack from the sea.

The cradle of civilisation was not there. It was in the alluvial plains of the Tigris-Euphrates valley and the rich, well-watered lands of the lower Nile. It was in Mesopotamia that the first city-states were built, and in Egypt that the greatest and longest-lived of ancient empires had its base. So Israel would almost invariably be a small country at the juncture of powerful empires, in a simultaneously strategic and vulnerable location on major trade routes.

The normal movement of population is from poor countries to rich ones, and from rudimentary to more advanced civilisations. The two great Jewish journeys, Abraham's from Ur of the Chaldees, and Moses' and the Israelites' from Egypt, were in the opposite direction. The explanation is, as I have said, that the Bible is a critique of empires. The critique is present in its sketch of the Tower of Babel, whose builders had the hubris that they could, unaided, reach heaven. It is there more explicitly in its portrait of pharaonic Egypt, which first welcomed the Hebrews, then enslaved them.

Israel is a land of small towns and small farms, whose ideal is the modest utopia envisioned by the prophet Micah:

> Every man will sit under his own vine
> and under his own fig tree,
> and no one will make them afraid,
> for the Lord Almighty has spoken. (Mic. 4:4)

The Israelites never aspired to be an Egypt, a colossus, a superpower. To the contrary, in one of the most glorious passages in the Bible, Isaiah imagines a day when God will love Israel's enemies as he loves his own people:

> In that day there will be a highway from Egypt to Assyria. The Assyrians will go to Egypt and the Egyptians to Assyria. The Egyptians and Assyrians will worship together. In that day Israel will be the third, along with Egypt and Assyria, a blessing on the earth. The Lord Almighty will bless them, saying, 'Blessed be Egypt my people, Assyria my handiwork, and Israel my inheritance.' (Isa. 19:23–5)

That is why it is so ironic that Israel should be called an imperialist power. Israel is the only nation to have ruled the land in the past four thousand years that has *not* been an empire and never sought to become one. Israel has been ruled by many empires: Egypt, Assyria, Babylon, Persia, the Ptolemies, Seleucids and Romans, the Byzantines, Umayyads, Abbasids, Fatimids, Crusaders, Mamluks and Ottomans. The only non-imperial power to rule the land was and is Israel.

This explains a much misunderstood sentence. It is sometimes said that the early Zionists claimed that Israel was 'a land without a people, for a people without a land', thus ignoring the non-Jewish population resident there. That was not the original proposition, which was made by a Christian, Lord Shaftesbury, in 1843. He said, 'There is a country *without a nation;* and God now in his wisdom and mercy, directs us to *a nation without a country,* His own once loved, nay still loved people, the sons of Abraham, of Isaac and of Jacob.'[6] The meaning is not that Israel was unpopulated but that Jews were the only nation to have a national, as opposed to individual, claim to the land. At all other times, it existed as, at best, an administrative district within an empire whose base was elsewhere.

The Land That Makes You Look to Heaven

There is another intriguing footnote, within the Bible itself, as to why this land is different. In a masterstroke of delayed information, Moses tells the Israelites as they are almost within sight of the land that there is a qualification to the description he has given previously, that it is 'a land flowing with milk and honey'. It *is* a good land but with one caveat:

> The land you are entering to take over is not like the land of Egypt, from which you have come, where you planted your seed and irrigated it by foot as in a vegetable garden. The land you are crossing the Jordan to take possession of is a land of mountains and valleys that drinks rain from heaven. It is a land the Lord your God cares for; the eyes of the Lord your God are continually on it from the beginning of the year to its end. (Deut. 11:10–12)

Israel is not the Nile delta or the Tigris-Euphrates valley. It is a land dependent on rain, and rain in that part of the world is not predictable. We knew this already: Abraham, Isaac and Jacob all have to leave the land temporarily because of drought and famine. We have merely lost sight of this during the narrative from Exodus to Deuteronomy in which our focus has been on Egypt and the desert. But the passage intimates a correlation between geography and spirituality. Israel is a place where people look up to heaven in search of rain, not down to earth and its natural water supply. It is a place where you have to pray, not one in which nature and its seasons are predictable.

That is part of a larger narrative. Because the terrain of Israel is such that it cannot become the base of an empire, it will constantly be at threat from larger and stronger neighbouring powers. Israel will always find itself outnumbered. It will need to rely on exceptional courage from its soldiers, and ingenuity in battle. That will take high national morale, which in turn will require from the people a sense of belonging to a just and inclusive society.

Commitment will be needed from every individual. They will need to feel that their cause is justified and that they are fighting for something worth preserving. So the entire configuration of the Torah's social ethics, whose guardians were the prophets, is already implicit in the kind of geo-political entity Israel is and will be. It would always be a small and highly vulnerable country, set in a strategic location at the junction of three continents, Europe, Africa and Asia.

There is a metonymic moment at which this is hinted for the first time. It occurs in the first battle the Israelites have to fight for themselves, against the Amalekites after the crossing of the Red Sea:

> So Joshua fought the Amalekites as Moses had ordered, and Moses, Aaron and Hur went to the top of the hill. As long as Moses held up his hands, the Israelites prevailed, but whenever he lowered his hands, the Amalekites prevailed. (Exod. 17:10–11)

The sages understood the symbolism. When the Israelites looked up, they won. When they looked down, they began to lose. Israel, within itself, would always seem to testify to something beyond itself. It would become the land whose history demonstrated the truth spoken by the prophet Zechariah: 'Not by power nor by might but by my spirit, says the Lord almighty' (Zech. 4:6). Its history would be unlike the usual laws of nations, in which victory goes to the strong, the weak are vanquished and great powers rise, bestride the narrow world, and then decline, their place to be taken by another and younger power. Israel would survive, but it would do so against the odds. As with its agriculture, so with its battles: Israel is a people that must lift its eyes to heaven.

The Perpetual Journey

The journey to the land was never easy. Almost as soon as Abraham arrived, he was forced by famine to leave. Jacob and his family went into exile in Egypt, where, generations later, they were enslaved. In the days of Moses, the Israelites made the second great journey to the land. It should have taken weeks, but it lasted forty years. Moses himself died without entering it.

Centuries later, the Assyrians conquered the north, then the Babylonians did the same to the south, destroying the Temple and taking many of the people captive. It might have been the end of Jewish history. But it was there that a great determination was born. In words engraved on the Jewish soul ever since, the exiles vowed never to forget the country to which God had first called them, the place they called home. Though they no longer lived in the land, the land lived on in them. By the waters of Babylon, they made a pledge:

> If I forget you, O Jerusalem,
> may my right hand forget its skill.
> May my tongue cling to the roof of my mouth
> if I do not remember you,
> if I do not consider Jerusalem
> my highest joy. (Ps. 137:5–6)

They came back, reorganised their society, rebuilt the Temple and in the days of Ezra and Nehemiah solemnly renewed their covenant with God. They were conquered again, first by the Greeks, then by the Romans. As long as they were free to practise Judaism, they did not take up arms against their rulers, but they were not always free. That led to three rebellions, the first against the Seleucid Antiochus IV in the second century BCE, then against Rome in the first century CE, and a third time under Bar Kochba in 132 CE.

The first revolt was successful, but the second and third were disastrous. The Temple was destroyed. Jerusalem was levelled to the ground and rebuilt as a Roman *polis,* Aelia Capitolina. Jews were forbidden to enter except on one day of the year, the Ninth of Av, when they mourned the loss of the Temple as if a member of the family had died. The Hadrianic persecutions, after the Bar Kochba rebellion, were so draconian that the Talmud says there were rabbis who argued that Jews should no longer marry and have children, with the result that the Jewish people would cease to be. Slowly, Jewish life moved back to Babylon and elsewhere. The longest exile had begun.

Yet Israel remained the focus of Jewish hopes. Wherever Jews were, they built synagogues, each of which was a symbolic fragment of the Temple in Jerusalem. Wherever they were, they prayed about Jerusalem, facing Jerusalem. They remembered it and wept for it, as the psalm had said, at every time of joy. They never relinquished their claim to the land, and there were places, especially in the north, from which they never left. The Jewish people was the circumference of a circle at whose centre was the Holy Land and Jerusalem the holy city. For centuries they lived suspended between memory and hope, sustained by the promise that one day God would bring them back.

Throughout the Middle Ages, until modern times, when they could, they returned. Judah Halevi set sail to go there in 1140, though we do not know if he reached his destination. Maimonides and his family went there in 1165, though they were unable to stay in a land ravaged by the Crusaders and were eventually forced to leave and go to Egypt. Nachmanides went in 1267 and revived the Jewish community in Jerusalem.

In the fifteenth and sixteenth centuries, exiles came from Spain and Portugal, turning the community in Safed into the world centre of Jewish scholarship and mysticism. In the seventeenth century, they came from the Ukraine after the massacres of 1648. In the eighteenth century, disciples of both the Baal Shem Tov and the Vilna Gaon made their way there. In the nineteenth century, as travel became easier, more Jews came.

In 1798, Napoléon began his campaign in the Middle East, landing first in Egypt, then in Palestine. With his strong sense of history, he realised that this could herald the return of Jews to the land from which they had been exiled for so long. He called on them to take up the challenge, but his own campaign foundered and nothing came of the offer. Soon thereafter, the French historian Chateaubriand visited Jerusalem. There he found a tiny Jewish community whose persistence filled him with awe. Speaking of the Jewish settlement, he wrote:

> It has seen Jerusalem destroyed seventeen times, yet there exists nothing in the world which can discourage it or prevent it from raising its eyes to Zion. He who beholds the Jews dispersed over the face of the earth, in keeping with the Word of God, lingers and marvels. But he will be struck with amazement, as at a miracle, who finds them still in Jerusalem and perceives even, who in law and justice are the masters of Judea, to exist as slaves and strangers in their own land; how despite all abuses they await the king who is to deliver them . . . If there is anything among the nations of the world marked with the stamp of the miraculous, this, in our opinion, is that miracle.[7]

It was the wave of European nationalism in the nineteenth century that led Jews, as well as non-Jews such as George Eliot and Lord Shaftesbury, to believe that the time had come to re-establish a Jewish state. The first Jewish Zionists, in the mid-nineteenth century, were religious figures, Rabbis Yehudah Alkalai and Zvi Hirsch Kalischer, who heard, in the mood of the age, a divine call to re-establish themselves as a nation in their land.

Soon, though, another force began to emerge: antisemitism. The first to detect it was the erstwhile colleague of Karl Marx, Moses Hess, whose *Rome and Jerusalem* (1862)[8] was the first document of secular Zionism. This was followed by Judah Leib Pinsker's *Auto-Emancipation*[9] after the 1881 Russian pogroms, and then Theodor Herzl's *The Jewish State* (1896)[10] after the

Dreyfus trial in France led him to conclude that Europe was now unsafe for Jews.

With Herzl, the long-standing programme of *aliyah* and settlement became a political movement. The 'return to Zion', a dream as old as the prophets, had become Zionism. Its great achievement was the Balfour Declaration of 1917, a commitment on the part of the British government, by then the dominant power in the Middle East, to establish, in Palestine, a 'national home for the Jewish people'.

Then came 1933, and the rise to power of Hitler. No one who had read or heard his words could doubt the danger. Antisemitism was at the heart of his programme, and laws against Jews were among the first of his acts. Gradually, inexorably, Jews were deprived of their rights, their jobs, their freedoms; they were spoken of as lice, vermin, a cancer in the body of the German nation that had to be surgically removed.

A major humanitarian catastrophe was in the making and many people knew it. In July 1938 world leaders gathered in the French town of Evian to discuss ways of saving the Jews. None was forthcoming. Nation after nation shut its doors. Millions of Jews were in danger and there was nowhere they could go. Jews discovered that on the whole surface of the earth there was not an inch they could call home in the sense given by the poet Robert Frost as the place where, 'When you have to go there, they have to let you in.' From that moment a Jewish homeland, promised twenty years earlier, became a moral necessity.

As the smoke of war cleared in 1945, as the Russians entered Auschwitz and the British Bergen-Belsen, slowly people began to understand the enormity of what had happened. A third of world Jewry had gone up in flames. One and a half million children had been murdered, not just because of their faith, or their parents' faith, but because one of their grandparents had been a Jew. When the destruction was over, a pillar of cloud marked the place where Europe's Jews had once been, and a silence that consumed all words.

Even then, the Jewish situation remained tense. Refugee ships carrying Holocaust survivors to Mandatory Palestine were turned back. There was violence in the land. Britain turned to the United Nations and on 29 November 1947 the historic vote for partition took place. It passed by thirty-three votes to thirteen with ten abstentions, among them Britain: one of the few occasions during the Cold War period that America and Russia voted together, both supporting the motion. There were to be two states, one Jewish, one Arab. Two thousand years of Jewish powerlessness were at an end. On the 5th Iyar 5708, 14 May 1948, the state of Israel was proclaimed. The land promised to Abraham was to be theirs again.

In Search of Peace

On the day of its birth, Israel was attacked by the armies of five states, Egypt, Syria, Lebanon, Jordan and Iraq. A country of a mere six hundred thousand people, many of whom were refugees or Holocaust survivors, faced the full force of nations whose population was 45 million. From then on, Israel was never far from the threat of war or terror.

In 1967, Arab armies gathered in force on Israel's borders. The Egyptian president Abdul Nasser closed the straits of Tiran and spoke of driving Israel into the sea. Israel won a stunning victory in what came to be known as the Six Day War. Seven years later, while most Israelis were in synagogue on Yom Kippur, the holiest day of the Jewish year, Egypt and Syria attacked again, making rapid and devastating advances. For those of us watching these events from afar, on both occasions it seemed as if a second Holocaust was in the making. Eventually Israel drove the invading forces back, and survived.

From then on, the entire nature of the struggle changed. The assault on Israel switched from war to terror, and from nation-states to sub-national groups, spearheaded by the PLO under Yasser Arafat, later succeeded by Hamas and Hezbollah. At the national level, Israel concluded a peace agreement with Egypt in 1979, and with Jordan in 1994. Meanwhile, accompanying the shift to terrorism, an international campaign of delegitimisation began. Its first victory was the 1975 United Nations resolution equating Zionism with racism, a motion Kofi Annan, its General Secretary, was later to call the 'low point' in its history as an institution. The motion was not repealed until 1991.

Israel has often been accused of being a threat to peace. In fact, of the many partition (*i.e.*, two-state) proposals between the Balfour Declaration and today, Israel has accepted them all; its neighbours have rejected them all. Israel agreed to the Peel Commission proposals in 1937; the Arabs rejected them. It accepted the 1947 United Nations resolution; again the Arabs rejected it. In 1948, in the Declaration of Independence, Ben Gurion called for peace; the Arab response was war. In 1967, after the Six Day War, Israel made an offer to return territories in exchange for peace. The offer was conveyed on 16 June 1967. On 1 September 1967, the Arab league meeting in Khartoum gave its reply, the 'Three No's': no to peace, no to negotiation, no to recognition.

In 1969, Golda Meir became Prime Minister. Her first announcement was a call to Israel's neighbours to begin peace negotiations. Within three days, Egypt's President Nasser delivered his rejection with the words, 'There is no call holier than war.' In June 1969, Mrs Meir offered to go personally to Egypt to negotiate an agreement. A Jordanian newspaper commented that she apparently believed 'that one fine day a world without guns will emerge in the Middle East. Golda Meir is behaving like a grandmother telling bedtime stories to her grandchildren.'[11]

Between 1993 to 2001, during the Oslo peace process, Israel made its most generous offers, reaching the point at Taba of offering the Palestinians a state in all of Gaza, some 95–97 per cent of the West Bank, with compensating border adjustments elsewhere, and with East Jerusalem as their capital. Again, the answer was 'no'. Prince Bandar bin Sultan, the Saudi ambassador to the United States and an active participant in the talks, said in December 2000, 'If Arafat does not accept what is available now, it won't be a tragedy, it will be a crime.'[12]

The story of the negotiations has been told in several books. I had the privilege of private meetings with both President Clinton, who led the peace process, and Dennis Ross, chief negotiator for Clinton and his predecessor, George H. W. Bush. Both blamed Arafat for the failure of the talks. Clinton used a striking sentence: 'Ehud Barak [the Israeli Prime Minister] offered the Palestinians more than I thought he would, and more than I thought he should' (I took this to be a reference to Barak's offer to the Palestinians of sovereignty over the Temple Mount). As Ross put it in his book *The Missing Peace,* Rabin and Peres 'had made a historic choice'; Arafat 'made only a tactical move'. Worse, during the peace process 'he continued to promote hostility to Israel'. His failure to condemn violence was, Ross says, a 'travesty'.[13]

Yitzhak Rabin paid for his pursuit of peace with his life, as did Egyptian President Anwar el-Sadat. Both were brave men. I came to know Rabin a little in those years, and gave my public support to the peace process. In October 1995, I became anxious about the growing opposition he faced within Israel itself. I wrote to him privately, urging him to spend more time in talks with the settlers. He wrote me back a moving and deeply personal letter, telling me of his efforts and hopes. In it he said:

> I know that there is no long-term answer to our security problems, and to our co-existence with our neighbours, other than peace. For the sake of our children and grandchildren we cannot forfeit this historic opportunity. I have said many times that we did not pray for nearly two millennia for the return to Zion only to find ourselves ruling over two million Palestinians or creating a bi-national State. I know that you share this view.

The letter was dated 18 October 1995. Our office received it shortly thereafter in cable form. For some reason, however, the letter itself with his signature was delayed and only arrived at the Israel embassy on Tuesday 7 November. That day I had returned from his funeral in Jerusalem and was visiting the embassy to pay my condolences to the ambassador. We opened the letter and read it together in ghostly silence. It felt like a voice from the grave. The Hebrew language has two words for strength, *koach* and *gevurah*. *Koach* is the courage to wage war. *Gevurah* is the courage to make peace. Israel has not lacked either.

What is often not understood is how the Palestinians have checkmated every Israeli move to establish peace. The Oslo peace process led to suicide bombings. Israel's withdrawal from Lebanon led to the Katyusha attacks by Hezbollah—attacks which caused as many Palestinian as Israeli casualties, since in the north of Israel the two populations are roughly equivalent in size. The 2005 withdrawal from Gaza led to the rise of power of Hamas and the sustained missile attacks on Sederot and surrounding towns.

Every Israeli offer, every withdrawal, every hint at concessions has been interpreted by the Palestinians as a sign of weakness and a victory for terror, and has led to yet greater terror. If every Israeli gesture towards its neighbours is taken as an invitation to violence, then peace becomes impossible, not because Israel does not seek it, but because, simply and quite explicitly, Hamas and Hezbollah do not seek peace with, but the destruction of, Israel. What any nation sincerely committed to peace can do in such circumstances, it is hard to know, other than to settle for a long period of conflict limitation.

What is also often forgotten is that Jordan could have created a Palestinian state on the West Bank, which they ruled between 1948 and 1967. They did not. Egypt could have offered the Palestinians a state in Gaza, which they ruled during the same period. They did not. Jordan massacred Palestinians in 1970, forcing them into Lebanon. The Syrians massacred their sympathisers, the Muslim Brotherhood, in Hama in February 1982. In September 1982, there was a massacre, by Phalangists, of Palestinians in Lebanon. During the first Gulf War in 1991, Kuwait expelled all three hundred thousand Palestinians. No Arab country except Jordan offered citizenship to Palestinian refugees. The only nation ever to have offered the Palestinians a state has been Israel.

One of the most debated claims is that in 1948 Israel created the problem of Palestinian refugees. The debate is a live one in Israel itself, with some historians claiming that Israel encouraged some Palestinians to leave. The historical facts are complex. Some fled. Others left voluntarily. Many left at the prompting of the Arab states themselves, urging them to leave while they destroyed the Jewish state, after which they would return triumphant. At the time, Jamal Husseini, vice-president of the Arab Higher Committee, complained to the Syrian representative at the United Nations that the Arab armies 'did not enable the inhabitants of the country to defend themselves, but merely facilitated their escape from Palestine'. After a fact-finding mission to Gaza in June 1949, the head of the British Middle East office in Cairo, Sir John Troutbeck, reported that the refugees 'express no bitterness against the Jews'. Their anger was directed solely at the Egyptians and other Arab states: ' "We know who our enemies are," they will say, and they are referring to their Arab brothers who, they declare, persuaded them unnecessarily to leave their homes.' Some said that they 'would give a welcome to the Israelis if they were to come in and take the district over'.[14]

Also sometimes forgotten is that at the same time some seven to eight hundred thousand Jews were forced to leave Arab states, among them Iraq, Egypt, Yemen, Algeria, Lebanon, Syria, Morocco, Tunisia and Libya, in many of which they had lived for far longer than had the non-Jewish population of Palestine. The plight of the two groups was quite different. The Jewish refugees were absorbed immediately, most by Israel itself. The Palestinian refugees were denied citizenship by every Arab country except Jordan, to be used as pawns in the political battle against Israel. I heard from Bill Clinton himself an extraordinary remark. He said that once Yasser Arafat himself had said to him in a moment of candour: 'Do you think I do not know that you [the Americans] care more about Palestinian children than our Arab friends do?'

I believe that the Palestinians should have a state. So do the overwhelming majority of Israelis. I believe that they should have freedom and dignity, that their children should have a future, that there should be an end to the terrible suffering that has existed since 29 September 2000 because of the collapse of the peace process. Their fate has been a tragic one, and no one with the slightest humanitarian instincts could wish it to continue.

Jews did not return home to deny others a home. That was neither the intent of the early settlers nor the language of the Balfour Declaration or the United Nations resolution. The tragedy is that Israelis can understand the plight of the Palestinians better than any other people on earth. They know what it is to eat the bread of affliction and the bitter herbs of suffering. They know that Jews are commanded to love the stranger.

At the end of his magisterial law code, Moses Maimonides wrote about the messianic age: 'The sages and the prophets did not long for the days of the Messiah so that Israel might exercise dominion over the world, or rule over others, or be exalted by the nations.'[15] All they sought was to live at peace, to find a place where they could worship the free God in freedom and be a blessing to the families of the earth. That Israel has been forced, in self-defence, into acts and attitudes no Jew would have wished for is part of the tragedy.

The broad shape of a solution to the problem of Israel and the Palestinians has never been in doubt. It was implicit in the Balfour Declaration in 1917, explicit in the 1947 United Nations resolution on partition, and set out in detail in all peace proposals since: two states for two peoples, a political solution to a political problem. As Shimon Peres said when someone asked him whether he could see light at the end of the tunnel: 'I can see the light. The problem is, there is no tunnel.' The solution is clear. The question has always been how to get from here to there.

The words that echo in the mind go back to the dawn of Jewish history, when there was a quarrel between Abraham and his nephew Lot: 'Please let there be no strife between you and me and between my herdsmen and your herdsmen; for we are brethren. Is not the whole land before you? Please separate from me. If you take the left, then I will go to the right; or, if you go to the right, then I will go to the left' (Gen. 13:8–9). Abraham was willing to make concessions for the sake of peace. So must Israel, and so most of its population still believe.[16]

A fundamental falsehood permeates almost every discussion of the Israel–Palestine conflict, namely that it is a zero-sum game in which one side loses and the other side wins. That is precisely what it is not. From peace both sides gain. From violence both sides suffer. That is why not only Israelis but also those who genuinely care for the Palestinians and for their children's right to a future must give their support to peace.

Choosing Life

I have tried in this chapter to say what Israel means to me and why I have consistently defended it, sometimes to a hostile British public. No nation is perfect. None can avoid mistakes. Criticism of Israel is legitimate; denial of its right to exist is not. My attachment to it is not political but religious. Israel is the land where Judaism was born, almost four millennia ago, when Abraham and Sarah began their journey. Judaism gave rise in turn to Christianity and Islam, both of which literally or metaphorically claim descent from Abraham and Sarah. Today there are 120 countries in which the majority of the population is Christian.[17] There are fifty-seven member states of the Organisation of the Islamic Conference.[18] There is only one Jewish state, a tiny country, one-quarter of one per cent of the landmass of the Arab world.

Israel has done extraordinary things. It has absorbed immigrants from 103 countries, speaking 82 languages. It has turned a desolate landscape into a place of forests and fields. It has developed cutting-edge agricultural and medical techniques and created one of the world's most advanced high-tech economies. It has produced great poets and novelists, artists and sculptors, symphony orchestras, universities and research institutes. It has presided over the rebirth of the great Talmudic academies destroyed in Eastern Europe during the Holocaust. Wherever in the world there is a humanitarian disaster, Israel, if permitted, is one of the first to send aid. It has shared its technologies with other developing countries. Under immense strain, it has sustained democracy, a free press and an independent—some say too independent—judiciary. Had my great-grandfather, or, for that matter, George Eliot, been able to see what it has achieved, they would hardly believe it. In truth, I hardly believe it when I read Jewish history and begin to understand what Jewish life was like when there was no Israel. For me, more than anything else, Israel is living testimony to the power of Moses' command, 'Choose life.'

Twenty-six centuries ago, in exile in Babylon, the prophet Ezekiel had the most haunting of all prophetic visions. He saw a valley of dry bones, a heap of skeletons. God asked him, 'Son of man, can these bones live?' Ezekiel replied, 'God, you alone know.' Then the bones came together, and grew flesh and skin, and began to breathe and live again. Then God said, 'Son of man, these bones are the whole house of Israel. They say, "Our bones are dried up, our hope is lost *[Avdah tikvatenu]*." Therefore prophesy and say to them: "This is what the Lord says: My people, I am going to open your graves and bring you up from them; I will bring you back to the land of Israel" ' (Ezek. 37:1–14).

It was this passage that Naftali Herz Imber was alluding to in 1877 when he wrote, in the song that became Israel's national anthem, *Hatikva,* the phrase *od lo avdah tikvatenu,* 'our hope is *not yet* lost'. Little could he have known that seventy years later, one-third of the Jewish people would have become, in Auschwitz and Treblinka, a valley of dry bones. Who could have been blamed for saying, 'Our bones are dried up, our hope is lost'?

Yet a mere three years after standing face-to-face with the angel of death, the Jewish people, by proclaiming the state of Israel, made a momentous affirmation of life, as if it had heard across the centuries the echo of God's words to Ezekiel: 'I will bring you back to the land of Israel.'

And a day will come when the story of Israel in modern times will speak not just to Jews but to all who believe in the power of the human spirit as it reaches out to God, as an ever-lasting symbol of the victory of life over death, hope over despair. Israel has taken a barren land and made it bloom again. It has taken an ancient language, the Hebrew of the Bible, and made it speak again. It has taken the West's oldest faith and made it young again. It has taken a shattered nation and made it live again.

More than a century ago, a young Jew from Lithuania, my great-grandfather, built a house on land never before cultivated, and the settlers gave it a name from a verse in the book of Hosea in which God said, 'I will turn the valley of trouble into a gateway of hope.' That remains the Jewish dream. Israel is the gateway of hope.

8

A New Zionism

On 20 January 2009, a bright crisp winter morning, Barack Obama was sworn in as the forty-fourth President of the United States of America, the first African-American to hold that office. It was a historic moment, and the almost two million people who crowded the Mall from the Capitol to the Washington Monument—the largest crowd ever gathered in America for a political event—were intensely aware of it. The nation that had fought a civil war over the abolition of slavery had finally conferred its highest office on, as Obama put it, 'a man whose father less than sixty years ago might not have been served at a local restaurant'. It was a redemptive moment.

His inaugural address touched on the many problems facing America and the world. It was sombre, untriumphant. Four times he used the word 'crisis'. It was a quintessentially twenty-first-century speech. But at the same time it followed the protocol—the language, imagery and key ideas—of almost every other presidential inaugural address since Washington's first in 1789. What Barack Obama was doing was something that sets America's political culture apart from all others in the contemporary world. He was *renewing the covenant*, a form of politics born in the Hebrew Bible.[1]

Covenant had been part of America's self-definition since the beginning. It was present in the Mayflower Compact (1620), whose signatories agreed to 'Covenant and Combine ourselves together into a Civil Body Politic'. It was the theme of John Winthrop's speech to his seven hundred fellow Puritans aboard the *Arabella* in 1630. 'Thus stands the case between God and us,' he said. 'We are entered into a covenant with him for this work.' The people must pledge themselves to 'follow the counsel of Micah, to do justly, to love mercy, to walk humbly with our God'. Then 'we shall find that the God of Israel is among us'. 'We shall be', he added, in a phrase revived by John F. Kennedy, 'as a city upon a hill.'[2]

The biblical story of exodus and redemption, freedom and responsibility, became the American narrative. Americans saw themselves as the new Israel, and America as the promised land. Like the Israelites in the days of Moses, they had escaped from their own Egypt, England, and from a tyrannical pharaoh, George III. They had crossed their Red Sea, the Atlantic, and, like the Israelites, they were about to found a new kind of society, one that would serve as a moral example to the world.

Virtually every American president has explicitly or implicitly rehearsed that story at his inauguration. Jefferson did so in 1805: 'I shall need, too, the favour of that Being in whose hands we are, who led our fathers, as Israel of old, from their native land and planted them in a country flowing with all the necessaries and comforts of life.' So did Lyndon Baines Johnson in 1965: 'They came here, the exile and the stranger . . . They made a covenant with this land.' In 1997, Bill Clinton said: 'Guided by the ancient vision of a promised land, let us set our sights upon a land of new promise.'[3] In my address to the European Parliament on 21 November 2008, two months before the inauguration, I predicted, 'I do not know what Barack Obama will say when he makes his inaugural speech, but he will either mention or allude to the concept of covenant.'[4]

So he did, in textbook manner. There was the reference to the exodus, a journey through the wilderness that involved crossing a sea: 'They packed up their few worldly possessions and travelled across oceans.' There was the covenant itself: 'Our founding fathers . . . drafted a charter to assure the rule of law and the rights of man.' There was the key covenantal virtue, in Hebrew *emunah*, meaning faithfulness to one's promises: 'We the people have remained faithful to the ideals of our forebears and true to our founding documents.' There was the idea, central to covenant, of a commitment handed on by parents to children: 'to carry forward that precious gift, that noble idea, passed on from generation to generation: the God-given promise that all are equal'. There was the covenant idea that nations flourish not by the power of the state but by the duty and dedication of their citizens: 'For as much as government can do and must do, it is ultimately the faith and determination of the American people upon which this nation relies.' The ending was biblical in language and cadence: 'Let it be said by our children's children . . . that we did not turn back nor did we falter; and with eyes fixed on the horizon and God's grace upon us, we carried forth that great gift of freedom and delivered it safely to future generations.'[5]

No other country uses language of this kind, drawn as it is from the books of Exodus, Deuteronomy and the prophets, certainly not Israel, whose political culture is secular and drawn from other sources. In early Zionist thought, Marx tended to be more influential than Moses, Nietzsche than Nehemiah and Tolstoy than Torah. There was a moment just prior to Ben-Gurion's Declaration of Independence in May 1948 that became emblematic of much that was to follow. The religious Zionists insisted that at this historic moment there must be a reference to God. How could Jews witness the realisation, after two thousand years, of the prophetic dream, without thanking God who had brought them back to Zion as he said he would? The secularists refused on principle. For two thousand years Jews had prayed to God to bring them back to the land, and nothing had happened. Only when Jews *stopped* believing in God and started acting for themselves did the Zionist dream become a reality.

There was a stand-off, each side refusing to back down, until a diplomatically minded rabbi, Judah Leib Maimon, proposed the phrase 'Rock of Israel'. To the religious, it meant God. To the secularists, it meant the flint-like strength of the Jewish people. To Ben-Gurion himself, a secularist but also a passionate scholar of the Bible, it had the advantage of being a biblical quotation

(2 Sam. 23:3) taken from the last words of Israel's greatest king, David. The crisis passed, but the tensions remained.

The supreme irony of contemporary politics is that *the United States of America has a Judaic political culture; the state of Israel does not.* I believe that the time has come for this to change. Israel has ignored its own finest gift to politics, the concept of covenant and all that goes with it. It was this idea, taken up in the seventeenth century by thinkers like Thomas Hobbes, John Milton and John Locke, that led to the new birth of freedom in the modern world. It is a remarkable idea, dedicated, as Lincoln said in the Gettysburg Address, to the proposition that all men are created equal, a notion Plato and Aristotle would have found absurd.

This is not a minor matter. Israel is a deeply divided nation, split along lines of religion, ethnicity and culture. At times of relative peace it has known that its future may be more threatened by schisms within than by enemies without. President Chaim Herzog said so in 1986, and opinion polls at various times have shown that a significant proportion of the Israeli public believe likewise. In particular, religion is a divisive rather than a unifying force within Israel itself, and it is precisely this to which the concept of covenant offers a solution, as I hope to show.

The story I tell in this chapter is not simple. I have written about it in other books (*The Politics of Hope* and *The Home We Build Together*), in a secular, non-Jewish and non-Israeli context, but I believe it to be essential to Israel's political future. The prophets who lived and taught two and a half millennia ago were right. They were moral idealists but political realists. They understood that Israel's survival depended less on military strength than on moral conviction, social justice and a cohesive sense of national identity. They also knew that Israel's political culture was meant to be unlike any other, but that the people and their rulers often forgot this, with disastrous consequences.

If I am right, the conclusion is stark: the first challenge of Zionism, the creation of a Jewish *state,* has been brilliantly achieved. The second challenge, the creation of a Jewish *society*, has hardly been tackled at all.

Social Contract

The story begins some three thousand years ago in the eighth chapter of the first book of Samuel. The Israelites had conquered and settled the land. For several centuries they had existed as an amphictyony, a loose confederation of tribes. From time to time when the need arose—usually the prospect of war—a charismatic figure would emerge and lead the people in battle. They were known as judges, though not in the judicial sense: they tended to be military leaders. Every so often there would be a suggestion of formalising the role into a permanent position of leadership, but the general consensus was well expressed by Gideon when the people wanted to make him king: 'I will not rule over you, nor will my son rule over you. The Lord will rule over you' (Judg. 8:23).

The system was fraught with the possibility of anarchy: 'In those days there was no king in Israel: everyone did what was right in their own eyes' (Judg. 17:6; 21:25). So, towards the end of the life of the priest-judge Samuel, the people came and asked him to appoint a king. This displeased him—he took it as a rejection of his leadership—and displeased God even more. 'It is not *you* they have rejected,' he told Samuel, 'but they have rejected *me* as their king' (1 Sam. 8:6–7). Nonetheless, God told Samuel to tell the people what the implications and consequences of appointing a king would be, and if they persisted in wanting one, then their request should be granted.

Samuel's speech to the people is a masterpiece of discouragement:

> This is what the king who will reign over you will do: He will take your sons and make them serve with his chariots and horses, and they will run in front of his chariots . . . He will take your daughters to be perfumers and cooks and bakers. He will take

> the best of your fields and vineyards and olive groves and give them to his attendants . . . He will take a tenth of your flocks, and you yourselves will become his slaves. When that day comes, you will cry out for relief from the king you have chosen, and the Lord will not answer you in that day. (1 Sam. 8:11–18)

The people refused to be dissuaded, and their wish was granted. Samuel appointed Saul as Israel's first king.

The entire episode is puzzling. Moses had already told the people in one of his closing addresses that they should appoint a king: 'When you enter the land the Lord your God is giving you and have taken possession of it and settled in it, and you say, "Let us set a king over us like all the nations around us," be sure to appoint over you the king the Lord your God chooses' (Deut. 17:14–15). Why, if God was in favour then, is he against it now? Does the Bible generally regard monarchy as a good or bad thing? If good, why does God consider the people's request a rejection of him? Why does Samuel try to discourage the people from going ahead with the idea? And if bad, why does God give his command in Deuteronomy and his consent here?

The ambiguities and ambivalences of the key texts led to differences of opinion between the medieval commentators. Maimonides held that the appointment of a king is both a positive value and a command. Abrabanel, a statesman who spent his life in the service of kings and princes, held it to be a mere concession to the sinful nature of human beings.

The thinker who decoded the mystery was the nineteenth-century Talmudist Rabbi Zvi Hirsch Chajes.[6] His argument is that the entire passage is a social contract on Hobbesian lines. According to Hobbes, in a 'state of nature', that is, in a land without government of any kind, there is unmediated conflict. I want what is yours, you want what is mine, and the result is anarchy and bloodshed, a 'war of every man against every man'. No one is safe. If you hire bodyguards, you have no guarantee that they won't try to rob you. Even if they don't, others can muster yet greater forces to challenge your supremacy. Under this condition, familiar to anyone who has lived where the rule of law has broken down, life is 'solitary, poor, nasty, brutish and short'.[7]

It is therefore in each individual's interest to hand over some of his or her powers of freedom of action to a supreme authority who will make laws and administer them. That authority, whether it was a monarch or some other form of government, he called 'the great Leviathan'. The creation of a central authority was the birth of the state, and thus of political society.

That, says Chajes, is what happened in the days of Samuel. The people, conscious of the weakness of a tribal federation without a central ruler, decided that they needed a leviathan of their own, not so much to ensure the rule of law within as to create a unified defence against enemies without. To be sure, they might have placed their entire faith in God and done without a political structure. But they still had to fight battles, they still had to create national unity, and God was not in principle opposed. If they wished to hand over some of their rights to a king, so be it, within the limitations set out in the book of Deuteronomy (the king must not accumulate wealth, multiply wives or buy horses from Egypt). Samuel's speech sets out precisely the nature of the social contract and the loss of liberty it will entail.

The people assent to the terms, and the arrangement is made. A number of consequences follow. First, from the outset, Israel accepted only the idea of constitutional monarchy. There is no 'divine right of kings': the monarch had no absolute power; his authority was limited to those matters which were in the interests of the nation as a whole. That is why, for example, Elijah challenged King Ahab on his seizure, for personal advantage, of Naboth's vineyard.[8] Second, sovereignty resides with the people. This was especially important when it came to the modern state of Israel. Rav Kook, Chief Rabbi of pre-state Israel until 1935, explained that when there is no king, power reverts to the people who then have the right to choose how they wish to be governed, which may be by a democratically elected parliament, a Knesset.[9] Third, Judaism has a predisposition to *limited* government, since every transfer of power to a central authority involves a sacrifice of liberty and, ideally, the more freedom we have to serve God, the better.

Implicit in the whole account and the subsequent history of the monarchy in Israel is that politics involves risk. Power corrupts both the powerful and the powerless. Thus emerged the unique biblical institution of the prophet, the man or woman empowered by God to speak truth to power. If Chajes' interpretation is correct, it follows that 1 Samuel 8 is a political text of the highest importance. The question was asked in the seventeenth and eighteenth centuries as to whether the social contract ever actually happened, or whether it was a theoretical construct. It did happen, in the days of Samuel.

Social Covenant

It is just here that the unique structure of biblical politics becomes visible. For the birth of Israel's monarchy, its social contract, was *not* its birth as a body politic. It was the *second* foundational event in Jewish political history, not the first. In this respect, biblical politics is different from every other account given in Western thought.

The first event took place at Mount Sinai in the days of Moses. It was there that God proposed a covenant with the people:

> You have seen what I did to Egypt, and how I carried you on eagles' wings and brought you to myself. Now if you obey me fully and keep my covenant, then out of all nations you will be my treasured possession, though the whole earth is mine. You will be for me a kingdom of priests and a holy nation. (Exod. 19:6)

God tells Moses to take this proposal to the people, to see whether they are willing to agree. Moses does, and the people give their consent, both before and after the revelation when they hear the Ten Commandments. Before: 'The people all responded together, "We will do everything the Lord has said" ' (Exod. 19:8). After: 'They responded with one voice, "Everything the Lord has said we will do" ' (Exod. 24:3). This was Israel's great foundational moment, its birth as a body politic, a nation under the sovereignty of God.

What was transacted at Sinai was not a *contract*. It was a *covenant*. In a contract, two or more individuals, each pursuing their own interest, come together to make an exchange for mutual benefit. So there are commercial contracts that create the market, and there is the social contract that creates the state. A covenant is something different, more like a marriage than a deal. In a covenant, two or more individuals, each respecting the dignity and integrity of the other, come together in a bond of love and trust, to share their interests, sometimes their lives, by pledging their faithfulness to one another, to do together what neither can achieve alone.

A contract is a *transaction*. A covenant is a *relationship*. A contract is about interests. A covenant is about identity. It is about two or more 'I's coming together to form a 'We'. A contract can be terminated by mutual consent when it is no longer in the interests of the parties to continue. A covenant binds the parties even in—especially in—difficult times. That is because a covenant is not about interests but about loyalty, fidelity, holding together when everything else is driving you apart. That is why contracts *benefit*, but covenants *transform*.

The key element in contract is power. Contracts exist because there is an agency—the law, the police, the courts—to enforce them. Covenants are not about power at all. They are about a mutually binding promise, a moral commitment. The great statement about Jewish covenantal responsibility is the principle—post-biblical but implicit throughout the Hebrew Bible—that *kol Yisrael arevin zeh bazeh*, 'all Israel are responsible for one another'.[10] Covenantal politics is a politics not of power but of the *word:* the word given, the word received, the word honoured in trust.

In one sense, covenants were a recognised feature of politics in the Ancient Near East. They were secular treaties, usually between a strong nation and a weak one. They set out the terms of a relationship. The strong power would protect the weak, in return for which the weak would pledge its loyalty and fealty to the strong.

The Bible took this idea and transformed it in a revolutionary way. It was now conceived of as a partnership between God and a people. God will protect them. He has already rescued them from slavery. In return, they pledge themselves to God, obeying his laws, accepting his mission, honouring his trust. The people are free to choose whether or not to enter into this agreement. God commands Moses to tell them of the proposal and ask them to decide whether they accept it or not. The fact of choice is fundamental, for the Bible portrays God not as an overwhelming force but as a constitutional sovereign. The supreme power, God, grants his people the freedom to decide whether or not to enter into the covenant. Thus was born the first principle of a free society: there is no justified government without the consent of the governed, *even if the governor is creator of heaven and earth.*[11]

No less essential is the participation of the whole people, for each must give his or her consent. It is a point the Bible emphasises twice: '*All the people* responded as one' (Exod. 19:8); '*All the people* responded with one voice' (24:3). This is not democracy in the modern or even the Greek sense, but it is a corollary of the idea that the human person as such is in the image of God. In covenant as the Bible understands it, each individual has significance, dignity, moral worth, the right to be heard, a voice.

Even more significant is the geographical setting. The covenant is made, not accidentally but essentially, in the wilderness. It turns the Israelites from a group of escaping slaves into an *edah,* a body politic, a 'civil society'. But they have, as yet, no country, no territory, no home. They are in the desert. They have not entered the land. In the history of every other known polity, first comes the territory, then, many centuries later, come the laws. In the case of the Bible, the laws precede the land.

What makes biblical politics unique is this dual theory of how individuals come together to order their collective life. The book of Samuel tells of the birth of Israel as a *kingdom*. The earlier book of Exodus tells of its birth as a *nation*. One is a story about rulers, courts, government and the distribution of power. The other is about commandments, relationships, morality and the sharing of responsibility. What does this mean in political terms?

The Difference Between State and Society

Overwhelmingly, the history of political theory has been about the *state,* about how a nation is governed: who rules whom, and how. The great political struggles have been about power. The Bible is full of such stories, as are most other works of history. What is unusual about the Bible considered as a political text is that it regards this as a secondary issue altogether, a distraction from the core business of human interaction. Its primary interest is *society.* It is there that the great ideals are tested: justice, compassion, human dignity, welfare, relations between employer and employee, the equitable distribution of wealth, and the social inclusion of those without power—the widow, the orphan and the stranger. That, suggests the Bible, requires a different base, another kind of logic. To these issues, social contract is irrelevant. What matters is social covenant. To put it at its simplest: *Social contract creates a state. Social covenant creates a society.*

The first person in modern times fully to understand and articulate this difference was one of the most colourful characters England has produced, the only figure to have had a front-row seat in both the American and French Revolutions, the man Barack Obama quoted at the culmination of his inaugural address: Thomas Paine. What Paine understood earlier and more clearly than others was the distinction between the two modes of human association. Here is how he set it out at the very beginning of his first great work, *Common Sense:*

> Some writers have so confounded society with government as to leave little or no distinction between them; whereas they are not only different, but have different origins. Society is produced by our wants and government by our wickedness; the former promotes our happiness *positively* by uniting our affections, the latter *negatively* by restraining our vices . . . Society in every state is a blessing, but government, even in its best state, is but a necessary evil . . . Government, like dress, is the badge of lost innocence; the palaces of kings are built upon the ruins of the bowers of paradise.[12]

Society is one thing, the state—governments, kings, the lineaments of power—is another. Society, says Paine, emerges naturally out of the inability of each of us to supply our wants and needs alone. So we co-operate, divide our labours, trade, form friendships and associations, and establish relationships of trust. Were everyone to play his or her part, there would be no need for government at all. But not everyone does. Some cheat. Some steal. Some invade the territory of others. That is when governments become necessary and social contracts are made.

Common Sense was published in 1776, the year of the American Revolution. It was an immediate best-seller: a hundred thousand copies were bought in the first three months. So great was its influence that Paine is sometimes called 'the Father of the American Revolution'. Before Paine, the words 'covenant' and 'contract' were often used interchangeably, and the phrases 'civil society' and 'political society' were thought of as the same thing. In the nineteenth century, others began to write about civil society, most notably Alexis de Tocqueville. In *Democracy in America* he was the first to show how democratic freedom makes demands not only of governments but also of people in their dealings with one another: in families, communities and voluntary organisations, each an exercise in the 'art of association', without which, he believed, democratic societies would eventually fall to the sickness of individualism.[13]

But Paine saw it first—and did so precisely on the basis of a close reading of the Hebrew Bible, which is how he develops the argument in his book. Paine, a natural rebel and a sceptic, was able to read the Bible in a way the more godly did not: as a political document. What he discovered was that the true heroes of the biblical narrative were not kings (government) or priests (organised religion) but prophets: the voice of conscience, the ethical imperative, the people who spoke about the quality of relationships within society. Politics, in the sense of governments and the use of power, is secondary in the Bible. It is a necessary evil. It brings in its wake great dangers, but without it there would be anarchy. Political leaders can rise to greatness: the supreme example in the Bible is King David. But the real arena of collective grace lies with us, the us-together that we call not the state but society.

We can now understand a phenomenon that would otherwise be wholly unintelligible: how Jews survived in exile for two thousand years. They did so because *they were a society before they were a state*. They had laws before they had a land. They had a social covenant before they had a social contract. So, even if the contract failed, the covenant remained. Even if they lost their state, they were still bound together as a covenanted nation. Even if they lost the land, they still had the laws. No other nation has had this dual political structure. No other nation could survive the loss of its land. Though the survival of Jews as a people has seemed to many, among them Augustine, Pascal and Rousseau, to be a miracle, it has a structural explanation. It lay in the unique feature of biblical politics: the priority of covenant over contract, society over state.

Ben-Gurion and the Culture of the State

Covenant is one of the primary forms of society. The others are *organic* and *hierarchical* societies. Organic societies exist when a people have had a long history of living together in the same territory. They tend to be tradition-directed societies in which people do what they do because that is what their ancestors have done 'since time immemorial'. Hierarchical societies are usually the result of conquest and they are always based on status, class or caste, usually though not always conferred by birth. Covenantal societies, today rare, come about when people feel the need to make a new beginning, a 'more perfect union', a 'new birth of freedom'.

Covenant played a decisive part in European history, especially in Switzerland and Holland in the sixteenth century, England and Scotland in the seventeenth. However, as we have seen, it was in America that covenant remained central from the Mayflower Compact to today. America is one of the few polities to have had, as did biblical Israel, a dual founding. Its covenant, setting out fundamental values, was the Declaration of Independence in 1776. Its contract was the Constitution of 1787.

The history of Zionism, by contrast, was dominated from the outset by the idea of state rather than society. This was understandable, given its historical origins. Jews in the Diaspora had, if not a society, then at least a community of communities. What they lacked was political *power,* sovereignty, a state. It was the birth of the European nation-state that created modern antisemitism, because for the first time the question was asked: are Jews really Frenchmen or Germans, or are they merely Jews residing in Germany and France? Herzl understood that if the nation-state created the problem, it also contained the solution. Jews must have a nation-state of their own.

So it was not accidental that the most powerful effort to create a national culture, that of Israel's first Prime Minister David Ben-

Gurion, was called *mamlachtiut*, 'statism', placing the state at the heart of identity. Ben-Gurion sought to create national cohesion. He saw that Israel had to move beyond what he called the 'Diaspora customs of disintegration, anarchy, lack of national responsibility, and unity'. His focus was on the institutions of the state itself, the Knesset, government-owned or -funded bodies, above all the Israel Defence Forces. For Ben-Gurion, *mamlachtiut* was at the heart of the transformation he felt necessary if Jews were to be able to exercise political sovereignty and power, having lacked it for two thousand years.[14]

The essence of *mamlachtiut* was the primacy of the state over civil society, secular law over tradition and custom, government institutions over voluntary bodies. As one observer has written:

> With the establishment of the state, many functions and services—which had hitherto been performed by voluntary organizations—came under the control of central state agencies and governmental ministries. The transfer of authority was accompanied by changes in social values. The establishment of a sovereign state, after so long a period of life in the Diaspora, placed an even greater emphasis on the state as a symbol of national survival.[15]

This involved massive centralisation and secularisation. Nowhere was this more evident than in the army, which was charged not only with the task of military defence but also with the integration of minorities, education, culture, settlement and the absorption of new immigrants. There were those who placed the army in the role once reserved for God. One banner carried by soldiers in a parade in Haifa used the biblical phrase 'Israel, trust the Lord, he is your help and saviour', but for 'the Lord' substituted 'Israel's Defence Forces'. A banner in an army base read, 'In the beginning, the IDF created the soldier, and the IDF created the nation.'[16]

Mamlachtiut rode roughshod over the traditions, mainly religious, of Jews from Arab lands, who were forcibly socialised and secularised in immigration camps and the state school system. Ben-Gurion said about these oriental, Sephardic Jews that they were 'from a Jewish point of view, dust of man, without language, without tradition, without roots, without an orientation to the life of statehood, without the customs of an independent society'.[17] This left lasting resentments until this group organised itself politically in the form of the Shas party in the mid-1980s.

The result was that, though Israel managed remarkably the transition from powerlessness to power, it did so at the cost of weakening the very institutions that had been the source of Jewish strength in the past: communities, charities, voluntary associations and community-based schools. Even religion became a branch of the state. So, while the state grew strong, society grew weak. Instead of an *edah,* there were *edot* in the plural: in place of a single national community, there was an endless proliferation of local communities, differentiated by ethnicity, culture and their place on the religious-secular spectrum. Each had its own political party or parties. Every battle was fought in the political arena.

Philosophical issues became ideological, translated into budget allocations and legislation. Israel's curious electoral system—proportional representation based on party list—maximised the fragmentation of public life. Matters reached a point where Israelis of different persuasions communicated with one another by bumper stickers—brilliantly satirised by novelist David Grossman's 'Sticker Song'.[18] Had it not been for the fact that Israel has, since its birth and for twenty years before, faced a set of common enemies, it might well have split apart along any of a number of fissures. Hence the proposition at the core of this chapter: the first challenge of Zionism, the creation of a Jewish state, has been achieved. The second, the creation of a Jewish society, has hardly begun. What would this involve?

In Search of a Narrative

First, the construction of a national narrative. Even to suggest such a thing sounds absurd. The Bible more or less invented the concept of a national narrative: the story of the exodus, endlessly repeated on Passover, when bringing firstfruits to the Temple and, once the synagogue was established as an institution, as part of the morning and evening daily prayers. Jews were a people of memory—the first people, as Yosef Hayim Yerushalmi has reminded us, to see remembering as a religious obligation.

Yet there is no single national narrative accompanying the modern state of Israel. Instead, there has been a succession of them. The earliest invoked scenes of heroic resistance, from Massada to the defence of Tel Hai and Yosef Trumpeldor's last words (taken from Roman, not Jewish, sources), 'It is good to die for our country.' Then came Ben-Gurion's narrative of a people whose history is recorded in the Bible, read not as sacred scripture but as national literature. This told the story of a people that once made history as a nation in its land, then disappeared from history, living in suspended animation for two thousand years, before coming to life again in the twentieth century.

In the 1960s, after the Eichmann trial brought the Holocaust into Israeli discourse, came the story of *Shoa u-Gevurah,* destruction and rebirth. As Israel began the long peace process of Oslo, yet another voice began to be heard, that of post-Zionism, meaning an Israel without Jewish identity, a liberal democracy with procedures but no traditions. The one voice that might have supplied an enduring narrative, Judaism itself, was more or less ruled out in principle, because Judaism is a religion, and Israel is a secular state.

Again we are in the presence of surpassing irony, for it is the United States, whose political system is predicated on the separation of church and state, that evolved a national narrative based on the biblical idea of covenant. Here, for instance, is John Schaar's account of what America meant to Abraham Lincoln:

> We are a nation formed by a covenant, by dedication to a set of principles and by an exchange of promises to uphold and advance certain commitments among ourselves and throughout the world. Those principles and commitments are the core of American identity, the soul of the body politic. They make the American nation unique, and uniquely valuable, among and to the other nations. But the other side of the conception contains a warning very like the warnings spoken by the prophets to Israel: if we fail in our promises to each other, and lose the principles of the covenant, then we lose everything, for they are we.[19]

This is not a 'civil religion' in the sense given by Jean-Jacques Rousseau. It is not about the state. It is about values higher than the state. This is what Barack Obama meant when he said at his inauguration: 'For as much as government can do and must do, it is ultimately the faith and determination of the American people upon which this nation relies.' And as Schaar noted, it is essentially the vision of ancient Israel's prophets.

The absence of an Israeli national narrative was underscored for me at one significant occasion in Jerusalem. I had officiated at the funeral of a distinguished British Jew, Dorothy de Rothschild. As an eighteen-year-old, she had been Chaim Weizmann's assistant at the time of the Balfour Declaration. When the state of Israel was born, she and her husband, James, donated the money to build the Knesset, Israel's parliament. In her will, she donated the money necessary to construct a new building for Israel's Supreme Court, a project overseen by her nephew Lord (Jacob) Rothschild. Described in the *New York Times* as Israel's finest building,[20] it was opened in 1992. I was present at the ceremony.

It was a biblical moment. The verses almost cried out to be quoted: Isaiah's 'Zion will be redeemed with justice' (1:27), and the psalmist's 'Jerusalem built as a city bound firmly together . . .

There the thrones for judgement stand' (Ps. 122:5). Yet in the many speeches, by Israel's President, Prime Minister and the President of the Supreme Court, there was no reference to the Bible or the significance of justice in Israel's history. The only exception was Dorothy de Rothschild herself, whose letters were quoted by her nephew. She, an English Jew, had understood the biblical resonances of the words *Jerusalem* and *justice;* the leading Israelis had not. If the United States needs a national narrative, and borrows biblical Israel's for the purpose, should Israel itself not do so?

Nor need the narrative be exclusive to Israel's Jewish citizens. George W. Bush, at his second inauguration (2005), became the first President to refer to Islam in an inaugural address, while at the same time invoking the classic American value of civil society: 'Self-government relies, in the end, on the governing of the self. That edifice of character is built in families, supported by communities with standards, and sustained in our national life by the truths of Sinai, the Sermon on the Mount, the words of the Koran, and the varied faiths of our people.'[21] National narratives can be, indeed must be, inclusive.

What has not been noted is that the very institution of American presidential inaugurals is an adaptation of a biblical command, the 612th, known as *Hakhel,* the command that every seven years the king should 'Assemble the people—men, women and children, and the strangers living in your towns—so they can listen and learn to fear the Lord your God and follow carefully all the words of this law' (Deut. 31:12). The Hebrew Bible contains historical accounts of such gatherings in the days of Joshua, Josiah, Ezra and Nehemiah. In effect, these were national covenant renewal ceremonies, in which leaders recalled the nation's history, gave thanks to God and rededicated themselves to the terms of their vocation. That is what Barack Obama was doing on that winter morning in January 2009. The American example shows that it can be done, and done inclusively, even in a secular state.

Civil Society

The second challenge is to re-empower civil society. The extraordinary fact is that for twenty centuries without a state, Jewish communities throughout history managed to create their own educational, health and welfare systems, all run on purely voluntary lines. Few if any would suggest today that in Israel education, healthcare and welfare should be privatised, but this entire tradition of voluntary self-help was Jewry's greatest strength in the past, and it has been twice threatened in Israel. The first time, the threat came from *mamlachtiut* itself, the belief that whatever was to be done for the common good should be done by the state, a view that owes more to East European socialism than to Judaism. The second time it came from the adoption of Thatcherism and Reaganomics and reliance on the market rather than on the state. The result was the growth of consumerism and what J. K. Galbraith called private affluence and public poverty. Neither of these is the covenantal way.

The state and the market have a different logic from that of covenant. The state is about the concentration and application of power. The market is about the production and distribution of wealth. These are two primary modes of human organisation. We get people to act in the way we want, either by forcing them to—the way of power—or by paying them to—the way of wealth.

There is, though, a third way, as we can see by a simple thought experiment. Imagine you have total power, then you decide to share it with nine others. You are left with one-tenth of the power with which you began. Suppose you have a thousand dollars and decide to share it with nine others. You are left with one-tenth of the money with which you began. Now suppose that you decide to share not power or wealth but love, or friendship, or influence, or even knowledge, with nine others. You are left not with less but with more.

The reason is that love, friendship and influence are things that exist only by virtue of sharing. I call these *covenantal goods*—goods such that the more I share, the more I have. In the short term at least, wealth and power are zero-sum games. If I win, you lose. If you win, I lose. Covenantal goods are non-zero-sum games, meaning that if I win, you also win. Wealth and power, economics and politics, the market and the state, are arenas of *competition*. Covenantal goods are arenas of *co-operation*. The home of covenantal goods is not the state or the market but civil society: families, communities, schools, congregations, fellowships *(chevrot)*, communities and society itself, once we have clearly differentiated society from state. Covenantal goods exist wherever human relationships are structured not around wealth or power but around collective belonging and shared responsibility, around, in other words, the principle of 'All Israel are responsible for one another.'

The first philosophers of civil society were the prophets. Unlike the priests, who spoke in terms of holy and profane, permitted and forbidden, pure and impure, the prophets spoke the language of the covenantal virtues: righteousness *(tzedek)*, justice *(mishpat)*, loving-kindness *(chessed)* and compassion *(rachamim)*. Insofar as one can summarise the message of Elijah and Elisha, Amos and Hosea, Isaiah and Jeremiah, and translate it into secular terms, it would be this: Israel is a small nation surrounded by empires. To survive it needs the strongest possible cohesion and morale. People must feel that they are fighting for something precious, a society whose manifest justice and graciousness are apparent to all. Thus motivated, they will defeat powers greater than themselves. If, however, Israel worships the idols of power or wealth, it will lose its corporate identity. The poor will resent the rich; the weak will feel exploited by the strong. The nation will be divided, and a house divided against itself cannot stand.

The shape of Israel's civil society is set out in Psalm 146 as the way of God: 'He secures justice for the oppressed. He gives food to the hungry. The Lord sets captives free. The Lord gives sight to the blind. The Lord raises those bowed down. The Lord loves the righteous. The Lord protects the stranger. He gives courage to the orphan and widow.' It is there in every syllable of Diaspora Jewish life, in the social infrastructures Jews created voluntarily because they had no state to turn to. It is there in the basic idea of the Jewish polity, namely a society of equal dignity in which no one is condemned to poverty or solitude, in which Jews sustain one another through the thousand filaments of connectedness, caring for the sick, visiting the lonely, comforting the bereaved, giving hospitality to strangers: the vision of what Aharon Lichtenstein called 'societal beatitude' which was Jewry's greatest contribution to the moral vocabulary of humankind.

A Judaic civil society depends on the highest priority being given to education. Judaism created the world's first system of universal education, and remains the supreme example of a civilisation predicated on schools and houses of study. Education, in Judaism, is the keystone of the social structure. It is the best way of securing equality and human dignity. It must be the top item in any budget. Jews knew that to defend a country you need an army, but to defend a civilisation you need schools. Education is the Jewish ministry of defence.

Equally, it is here at the level of civil society that Israel must integrate the entire population, Jewish, Muslim or Christian, as equal citizens, 'the stranger in your midst', giving non-Jews precisely the level of dignity and respect that Jews would wish for, were the roles reversed: 'Do not oppress the stranger because you know what it feels like to be a stranger' (Exod. 23:9).

Religion and State, or Religion and Society?

The third proposition is the most controversial but the most necessary. It concerns the relationship between religion and politics, 'church and state'. The role of religion in the United States surprised and intrigued a young French diplomat who travelled there in 1830 and 1832 and wrote one of the finest books ever written about it. The traveller was Alexis de Tocqueville and the book he wrote, *Democracy in America,* remains a classic. In it he described one of the major differences between America and France. In France, religion had power but not influence. In America, religion had no power at all. The First Amendment constitutionally enshrined the separation of church and state. But its influence was immense. Tocqueville discovered to his surprise that though in France religion and liberty were opposed to one another, in America they walked hand in hand.[22]

At first he could not understand why, and he spent considerable time talking to religious leaders to understand what it was about them that made them different. What he discovered, again to his surprise, was that as a matter of principle they did not get involved in politics. Politics by its nature is divisive. The religious leaders understood that if they became involved in politics, they too would become a divisive force in American life, which is not what they wanted at all. So they concentrated on the moral and social aspects of life. They built communities. They created charities. They built schools. Above all they strengthened the institutions of marriage and the family. These had nothing to do with politics but everything to do with the culture in which politics takes place. Tocqueville understood, more than most, that if you want to sustain a democracy, you have to build a society of responsible, public-spirited individuals. That is what religion did, and for that reason he called it 'the first of America's political institutions'.

Religion in Israel does not function in that way. Many, perhaps most, of the early Zionists were not religious. Some were strongly anti-religious. Zionism itself required a certain secularisation of the mind, if Jews were to act on the dream of the return to Zion, rather than wait for God to bring it about. Some were inspired by Nietzsche, others by Tolstoy, yet others by Marx. As for the religious, the book that shaped their thinking was the Babylonian Talmud, which has relatively little to say about politics because it was written in Babylon, where Jews formed communities but had no political power.

The early battles over the character of modern Israel were fought in the arena of the state. They concerned such things as the Sabbath as the day of rest, *kashrut* (Jewish dietary laws) in state institutions, the role of the rabbinate in family law and the national education system. The latter in particular led to the most serious division, because tensions between religious and secular were so deep that they could be resolved only by the creation of two national networks, state-secular *(mamlachti)* and state-religious *(mamlachti-dati)* schools. The result was to socialise young Israelis into a permanent religious-secular culture divide. And because the issues all related to the state, the result was the formation of religious political parties, which exist to this day.

The result is precisely what Tocqueville foresaw. *If religion enters politics, it becomes a divisive, not a uniting, force.* If it seeks power, it will forfeit influence. If it is priestly, it will fail to be prophetic. If it fails to speak on behalf of the nation as a whole, it will fracture into a hundred sects instead of being the animating spirit of the nation. Judaism must be depoliticised and put back where it belongs, in civil society, far removed from all structures of power.

That is the challenge of Judaism in the state of Israel in our time. Its place is *not* in party politics, not as an arm of the state, not as a set of segregated enclaves, not as an 'adversary culture', and not as a territorial ideology. Its role is to create, shape, drive and motivate civil society. If religion is not seen by Israelis as a unifying force in society, if religious Jews are not admired for their work with the poor, the lonely and the vulnerable, if Judaism is not the voice of justice and compassion, then something is wrong in the soul of Israel. To be sure, some of this work happens already; there are admirable examples. But there is much more to be done. Judaism in Israel today has lost the prophetic instinct when it needs it most.

Judaism is about society, not the state. To be sure, Judaism *requires* a state, but it is conspicuous that its structures of governance came to it from the outside. The Torah itself says so. Its first structure of governance—leadership by delegation to heads of thousands, hundreds, fifties and tens—came not from Moses but from a Midianite priest called Jethro. Monarchy itself is described, in both Deuteronomy and the book of Samuel, as a borrowing: 'Let us set a king over us *like all the nations around us*' (Deut. 17:14; 1 Sam. 8:5, 20). Every society, according to Hobbes, has a social contract. Few have a social covenant, and those that do, like the United States, model themselves directly or indirectly on the covenant at Sinai.

The form of politics closest in spirit to Judaism at this time is liberal democracy. Liberal democracy is not Athenian democracy. In ancient Greece, the people existed to serve the state. In Judaism, and liberal democracy, the state exists to serve the people. Liberal democracy respects one of Judaism's most fundamental values: the priority of the personal over the political. It is limited government, of a kind Judaism favours. The liberal democratic state does not aspire to be a vehicle of redemption; it is there to keep the peace, establish the rule of law, and ensure non-violent transitions of power. Although Judaism does not recognise the concept of separation of church and state (neither, for that matter, does England, a liberal democracy with an established church), it recognises a no less fundamental idea, namely the separation of powers between king, priest and prophet, the 'three crowns' spoken of by the sages. The Hasmonean kings were criticised by the sages because they combined kingship and priesthood: in effect, they breached the separation between political and religious leadership. Any attempt to see the state as the highest value is, as the late Yeshayahu Leibowitz never tired of saying, a form of idolatry. Judaism exists to etch social relationships with the charisma of grace. That is not the task of politics.

Societies need hope. Covenantal societies need high moral aspiration. Israel faces a long and difficult struggle to find peace. There is a real and present danger of national despair. Peace is not something one side can achieve alone: it is always a duet, never a solo. There is nothing Israel can do to guarantee peace, but there is something it can do to recapture the moral energy that went into the building of the land. It can renew the social covenant. It can create a new civic Judaism, one that embraces religious and secular, Jew and Palestinian, alike. Zionism Phase 1 gave back to Jewry what it lacked in dispersion: sovereignty and a state. Zionism Phase 2 must reappropriate what Jewry had even when it lacked a state, namely a profound sense of responsibility to the weak, the poor, the socially marginalised, the neglected and unheard. That is the challenge for a new religious Zionism: to build a society worthy of being a home for the divine presence by honouring the divine image in all its citizens.

9
The Jewish Conversation

In 1995 I had the privilege of being awarded the Jerusalem Prize, conferred in Jerusalem on Jerusalem Day. After the ceremony, the then President of Israel, a secular Jew known for his forthrightness, held a reception and made a speech about the recipients of the prize. Turning to me, he said (in Hebrew), 'I see Rabbi Sacks has been given the award for his contribution to religious education in the Diaspora. Well, religious education is better than nothing, but . . .' and proceeded to deliver a tirade against religion, suggesting that what the Diaspora really needs is secular Jewish schools. It was an arguable point, but this was probably not the best time and place to raise it. When I returned to Britain, I recounted the scene to the Israeli ambassador and said, 'Now I understand why, after four thousand years, the Hebrew language still does not have a word that means "tact".' He thought and said, 'In Hebrew, "tact" is—*tact*.' If you want to say it, you have to use the English word.

The same applies to 'civility'. Some years ago, the secular Israeli novelist Amos Oz and I held a public conversation at Bar-Ilan University to show that it was possible for a secular Jew and a rabbi to have a serious, respectful interchange of views. Amos started brilliantly: 'I suspect that I will not agree with Rabbi Sacks about everything—but then, on most things, I do not agree with myself!' As I was looking at the flyer for the event, printed in Hebrew and English, I saw that it was being held under a 'Chair in Judaism and Civility'. To my surprise I saw that the word 'civility' had been translated as *Ezrachut,* which means 'citizenship', a different concept entirely.

Hebrew, a language spoken for longer than any other, lacks

indigenous words for *tact, civility, diplomacy* and *understatement*. In modern times it has had to borrow them. Why? The answer, I would suggest, is that these words arise in cultures that have long held power. To survive, they have had to soften the conflicts that arise in any society. They have had, in Robert F. Kennedy's phrase, to 'make gentle the life of this world'. They have had to lower the temperature and make it possible to disagree without being disagreeable. Lacking power for two thousand years, Jews did not learn the arts of conflict containment. That, today, is dangerous.

A people that dwells alone will eventually be full of people who dwell alone. Unable to construct relationships with others, it will eventually be unable to sustain relationships within its own ranks. It will fragment, religiously into a series of non-communicating sects, politically into a multiplicity of parties. It will suffer destructive divisions, internal wars of culture and creed. Even its communities will be unstable. They will give rise to disagreements they cannot resolve, and they too will split apart. Families will fragment. There will be high rates of divorce, even domestic violence. If these syndromes sound familiar, they are. All of them afflict the Jewish people today, in Israel and outside.

This would be tragic under any circumstances. It is doubly so because Judaism contains some of the most original thinking about relationships between self and other in the entire religious experience of humankind. Judaism is about relationships. The Greeks asked, 'What exists?' Jews asked, 'What is the *relationship* between the things that exist?' The book of Genesis, with its stories of Adam and Eve, Cain and Abel, Abraham and Sarah, Isaac and Rebecca, Jacob and his wives, Joseph and his brothers, is almost entirely about relationships: between husbands and wives, between parents and children and between siblings. The story of the creation of the universe, fundamental to philosophy and science, takes a mere thirty-four verses. The rest of the book is almost entirely about how human beings relate to one another and to God.

Judaism is also about conversation. It is the only religion known to me in which human beings talk, argue and remonstrate with God. Abraham argues with God. So do Moses, Jeremiah, Jonah and Job. There is nothing remotely like this in the sacred books of either Christianity or Islam. And Jews argue with one another. Judaism is the only civilisation whose key texts are *anthologies of argument*. In the Bible, not only do the heroes of faith argue with God. The prophets argue with the people and its leaders, its priests and kings. They speak truth to power, and history lies in the dialectic between prophetic word and human response.

The rabbinic literature continues the tradition. The standard form of a Mishnaic teaching is: Rabbi X says this, Rabbi Y says that. The standard form of Midrash—the literature of early Jewish biblical exegesis—is a series of interpretations, usually incompatible with one another, of the same words. The Talmuds, Babylonian and Yerushalmi, instead of softening the arguments, deepen and intensify them. Standard editions of the Babylonian Talmud have the text surrounded by conflicting commentaries, one by Rashi, the other by the Tosafists, many of whom were his own descendants. *Mikraot Gedolot,* the classic Jewish editions of the books of the Bible, come with multiple commentaries, Rashi saying one thing, his grandson Rashbam another, Ibn Ezra saying a third, Nachmanides explaining the views of others and then disagreeing with them all. Jews know what it is to argue: it is their primary form of discourse. But an argument is a collaborative activity, a conversation scored for many voices. It is not what people do alone. Judaism is a dialogue, not a monologue.

From time to time in Jewish history, movements have arisen to promote particular constellations of Jewish virtues. The Hassidei Ashkenaz, the German-Jewish pietists of the twelfth and thirteenth centuries, were one; the Hassidic movement in the eighteenth century was another; Rabbi Israel Salanter's Mussar movement in nineteenth-century Lithuania was a third. If I had another life, the movement I would initiate would be one that focused on the arts of listening and conversation. There is too much anger and vituperation in the Jewish world today; too much speaking and too little listening; too much condemnation and too little understanding; too much self-righteousness, too little humility; too much seeking respect and too little paying respect; too much preoccupation with our fears and pains, too little attention paid to other people's fear and pains.

These are moral failures. Ultimately they are spiritual failures. In her book *Jews and Power,* Ruth Wisse of Harvard uses the phrase *moral solipsism,* which she defines as 'a reckoning that is preoccupied with its own performance to the exclusion of everyone else's'.[1] Solipsism is the condition of thinking oneself to be alone. That may be the Jewish condition, but it is not the Jewish vocation. It is yet another negative consequence of believing Jews to be the people that dwells alone.

I want, in this chapter, to begin a conversation—a conversation *about* conversation. I want to show in this chapter what a theology of conversation might look like. I choose both words deliberately: *theology,* because what is at stake is more than manners or skills, etiquette or social grace. How we relate to other people shapes and is shaped by how we relate to God. To put it secularly, relationships are at the heart of what it is to be human. Fail there, and we will fail elsewhere. And I speak of *conversation,* not 'dialogue', because dialogue today is associated with formal, staged encounters in which the various sides come with prepared positions. We have a surfeit of dialogues: between faiths, between religion and science, between cultures and between civilisations. Dialogues are rarely genuine encounters.

Franz Rosenzweig once pointed out that Socrates' dialogues—the greatest of their kind in philosophy—are boring, because you know in advance where they will end.[2] Socrates will show that the person with whom he is talking does not really understand what he thinks he believes. The second person in the dialogue is essentially a foil for Socrates' genius, as the only person, according to the Delphic oracle, who knew he didn't know. A dialogue is pre-scripted; a conversation is not. You don't know where it will end. Sometimes you don't know where it will begin. But this you know, that in some sense it will change you, for you are opening yourself up to another mind, an alternative perspective. Conversation is interesting, and quintessentially Jewish, because it is an encounter with otherness. Here, by way of a beginning, are ten Judaic principles of the encounter with otherness.

1. God Lives in Language

Language is creative. God made the world through words: 'And God said, Let there be . . . and there was.' God's first gift to humankind was the power to give names to things: 'Now the Lord God had formed out of the ground all the beasts of the field and all the birds of the air. He brought them to the man to see what he would name them; and whatever the man called each living creature, that was its name' (Gen. 2:19). The Targum, the Aramaic translation of the Bible, reads the phrase in which the first man is made—'and the man became a living being'—as 'and man became a speaking spirit'.[3] When God sought to stop the people of Babel from building their tower, he 'confused their language' so that they no longer understood one another.

God made the natural world with words. We make or unmake the social world with words. The distinctive feature of Homo sapiens is our power of language. It is this that allowed human beings to communicate with one another and thus form collaborative groups. The rabbis said that 'evil speech' is worse than the three cardinal sins—idolatry, murder and incest—combined,[4] because evil speech (gossip, slander, character assassination) destroys the relationships of trust on which society depends.

So words are holy. In Judaism the holiest object is a Torah scroll, for it contains God's word, his greatest gift to humankind. Judaism is a religion of holy words, because it believes in a transcendental God, a God who cannot be seen, felt, touched, represented in images or icons, a God beyond the universe unlike anything within the universe. The only ultimate connection between an infinite God and finite human beings is language. In revelation God speaks to us. In prayer we speak to God. Language is the narrow bridge across the abyss between soul and soul, whether the relationship is between two people or between myself and the Self of the universe. Language is the redemption of solitude.

2. *By Discovering the Other, We Discover Ourselves*

Having created man, God sees him isolated, without an other, and says, 'It is not good for the man to be alone' (Gen. 2:18)—the first occurrence of the words *not good* in the Bible. Dwelling alone is not a blessing but a curse. God then, while the man is sleeping, makes the first woman. Waking and seeing her, the man utters the first poem in the Bible:

> Now I have found
> bone of my bone,
> flesh of my flesh.
> She shall be called 'woman' *[Ishah]*
> for she was taken from man *[Ish]*. (Gen. 2:23)

At the first reading, this sounds as if man is claiming ontological priority. First there was man; only afterwards was there woman. Man comes from God and woman comes from man. That is how the classic Christian theologians read the text. But the Hebrew contains a nuance missed in translation. Biblical Hebrew contains two words for 'man', *adam* and *ish*. Adam is the species. It means, roughly, Homo sapiens. *Ish* is the individual, the person. Until this point, the Bible has consistently used the word *adam*. This is the first occurrence of the word *ish*, and it comes after the word *ishah*, woman.

The Bible is here signalling a momentous proposition. Adam

has to pronounce his wife's name before he can pronounce his own. I have to say 'you' before I can say 'I'. *I have to acknowledge the other before I can truly understand myself.* Not only can I not live alone, I cannot think, know, understand alone.

Sociologists from George Herbert Mead to Peter Berger, and philosophers from Wittgenstein to Charles Taylor,[5] have pointed out that identity is born in conversation. That is because we exist as persons in relation. Without language there is no relationship, and without relationship there is no personhood. Emperor Frederick II was one of several who experimented with bringing up children in total isolation or total silence, to discover which language they would speak: Hebrew, Greek, Latin or Arabic. Of course, they spoke none at all.

There is a beautiful phrase in the Babylonian Talmud: *ein sichah elah tefillah,*[6] which I translate literally as 'conversation is a form of prayer'. Why? Because in conversation I reach out to the human other, just as in prayer I reach out to the Divine Other.

3. *When Words End, Violence Begins*

The story of Cain and Abel also contains a nuance missed in translation. Here is a literal translation:

> And Cain said to Abel
> And it came to pass when they were in the field
> That Cain rose up against Abel and killed him. (Gen. 4:8)

And this is how the first line is rendered in some contemporary translations:

> And Cain talked with Abel his brother . . .
> Now Cain said to his brother Abel, 'Let's go out to the field' . . .
> Cain had words with his brother . . .
> Cain said to his brother Abel, 'Let's go for a walk' . . .

None of them is even close to the Hebrew original, and the reason is obvious. The verse contains fractured syntax. It says, 'And Cain said,' but it does not say *what* he said. To turn it into a coherent sentence, translations are forced either to add words not in the original or to paraphrase the verb from 'said' to 'talked with' or 'had words with'. In so doing, however, they completely miss the point of the verse. Style mirrors substance. The fractured syntax represents fractured relationship. The conversation broke down. 'And Cain said'—but his speech got no further, and there was nothing but tension and silence. *When words fail, violence begins.* That is the point of the verse.

It is a point made elsewhere in the Bible. Early in the story of Joseph we are told that the brothers envied him because of his father's favouritism and the special cloak he wore. The text then says that the brothers 'hated him and could not speak a kind word to him *[lo yachlu dabro le-shalom]*', an unusual form of words which literally means 'they could not *speak him to peace*'. This means, according to Jonathan Eybeschutz, that had they been able to speak openly, had they undertaken to communicate, they would eventually have reached a state of peace.[7] In the event, they plotted to kill him, and finally sold him into slavery.

The theme recurs in the story of Amnon and Absalom in the book of Kings. Amnon had seduced, raped and then abandoned his half-sister, Tamar. Absalom, his brother, was appalled. The text, however, says: 'Absalom never said a word to Amnon, either good or bad; he hated Amnon because he had disgraced his sister Tamar' (2 Sam. 13:22). He silently nursed his vengeance for two years, then he assassinated Amnon and his entire group of associates. Maimonides cites this episode to illustrate the law (Lev. 19:17): 'Do not hate your brother in your heart. Rebuke your neighbour frankly so you will not incur guilt because of him.' The second sentence, says Maimonides, is the antidote to the first. If someone offends you, say so and do not be silent, for otherwise you will come to hate him in your heart.[8] That led, in the case of Absalom, to murder.

The point reappears in another principle of Jewish law. One who kills someone accidentally is given shelter in one of the cities of refuge against reprisal by a relative of the killed person, a blood avenger. But this protection is given only to those who kill by accident, not to those who 'hate' the victim, whose killing cannot be judged to be accidental. This poses an obvious problem for the court. How can human beings know whether the accused hated his victim or not? We cannot look into another person's heart. The law needs a behavioural criterion of hate. The sages ruled that it is deemed to be present if the killer was *not on speaking terms* with the victim ('he had not spoken with him for three days because of hatred,' says Maimonides).

Violence, Alan Brien once wrote, is the repartee of the inarticulate. If we can speak together, we will be able to live together. Speech heals hate; silence incubates it. Such is the verdict of Jewish narrative and law. Ironically, Sigmund Freud, so hostile to any religious expression of Judaism, created psychoanalysis, which is often called the 'speaking cure' but is in fact the *listening cure*.

4. *Listening Is a Religious Act*

Conversation is more than the act of speaking. It involves an act of listening. And here we come to the most fundamental difference between the two great civilisations of antiquity: Athens and Jerusalem, the ancient Greeks and the Israelites. The Athenians excelled at the visual arts—painting, sculpture, architecture, theatrical drama and the spectacle of the Olympic Games. These all involved watching, seeing, being a spectator.

Jews favoured none of these things. Their belief in an invisible God—Freud himself saw this as Judaism's most distinctive feature—led to a systematic devaluation of the visual. Heinrich Graetz, the nineteenth-century historian, summed up the difference between biblical Judaism and all other cultures of its time:

> The pagan perceives the Divine in nature through the medium of the eye, and he becomes conscious of it as something to be looked at. On the other hand, to the Jew who conceives God as being outside of nature and prior to it, the Divine manifests itself through the will and through the medium of the ear. He becomes conscious of it as something to be heeded and listened to. The pagan beholds his god; the Jew hears Him, that is, apprehends His will.[9]

Rabbi David Cohen, the disciple of Rav Kook known as 'the Nazirite', pointed out that this affects our most basic metaphors of knowing.[10] To this day, in English, almost all our words for understanding or intellect are governed by the metaphor of sight. We speak of insight, hindsight, foresight, vision and imagination. We speak of people being perceptive, and of making an observation. We say, 'It appears that . . .' When we understand something, we say, 'I see.'

The Babylonian Talmud, by contrast, consistently uses the metaphor of hearing. When a proof is about to be brought, it says *Ta shma,* 'Come and hear.' When it speaks of inference it says, *Shema mina,* 'Hear from this.' When someone disagrees with a proposition, it says *Lo shemiyah leih,* 'He could not hear it.' When it draws an inference it says, *Mashma,* 'From this it can be heard.' Maimonides calls the oral tradition *Mipi hashemua,* 'from the mouth of that which was heard'. In Western culture, understanding is a form of seeing. In Judaism, it is a form of listening.

It is a theme that runs through the Bible. Moses reminds the people that at Mount Sinai:

> The Lord spoke to you out of the fire. You heard the sound of words but saw no form; there was only a voice. (Deut. 4:12)

Even apparent counter-examples turn out not to be. So, for instance, Moses begins one of his addresses with the word *Reeh,* 'see'. Yet if we attend to the passage as a whole, we realise that it is about listening, not seeing:

> See, I am setting before you today a blessing and a curse—the blessing if you *listen* to the commands of the Lord your God that I am giving you today; the curse if you do *not listen* to the commands of the Lord your God. (Deut. 11:26–7)

That is why one of the key words of Torah, and the first word of Judaism's greatest prayer, is *Shema,* 'Listen'. The nuances of this complex and multifaceted word give rise to one of the strangest features of the Hebrew Bible. The Torah is, among other things, a book of commands. Tradition enumerates them as 613. *Yet biblical Hebrew has no word that means 'to obey'*. How can this be? Obedience stands to command as truth stands to assertion. You cannot have one without the other. But when Hebrew was revived in modern times as the language of the nascent state of Israel, there was a clear need for a verb meaning 'to obey': an army depends on soldiers obeying the orders of their officers. Searching for and not finding such a word, the architects of modern Hebrew had to borrow one from the Aramaic: *letzayet.*

The word the Torah uses instead of 'to obey' is the root *sh-m-a,* which means (1) to listen, (2) to hear, (3) to attend, (4) to understand, (5) to internalise, (6) to respond in action, and thus (7) to obey. This is a fact of the highest significance, because it tells us that the Torah is not what Spinoza, Kant and Hegel thought it was: a series of heteronymous (Other-given) commands that call for mere obedience. The many meanings of the verb *sh-m-a* signal that the divine command is not an arbitrary imperative but one that God issues in the expectation that we will understand, internalise and act accordingly. It is at the heart of what David Weiss Halivni calls Judaism's 'predilection for justified law', law that speaks to the mind and to human understanding.

Judaism is not a religion of seeing but of listening. That—not sexual desire or any of the other fanciful explanations that have been given of it—is the real drama of the sin of Adam and Eve in eating the forbidden fruit. Eve *sees:* 'The woman *saw* that the fruit of the tree was good for food and pleasing *to the eye*' (Gen. 3:4). What neither Eve nor Adam do is to *hear-and-heed* (in Elizabethan English, *hearken,* the closest English came to a word with the same senses as *shema*) the command not to eat it. The story of the first sin is about the tension between a visual culture and an oral-aural one.

5. *To Hear, You Have to Listen*

There is a famous story in the book of Kings (1 Kgs. 18) whose significance is lost on us because we fail to realise that its ending comes later. It is about the confrontation between the prophet Elijah, a zealot, and the false prophets of Baal in the reign of King Ahab and Queen Jezebel. Elijah summons the Baal prophets to Mount Carmel and proposes a simple test that will decide once and for all who is the true God. Let us both prepare sacrifices and call on our deity, he says, and let us see who answers by consuming the sacrifice with fire.

It is, or so it seems, a perfect test, a controlled experiment. The event proceeds. The Baal prophets prepare their offering and call on their God. Nothing happens. They intensify their devotions, but still nothing happens. They work themselves into a frenzy, goring and lacerating themselves, but to no avail. Elijah for once cannot resist a touch of humour: 'Cry louder. Maybe your God is having a sleep.' Eventually they give up, defeated.

Elijah then utters a few words of prayer, and fire descends. He has proved his point, and everyone knows it. The assembled Israelites, awed and convinced, cry out, 'The Lord is God, the Lord is God.' In any other literature, this would be the end of the story. But the Hebrew Bible is anything but a simple-minded book.

The trial is the end of Elijah's encounter with the false prophets but only the beginning of his encounter with God. Unpopular with the king and queen for his treatment of what has become the court religion, a warrant is out for his arrest. He hides. Eventually he finds himself on Mount Horeb, another name for Mount Sinai where, centuries before, the Israelites had received their great revelation of God. There a famous scene takes place (1 Kgs. 19:11–13).

God tells Elijah to stand on the mountain, 'for the Lord is about to pass by'. Suddenly there is a great and powerful wind that tears the mountains apart and shatters rocks. But God is not in the wind. Then there is an earthquake. But God is not in the earthquake. Then there is a fire. But God is not in the fire. Then comes a still, small voice *(kol demamah dakah)*. God is in the voice.

There are many ways of translating the Hebrew phrase usually rendered as 'a still, small voice', or 'a gentle whisper'. Literally it means 'the sound of a thin silence'. My own interpretation is that God's voice is *a sound you can hear only if you are listening.* What God was saying to Elijah was, in effect: your trial was based on error. The prophets of Baal believe that God is power, and you showed them that I am a greater power. But the idea that God is power is pagan. God does not impose himself on humankind. He is always there, but only if we seek him. His word is ever-present, but only if we listen. Otherwise we will not hear it at all. God exists in the silence of the soul when we make space for his voice. The religious encounter, like a true human encounter, requires *active listening.*

6. *Without Argument, There Is No Justice*

As mentioned earlier, there is a phenomenon in the Hebrew Bible that has no parallel: the *argument* between humans and God. It makes its first appearance in the great dialogue between God and Abraham about the fate of the cities of the plain. God announces his intention of destroying them, for their inhabitants are wicked. Abraham, confessing himself 'mere dust and ashes', challenges the verdict. What if there are fifty righteous people, or forty, or ten? Will God punish the innocent along with the guilty? 'Shall the judge of all the earth not do justice?'

It is an astonishing passage and one that seems to make no sense. Does Abraham know something that God does not? Are his standards of justice more exacting? The suggestions are absurd. The text is only intelligible in the light of the prologue in which God says:

> Shall I hide from Abraham what I am about to do? Abraham will surely become a great and powerful nation, and all nations on earth will be blessed through him. For I have chosen him, so that he will direct his children and his household after him to keep the way of the Lord by doing what is right and just, so that the Lord will bring about for Abraham what he has promised him. (Gen. 18:17–18)

This speech, meant to be heard by Abraham, is an *invitation to argument*. It cannot be understood any other way. The words 'Shall I hide from Abraham' tell us that God seeks Abraham's opinion. He wants him to be part of the judicial process. God even gives Abraham the key words of the conversation he wants to ensue: *right (tzedek)* and *just (mishpat)*—which do indeed become key words in Abraham's speech.

What is at stake in this extraordinary encounter? It is not that Abraham knows anything God does not. Nor is it that Sodom and its neighbouring towns harbour righteous individuals. Something else altogether is involved. Justice, in the Hebrew Bible, is a transcendental quality to which God himself is answerable. No power, even divine power, is self-authenticating. No force carries moral authority by virtue of might alone. Even God, ruler and creator of heaven and earth, is a constitutional monarch, bound by moral law.

For justice to be done and be seen to be done, both sides need to be heard. Until an argument for the defence is heard, there can be no guarantee that the verdict is correct. In Jewish law, if the Sanhedrin, the high court, is unanimous in deeming the accused guilty of a capital offence, the verdict is null and void. In the case of God, we have faith in the total justice of his decree. But in Judaism faith is not blind. Therefore there must be a trial, and that is what the dialogue between Abraham and God is. The plaintiff is God, representing justice. The accused are the people of Sodom. Abraham is cast, by God, in the role of counsel for the defence. The judge of all the earth cannot be seen to be performing justice until the case for the defence has been made.

God wants human beings to be agents of justice. That is why he invites Abraham to teach 'his children and his household after him' the principles of the right and the just. By involving Abraham in the deliberations over the fate of the city and its inhabitants, he is asking him to become God's co-participant in the administration of justice. The rabbis expressed this idea when they said, 'A judge who delivers a just verdict becomes a partner of the Holy One, blessed be he, in the work of creation.' God is the judge of all the earth, but we must be involved in that task if there is to be justice on earth.

Justice is process as well as product; deliberation, not just outcome. Both sides, plaintiff and accused, the prosecution and the defence, have a voice. Justice essentially involves the principle *audi alteram partem,* 'hearing the other side'.[11] It is not coincidence that a court session is called a 'hearing'. Justice is a conversation between conflicting points of view. That is an essential part of human dignity: the accused has a voice. The person accused of wrongdoing must be heard. Even Sodom, the place of wickedness, must have no less a figure than Abraham speaking in its defence.

7. *Argument for the Sake of Truth and Heaven*

The sages took this concept and applied it to their own deliberations, coining the phrase 'argument for the sake of heaven'. This is the passage in which it occurs:

> Any argument for the sake of heaven will have enduring value, but any argument not for the sake of heaven will not have enduring value. What is an example of an argument for the sake of heaven? The argument between Hillel and Shammai. What is an example of one not for the sake of heaven? The argument of Korah and all his company.[12]

Following Meiri and other medieval commentators, the sages are here distinguishing between an argument for the sake of *truth* and one for the sake of *victory*. Hillel and Shammai were arguing for the sake of truth, the determination of God's will. Korah, who challenged Moses and Aaron for leadership, was arguing for the sake of victory: he too wanted to be a leader.

In argument for the sake of truth, if you win, you win, but if you lose, you also win, because being defeated by the truth is the only defeat that is also a victory. We are enlarged thereby. In an argument for the sake of victory, if you lose, you lose, but if you win, you also lose, for by diminishing your opponents, you diminish yourself. Moses won the argument against Korah, but only at the cost of invoking a miracle in which the earth opened up and swallowed his opponents. Yet this did not end the argument. The next day the people gathered against Moses, saying: 'You have killed the people of the Lord' (Num. 16:41). In this kind of confrontation, there is no benign outcome. You can aim only at minimising the tragedy.

The entire thrust of postmodernism, inspired by Marx and Freud, is to develop a 'hermeneutics of suspicion' in which there is no truth, only victory. Every argument is a (concealed) exercise of power, an attempt to establish a 'hegemonic discourse'. Judaism rejects this idea, not because it is never true—in the case of an argument not for the sake of heaven, it is—but because we can always tell when it is and when it isn't. There is such a thing as truth, and collaborative argument in pursuit of it. That is the basis of trust on which all genuine communication depends.

8. To Reach Truth You Must Listen to the Other Side

The concept of 'argument for the sake of heaven' allowed the sages to reframe disagreement as a unifying, not just divisive, force. They went further still, in the yet more radical idea that each of two opposing opinions can represent 'the words of the living God'. This is how they characterised the famous disputes between the schools of Hillel and Shammai:

> For three years there was a dispute between the schools of Shammai and Hillel. The former claimed, 'The law is in agreement with our views,' and the latter insisted, 'The law is in agreement with our views.' Then a voice from heaven *(bat kol)* announced, 'These and those are the words of the living God, but the law is in accordance with the school of Hillel.'
>
> Since 'both these and those are the words of the living God', why was the school of Hillel entitled to have the law determined in accordance with their rulings? Because they were kindly and modest, they studied their own rulings and those of the school of Shammai, and were even so humble as to mention the teachings of the school of Shammai before their own.[13]

The sages are here making two different, equally fundamental points. The first is that there is an alternative to the principle of Aristotelian logic, the 'law of contradiction' that states, 'Either p or not-p': an assertion is either true or false. Not necessarily so, say the sages. Two contrary propositions may both be true, from different perspectives, or at different times, or under different circumstances. That both are true follows from the fact that they are both interpretations of a biblical verse. Both therefore represent 'the words of the living God'. And because God grants his people the authority to interpret his word, both views are mandated, though only one can actually become law. God gives his blessing to a multiplicity of perspectives and thus creates the phenomenon of non-zero-sum disagreement. Several views may be true, even if only one is authoritative as law.

The second point, flowing from the first, is that the greatest minds know that theirs is not the only truth. The school of Hillel knew that more than one interpretation can be given. That is why they studied the views of their opponents alongside, and even before, their own. They were 'kindly and modest' because they realised that truth is not an all-or-nothing affair. It is a conversation, scored for a multiplicity of voices. The intellectual arrogance of knowing that you are right, your opponents wrong, is ruled out from the beginning. In the search to know what God wants of us, here, now, every voice is part of the argument, and the argument itself is as important as its outcome.

9. *The Dignity of Dissent*

This means that dissident voices must not be excluded. The Hebrew Bible itself contains dissident voices: the book of Ecclesiastes with its scepticism, and the book of Job, a sustained questioning of divine justice. Nowhere, though, is this more poignantly stated than in a Talmudic passage about the third-century sages Rabbi Yochanan and Resh Lakish. The background to it is that, according to tradition, Resh Lakish was originally a robber or highwayman, who was persuaded by Rabbi Yochanan, the leading sage in the land of Israel at the time, to devote his life to Talmudic study.

One day, in the house of study, the question arose as to when instruments such as swords, spears, daggers and knives are considered complete, and thus capable of becoming ritually unclean. Rabbi Yochanan said they are complete when they have been tempered in a furnace. Resh Lakish said they are not complete until they have been quenched in water. In the heat of the argument, Rabbi Yochanan said, 'Trust a robber to be expert in his trade.'

Resh Lakish, wounded by the jibe, turned on Rabbi Yochanan

and said, 'What benefit have you conferred on me by persuading me to give up robbery and become a rabbi? There, among robbers, I was called master, and here in the house of study I am called master.'

Rabbi Yochanan responded, 'I conferred on you the benefit of bringing you under the wings of the divine presence.'

Scarred by this encounter, Resh Lakish became ill and eventually died.

Rabbi Yochanan grieved for him so much that the other sages feared for his health. They decided that he needed another study partner, and sent him Rabbi Elazar ben Pedat, known for his expertise in Jewish law. This is how the passage continues:

> Rabbi Elazar went and sat before Rabbi Yochanan. To whatever Rabbi Yochanan said, Rabbi Elazar said, 'There is a *baraita,* a rabbinic teaching, that supports you.' Rabbi Yochanan said, 'Do you think you are like Resh Lakish? Whenever I would state something, Resh Lakish would raise twenty-four objections, to which I would respond with twenty-four rebuttals, with the result that we more fully understood the tradition. But all you say is, "There is a *baraita* that supports you," as if I did not know on my own that my view was correct.'[14]

Here in all its depth and pathos is the rabbinic ethic of the pursuit of knowledge as an extended argument between differing views within a fellowship of learning. The text is candid about the dangers. In the heat of the moment, Rabbi Yochanan and Resh Lakish both say things they subsequently regret, with devastating consequences. But Rabbi Yochanan remains insistent that the search for truth can be no less important than the truth itself, that scholarship thrives on challenge, that, as the sages put it, 'rivalry between scribes increases wisdom'. Merely to be told that you are correct adds nothing. Understanding—*religious* understanding—comes from the willingness to be challenged.

The Harvard economic historian A. O. Hirschman wrote a

work titled *Exit, Voice, and Loyalty*. He argued that when any organisation faces problems, those who become aware of them face two options. They can leave and go elsewhere—the option of 'exit'. Or they can raise the problems with those responsible—the option of 'voice'. If the complaints are heeded, people will stay—the choice of 'loyalty'. If they are not, people will leave: 'exit'.[15]

Hirschman also points out that there is a fundamental difference in the way these processes work themselves out in economics and politics. In economics, the free market is built around the possibility of exit. If I do not like X's goods, I will choose to buy Y's. That is what makes the market free. In politics, though, exit is more difficult. It usually means emigration, leaving home and undergoing a fundamental change in loyalties. That is why voice is essential to politics in an open society. Loyalty is predicated on freedom of speech, on minorities being able to speak and have their concerns heeded even if, in the end, they are overruled.

The free society depends, in other words, on *the dignity of dissent*. Judaism itself is predicated on the dignity of dissent. That is what is happening in the dialogues between Abraham and God, and between Hillel and Shammai. Dismiss a contrary view, as R. Yochanan did to Resh Lakish, and you impoverish the entire culture. The book of Job is built on this idea. It is not about whether Job is right or wrong in his complaint about the injustice he feels has been done to him. It is that he has the right to speak, to challenge God, to be heard and (in some sense) to be answered. William Safire, a political journalist, perceptively called his book on Job *The First Dissident*.

10. Argument as a Mode of Conflict Containment

In chapter 2 I noted that at critical moments of their history, Jews have split apart, with disastrous consequences. Why? The most compelling explanation I have ever come across was given by Rabbi Moshe Avigdor Amiel, Chief Rabbi of Tel Aviv between 1936 and 1945. Amiel's thesis is that in Judaism, *the individual takes priority over the community.*[16] One example he gives is the case of the person found guilty of manslaughter. In biblical times the 'cities of refuge' were set aside as protected places for those who had killed inadvertently. So long as the person stayed within the city, he was protected, but if he left, he could be killed without legal reprisal. Jewish law rules that such a person remains within the city (until the death of the high priest) 'even if all Israel have need of him'. This proves, says Amiel, that in Judaism the rights of the individual take priority over the needs of the nation. The individual may never be sacrificed for the group.

This means that Judaism is, as a matter of principle, a highly individualistic culture, and this clashes directly with the principles of politics. As Amiel puts it:

> In order to enforce order, there must be some denial of the individual's rights in society, or sacrifice of the private to the public good. No government or political order in the world can always benefit every individual. Every form of government must strive for the public good, and if the individual must occasionally suffer, there is no great harm done. But the Jewish national character cannot bear this, for Jewish ethics preaches the absolute freedom of the individual, which cannot be abrogated on behalf of society.[17]

According to Amiel, there is a tension within Judaism between the integrity of the individual and the political process itself. He draws the following fascinating conclusion: *the principled individualism of Jews is the source of their greatest strength and their most serious weakness.* Their greatest strength is to have survived in exile. That happened, he says, because Jews refuse to bow to majority opinion. Since Jews were a minority everywhere, had they lacked this obstinate refusal, they would have assimilated into the majority culture and disappeared. However, the same attribute that constitutes Jewish strength in exile becomes a weakness when Jews seek to govern themselves:

> In the Diaspora, our stiff-neckedness is of great benefit—we do not give in when the majority is against us. On the other hand, in our own land this is a disadvantage, as the individual is not willing to submit to the national will of the people of Israel.[18]

The notorious tendency of Jews to split apart follows directly, says Amiel, from the Jewish view that the individual takes priority over the collective. Unless people are willing to submit to the majority, there can be no government, no state, no politics. But Jews are not willing to submit to the majority. Judaism, by its own principles, creates a culture in which 'Everyone considers himself qualified to judge the judges, and sets up his own altar, not accepting any authority.'

Only in this context can we fully understand why the rabbis so carefully constructed a culture of argument for the sake of heaven. Politics demands a measure of conformity, but Jews tend to be non-conformists. Social cohesion requires a degree of submissiveness, but Jews are described in the Mosaic books as a 'stiff-necked people'. They submit (eventually) to God but to almost no one else.

The sages had lived through the disaster of the great rebellion against Rome, in which the Temple was destroyed, and the in some ways even greater disaster of the Bar Kochba rebellion, the greatest human tragedy in Jewish history prior to the Holocaust. They knew they had been defeated because they were divided. How, then, could they continue? Should they encourage conformism and intellectual timidity? That was an option they rejected. What they did instead was to bring difference to the house of study, locate it within the protocols of 'argument for the sake of heaven', and thus create a culture in which strong individuals with strongly held beliefs could disagree without splitting apart. This is how they put it:

> Even a father and son, even a teacher and disciple, when they study Torah in the same gate [the same academy] become enemies to one another. Yet they do not move from there until they come to love one another, as it is written, *et vaheiv besufa* [an obscure phrase in Numbers 21:14]—read this to mean, 'There is love at the end.'[19]

Cohesion does not need agreement. It needs respect for difference under the overarching canopy of a shared culture. So the sages devised a culture of conflict containment in which every view is granted a voice, every opinion tested against the evidence of sacred texts, and even rejected views such as those of the school of Shammai were preserved and treated with respect. Thus was born—continuous with the character of the Hebrew Bible but in a non-prophetic age—a unique rabbinic culture of questioning, critical reflection and argument, containing without suppressing the differences of opinion that must characterise any group of people who think long and hard about the problems they face together.

There is a fine passage in the writings of philosopher Alasdair MacIntyre about the nature of a tradition. When it is in good order, he says, 'it is always partially constituted by an argument about the goods the pursuit of which gives to that tradition its particular point and purpose . . . Traditions, when vital, embody continuities of conflict.'[20] That, supremely, is what Judaism is.

Reviving the Conversation

The inability of Jews to contain their conflicts is a recurring tragedy, one that continues unabated to this day. Its contemporary manifestations have been documented in a spate of recent books, among them Samuel Freedman's *Jew Versus Jew,* Noah Efron's *Real Jews* and Milton Viorst's *What Shall I Do with This People?*[21] It remains Jewry's single greatest weakness. Time and again, Jews find themselves unable to speak with a single voice.

It leads, often, to Jews being their own worst enemies. In a world in which Jews are not short of enemies, this is devotion to divisiveness beyond the call of duty.

Listening is a form of conflict resolution. One of the most intractable problems of Jewish law today is the plight of the *agunah,* the woman unable to remarry because her husband refuses to grant her a *get,* a Jewish divorce. We were determined, in Anglo-Jewry, to resolve this problem, and we took every measure within our power: pre-nuptial agreements, government legislation and communal sanctions against recalcitrant husbands. These solved most of the problems but not all. Two apparently insoluble cases remained. We solved them both but not by Jewish law, English law or communal pressure. *We listened.* We kept listening to both sides until each felt thoroughly heard. I have mediated many conflicts, and always in the same way, by focused, reflective, sustained and concentrated listening. Judaism is a religion of law, so Jews often believe that every problem has a legal (halakhic) solution. Sometimes it doesn't. Sometimes the problem lies not in the law but in the people to whom it applies. That is when you have to listen, in humility and humanity, in total openness to otherness.

Jews have repeatedly brought disaster on themselves because, riven by conflict, they split apart. I began by noting that Hebrew lacked words for *civility, tact, understatement* and *diplomacy.* That is the mark of a people unused to power. It is very dangerous. The religious, cultural, ethnic and political fragmentation of Israeli society, the deep religious divisions of the Diaspora and the tenuous state of Jewish peoplehood are warning signals. When a divided force meets a united one, eventually it loses. The subjects I have addressed in this chapter are therefore anything but peripheral. I see a Jewish people today as divided as it was in the last days of the Second Temple.

The irony, I have argued, is that Judaism contains a unique set of ideas that speak directly to this problem: language as holy, conversation as a kind of prayer, listening as a supreme religious act, justice as the willingness to hear both sides, and argument for the sake of heaven as a way of orchestrating conflicting perspectives into complex harmonies. These ideas, essential to Judaism, are the only way a highly individualistic people with strong beliefs and deep disagreements can stay together in a state of collective grace.

Judaism is a conversation scored for many voices. In a metaphorical sense, that is what the Oral Law, keystone of rabbinic Judaism, is: the dialogue between earth and heaven. Conversation has religious value, but it also has human value, because where words fail, violence begins. And as A. O. Hirschman reminded us, without voice there is no loyalty; instead there is exit. We must learn to listen respectfully to those with whom we disagree. *Shema Yisrael,* 'Listen, Israel', is the greatest command.

If we do not wish to remain 'the people that dwells alone', one conversation in particular needs to be revived—the conversation between Judaism and the world, to which I now turn.

10

Torah and Wisdom: Judaism and the World

In 1756 Voltaire, self-proclaimed defender of liberty, published a virulently antisemitic essay about the Jews. They had, he said, contributed nothing to the civilisation of the world. They had produced no art, no science, no philosophy and no original thought, even in religion. 'In short,' he concluded, 'we find in them only an ignorant and barbarous people who have long united the most sordid avarice with the most detestable superstition.'[1]

Within two centuries after those words were written, Jews had given rise to a stream of geniuses who transformed the very foundations of Western thought: in physics Einstein, in sociology Durkheim, in anthropology Lévi-Strauss, in politics Karl Marx, in philosophy Bergson and Wittgenstein, in the philosophy of science Karl Popper and T. S. Kuhn, in music Mahler and Schoenberg, in literature Proust and Kafka, Bellow and Canetti, in law Brandeis and Cardozo, in art Bernard Berenson and Ernst Gombrich. They dominated the field of psychiatry, with figures such as Freud, Adler, Melanie Klein, Erich Fromm, Abraham Maslow, Erik Erikson and Viktor Frankl. Jews were among the iconic thinkers of postmodernism, among them Walter Benjamin, Theodor Adorno and Jacques Derrida. They spanned the spectrum from Irving Berlin to Isaiah Berlin.

Numbering one-fifth of one per cent of the population of the world, Jews have produced 39 per cent of Nobel Prize winners in economics, 26 per cent in physics, 28 per cent in medicine, 12 per cent in literature, nine winners of the Nobel Peace Prize, 47 per cent of world chess champions, 42 per cent of authors of the fifty most cited twentieth-century books, and 30 per cent of the twentieth century's hundred leading thinkers. It is an unparalleled achievement, so much so that a former editor of *The Times*, William Rees-Mogg, wrote that 'one of the gifts of Jewish culture to Christianity is that it has taught Christians to think like Jews,' adding, 'Any modern man who has not learned to think as though he were a Jew can hardly be said to have learned to think at all.'[2]

Yet it is an achievement tinged with sadness. Many of these figures either renounced Judaism or, like Marx and Wittgenstein, came from families who had already done so. Perhaps it was inevitable. In nineteenth-century Europe there were simply too many doors closed to Jews. Professor Daniel Chwolson, the nineteenth-century Russian-Jewish orientalist, was once asked whether his decision to join the Orthodox Church had been made out of conviction or expediency. 'Conviction,' he replied, 'the conviction that it is better to be a professor in the Academy in St Petersburg than a teacher in a *heder* [Jewish school] in Vilna.' Heinrich Heine called baptism his 'entrance-ticket to European culture'.

Jewish intellectuals in the age of antisemitism were, in effect, secular Marranos. They hid their identity. In some cases—again Marx and Wittgenstein are examples—they overcompensated by developing attitudes that were hardly less than antisemitic. In an essay published in 1919, Thorstein Veblen wrote about the intellectually gifted Jew that he (or she) achieved intellectual independence 'only at the cost of losing his secure place in the scheme of conventions into which he has been born, and at the cost, also, of finding no similarly secure place in that scheme of gentile conventions into which he is thrown'. He becomes 'a disturber of the intellectual peace, but only at the cost of becoming an intellectual wayfaring man, a wanderer in the intellectual no-man's land, seeking another place to rest, farther along the road, somewhere over the horizon.'[3] They were often highly conflicted individuals who sought, through their work, to overcome that conflict.

The paradigm case was Spinoza, the first modern Jew. Spinoza, as Yirmiyahu Yovel has reminded us,[4] came from a family of

Marranos, Jews who, under Spanish persecution, publicly embraced Christianity while privately remaining Jews. This left them doubly alienated, regarded with suspicion by Christians because they were ethnically Jewish, and by Jews because they had abandoned their people and faith. It is not surprising that they or their children sought to create through their work a world in which there were neither Jews nor Christians, just people. They placed their faith in the Enlightenment, science and a highly abstract form of reason. Only in a world purged of particular identities could they be free.

There are two kinds of atheist.[5] There are those who simply do not believe in God. But there are others who, with an almost religious fervour, seek to create a world in which there is no religion at all. Of the second kind, a disproportionate number have been Jews or ex-Jews, most notably Marx, Freud and Spinoza himself. Religion, above all that of their ancestors, had caused them grief. A bearable world would therefore have to be a world without religion. There was no god—and they were his prophet.

So for two hundred years Judaism lost the vast majority of its most gifted minds, at least those who sought to make a contribution in the world outside its walls. Paul Johnson once described Judaism as 'an ancient and highly efficient social machine for the production of intellectuals', but in the modern age the machine failed. The loss of that energy and creativity was immense, incalculable.

At the same time, the reverse also occurred. The great heartlands of Jewish religious life, the yeshivot and Hassidic sects of Eastern Europe, turned inwards, fearing or perhaps simply disdaining the larger intellectual currents of the time. Not wrongly, they recognised something deeply hostile in Enlightenment culture to religion in general and Judaism in particular. The universalism of the Age of Reason was a template into which the particularism of Judaism did not fit.

One of the symbolic moments of that inward turn came when the Volozhyn yeshiva closed its doors in the 1890s rather than accede to a government requirement to teach secular studies, though some have contested that reading of events.[6] There were three great exceptions, figures of immense stature who, at different times, in different places, genuinely engaged with the wider culture of their time: in nineteenth-century Germany, Rabbi Samson Raphael Hirsch; in pre-state Israel, Chief Rabbi Abraham HaCohen Kook; and in twentieth-century America, Rabbi Joseph Soloveitchik. Each had disciples, but the delicate balance they created tended to split apart after their deaths.

The same dissociation of sensibilities prevails today. There are more Jewish students enrolled in universities than ever before. In America, some 90 per cent of Jews attend university. There are also more Jewish students studying in yeshivot than at any time in the past, more than in the days of the great East European academies, Mir, Volozhyn and Ponevez, more even than in the days of the schools of Sura and Pumbeditha that produced the Babylonian Talmud. Yet the connection between these two types of institution is weak and growing weaker. Interchange was once common, certainly in the 1960s, perhaps the high point of modern orthodoxy in America. Today it is rare.

There is a form of cerebral lesion in which the right and left hemispheres of the brain are both intact, but the connection between them is broken. The result is dysfunction of the personality, a failure of mental integration. It would not be an exaggeration to say that the Jewish people are collectively suffering the same kind of cerebral lesion.

In the 1930s the Jewish historian Cecil Roth produced a book called *The Jewish Contribution to Civilization*.[7] It was, as he himself noted, more about the contribution of Jews than of Judaism. In some respects that was inevitable. There is no Jewish science or mathematics or chemistry. But in the arts and humanities, in philosophy and literature, even the social sciences, there is such a thing as a Jewish perspective, and it is of consequence not just to Jews but to the world.

The current alienation between the world of traditional Jewish learning and academic scholarship, between the yeshiva and the university, is an impoverishment of a dialogue that has much to offer both sides. There are notable exceptions, but a wider engagement is one of the real tasks for the future. To state my conclusion in advance: *if we are to apply Torah to the world, we must understand the world.* We need a new generation of Jews committed to the dialogue between sacred and secular if Judaism is to engage with the world and its challenges.

In this chapter I want to set out a general theory of the relationship between Judaism and the universal intellectual enterprise of humankind. I want to move beyond the historic forces that, for two centuries, created a rift between Western culture on the one hand and Jews and Judaism on the other. To do so, I go back to the Hebrew Bible and the early rabbinic literature, to understand the difference and connection between two intellectual categories, Torah and *chokhmah,* 'wisdom'. What we will discover is a theory of the Jewish mind in relation to human thought as a whole, still challenging in its implications.

From Universal to Particular

As already noted, the structure of the Hebrew Bible is unusual and significant. Its subject is the people of Israel, the descendants of Abraham and Sarah. Yet the Torah does not start with Abraham. It begins instead with universal archetypes of humanity as a whole. We read about Adam and Eve, Cain and Abel, Noah and the Flood, Babel and its builders. None of these is a Jew, a Hebrew, an Israelite. They are us in our universality: temptation and sin, sibling rivalry and violence, hubris and the desire for godlike powers. Only after this prologue does the Torah narrow its focus to one man, one family, eventually one nation and its highly specific destiny.

The Torah is a particularist text, but it begins with the universals of the human condition. Is this merely incidental? Are the first eleven chapters of Genesis, from Adam to Abraham, merely a prelude to the history of the people of the covenant, or does the Torah tell these stories for a reason, and for the sake of an enduring truth?

What is absolutely clear is that Genesis tells the story not of one covenant but of two. The first, with Noah after the Flood (Gen. 9), applies to all humanity. The second, with Abraham and his descendants (Gen. 17), does not. It is the covenant of one people, the people with whom God, many centuries later at Mount Sinai, makes a more highly articulated Covenant of Sinai with its 613 commands.

Judaism is built on a dual structure. It has a universal dimension and a particularistic one, neither of which negates the other. God has a general relationship with all humanity and a particular relationship with the children of Israel. Rabbi Akiva expressed this, simply and beautifully, in his statement in *Ethics of the Fathers:* 'Beloved is humanity, for it was created in God's image . . . Beloved are Israel for they are called God's children.'[8]

What is unusual about this movement, from the universal to the particular, is that it is in the opposite direction to the one normally taken in Western civilisation as a whole. Alfred North Whitehead called Western philosophy 'a series of footnotes to Plato', and for Plato the movement of thought is from the particular to the universal. As we mature intellectually, we move from recognising leaves to the concept of a leaf, from specific games to the concept of a game, and so on. Sensations, experiences, direct encounters are always with particulars: this tree, that flower, this garden. But thought is about universals, things that are true everywhere, at all times. The same happens as we come to understand our place in the world. First we recognise our parents, then our family, then friends, neighbours, the community, the town, the region, the nation, until we arrive at the idea of humanity as a whole. The whole thrust of intellectual development is from the local to the global, and from the parochial to the cosmopolitan. High civilisation, on this model, is always marked by its universality.

Judaism moves in the opposite direction, and this alone would be sufficient to mark it as the counter-voice in the conversation of humankind. For the things we love deepest are also the most particular: not people in general, but this person, my beloved; not children in general, but these children, 'bone of my bone, flesh of my flesh'; not places in general, but this place, where I grew up, or where my people was born. Love, loyalty, attachment, identity: these are all fraught with particularity. Can I belong to the world in general without having roots in some particular place? Can I love humanity in general without loving anyone in particular? Science is concerned with generalities and universal laws, but poetry sings the particular: Keats' nightingale, Blake's tiger, Hopkins' kingfisher, Yeats' long-legged fly. Judaism is about the poetry of being and the choreography of love.

All meaning takes place in language, but after Babel there is no one universal language: there are the six thousand languages spoken today, each with its own nuances and inflections. All order is predicated on law, but there are many legal systems, each with its own history and inner logic. All nations have histories and cultures, but none is reducible to others. All life—we now know from studies of DNA—derives from the most primitive eukaryotic cell, but there are some three million species of animal life, the loss of any of which is an impoverishment of our natural heritage. *The miracle of creation is that unity in heaven creates diversity on earth.* Without negating the universal, Judaism is a celebration of particularity.

There are human universals. We are all born. We will all die. We all have need of food, drink, clothing, shelter. We are social animals, and all societies have kinship systems, divisions of labour, leaders and followers, rules of ethics and etiquette, rituals and rites of passage, and so on. Since 1948 the United Nations has recognised a universal code of rights. That, in Judaism, is the nature of the covenant with Noah: a set of universal principles governing such things as the sanctity of life and the imperative of justice. But there are also particularities, one of which, the covenant with Abraham, defines the parameters of Jewish life. *The basic structure of Jewish thought is the movement from the universal to the particular.* That is the first thing we notice about the Torah.

The Two Names of God

The second is that God has two names. In fact, he has many, but throughout the Hebrew Bible, two predominate: the four-letter name which, following Jewish custom, we will call *Hashem* ('the name'), and the name *Elokim*. Why two names and what is the difference between them?

To Judaism's early sages, *Elokim* represents God as justice. *Hashem* is God as compassion and mercy. However, Judah Halevi, in his classic work *The Kuzari,* offered a quite different analysis.[9] The word *El* is a Canaanite term meaning 'a god'. In general in the ancient world, natural forces were often seen as gods, so there was a sun god, a god of the ocean, a god of thunder and rain, and so on. Since Judaism is a monotheism, it sees none of these forces as an independent power. Instead, God created all the forces operative in the universe, and that is what the term *Elokim* signifies. It means the force of forces, the cause of causes, the totality of all powers. *Elokim* is thus a plural, generic noun meaning 'powers'.

Hashem, according to Halevi, is a word of a different grammatical type. It is not a noun but a proper name. *Hashem* and *Elokim* stand to one another as do 'Elizabeth' and 'Queen of England', or 'Barack Obama' and 'President of the United States'. A proper name exists only where we speak of individuals, not classes or types of things. The primary bearers of proper names are *persons,* human beings. In general, we use a proper name, rather than a title or description, as a form of intimacy. It would be lèse-majesté to address the Queen of England as 'Elizabeth'. Though it would no longer condemn you to imprisonment in the Tower of London, it just isn't done. Only those we know well do we call by name. So the name *Hashem* implies closeness of relationship.

If we now look at the distribution of the two names within the Mosaic books, especially Genesis, we make an unexpected discovery. Even after God's choice of, and covenant with, Abraham, the Torah takes it for granted that those outside the covenant may also encounter God. He reveals himself to them and speaks to them. They may even speak to him. They exhibit no surprise. They speak of God, not of Baal, Chemosh, Ra or any of the other deities of the Ancient Near East. In almost all cases, the word used is *Elokim*. *Elokim* is, as it were, common ground between the patriarchal family and its neighbours.

So, for example, when Abraham is forced by famine to go to the land of the Philistines, he fears that he may be killed for the sake of his wife Sarah, and says that she is his sister. She is duly taken into the harem of the king, Abimelech. God *(Elokim)* then appears to Abimelech at night in a dream and warns him that she is in fact married to Abraham. A dialogue about justice then ensues between God and the pagan king, who protests his innocence—not unlike the encounter between Abraham and God over the fate of Sodom.

Similarly, when Abraham negotiates to buy a plot of land in which to bury Sarah, the Hittites call him 'a prince of God *[Elokim]* in our midst'. When Joseph is brought up from prison to interpret Pharaoh's dreams, he says, 'God *[Elokim]* will give Pharaoh the answer he desires,' evidently assuming that Pharaoh will understand the word. Indeed, Pharaoh himself uses it:

> Pharaoh asked [his officials], 'Can we find anyone like this man, one in whom is the spirit of God *[Elokim]*?' Then Pharaoh said to Joseph, 'Since God *[Elokim]* has made all this known to you, there is no one so discerning and wise as you.' (Gen. 41:39)

This is a long way from what we were taught as children: that Abraham grew up among idolaters, that he was a breaker of idols, and that his monotheism was sharply at odds with the culture of his day. To the contrary, Genesis contains no explicit polemic against idols (other than Laban's fetishes). Abraham and Joseph speak about God, but so do Abimelech, Pharaoh, Laban and the Hittites.

Likewise the phrase 'fear of God *[Elokim]*' seems to represent a kind of universal morality that can be assumed to be understood by everyone. So when Abimelech challenges Abraham as to why he said that Sarah was his sister, not his wife, Abraham replies, 'I said to myself, there is no fear of God *[Elokim]* in this place . . .' (Gen. 20:11). When Joseph refuses the advances of Potiphar's wife, he says to her, 'How then could I do such a wicked thing and sin against God *[Elokim]*?' (Gen. 39:9). The assumption is that the wife of an Egyptian official will understand both the phrase and the idea it expresses.

More dramatically, early in the book of Exodus we encounter the first recorded act of civil disobedience: the refusal of the midwives to obey Pharaoh's command to kill every male Hebrew child. The text says that they 'feared God *[Elokim]* and did not do what the king of Egypt had told them to do' (Exod. 1:17). This is particularly interesting since, by a subtle ambiguity, the phrase describing them may mean either 'the Hebrew midwives' or 'the midwives to the Hebrews', leaving it unresolved as to whether they were Hebrew or Egyptian.[10] The phrase *yirat Elokim* seems to refer to a universal moral sense, a 'natural law', presumed to be present in everyone unless corrupted.

The word *Hashem* is quite different. It almost invariably signals a closeness of relationship, and is used far more of the covenantal family. So, for example, whereas Joseph's pharaoh understands and uses the word *Elokim,* the pharaoh to whom Moses speaks says defiantly:

> 'Who is the Lord *[Hashem],* that I should obey him and let Israel go? I do not know the Lord *[Hashem]* and I will not let Israel go.' (Exod. 5:2)

Consistent with this distinction, the covenant with Noah (Gen. 9:8–17) uses the word *Elokim* throughout. In the key communications of God with Abraham—the command to leave his family (12:1), the promise of the land (12:7) and of children (15:4–6), and the covenant (15:18; 17:1)—the name *Hashem* is used. The general contrast in Genesis is therefore not between monotheism and polytheism, or even between true worship and idolatry. It is between *Elokim* and *Hashem,* God as he appears to people in general, and the intimacy of his encounters with those he loves in particular.

So we have yet another duality. *Elokim* is universal, *Hashem* is particular. An Egyptian, a Philistine, a Hittite, someone who stands outside the covenant, can understand *Elokim* as the cause of causes, the supreme power. But *Hashem,* God's proper name, the name by which he is called in intimate person-to-person relationship: that is not universal. It bespeaks closeness, singularity. This is the God of revelation and self-disclosure, the God of love who will one day say, 'My child, my firstborn, Israel' (Exod. 4:22).

Creation, Revelation, Redemption

We can state this more precisely in terms of the parameters of Jewish faith. Maimonides articulated thirteen principles of faith. Rabbi Shimon ben Tzemach Duran reduced them to three, which Franz Rosenzweig called creation, revelation, and redemption.[11] The relationship between God and the universe is creation: the *work* of God. Between God and humanity it is revelation: the *word* of God. When we apply revelation to creation, the word of God to the work of God, the result is redemption.

We can now define the difference between *Elokim* and *Hashem.* *Elokim* is God in creation. The entire creation narrative of Genesis 1:1–2:3 is constructed around the name *Elokim*. It is *Elokim* who made the universe and all it contains, *Elokim* who spoke and brought the world into being, *Elokim* who said, 'Let us make man in our image, after our likeness.' *Elokim* is the God of space, the stars and the planets, the God of life and the human genome, the God of nature and science, the God of Newton and Einstein.

When it comes to revelation, the word the Torah uses is *Hashem*. It was *Hashem* who warned Cain against sin, who summoned Noah to enter the ark, who called to Abraham, telling him to leave his land, his birthplace and his father's house; *Hashem* who promised him children and a land; *Hashem* who spoke to Moses at the burning bush, who rescued his people from Egypt, who made a covenant with them at Mount Sinai, who gave them the Ten Commandments and the laws of life.

So we begin to see a new way of understanding the intellectual project of the Torah. It deals with the multiplicity of gods in the ancient world by gathering them together into a single entity named *Elokim*, a plural noun. There are many forces at work in the universe, but they are not disparate, random or clashing. They are part of a unified structure, the result of a single directing will. It was this intellectual leap that overcame mythology, preparing the way for science, and for science's holy grail, the unified field theory, the grand theory of everything. That is *Elokim*, God as the totality of forces operative in the universe.

We can all encounter *Elokim*, Jew and non-Jew alike. That is common language shared by Abraham's family and their contemporaries. Yet there is a another dimension to God altogether. The heroes of the Hebrew Bible do not encounter God merely as Dylan Thomas' 'force that through the green fuse drives the flower', or as Matthew Arnold's 'the eternal not ourselves that makes for righteousness'. They meet him as personal presence, the One who hears our cry, notes our deeds, who calls to us and who listens when we call to him. That is *Hashem*, the God of revelation and particularity, the God of the priests who summons Israel to become a holy nation, and of the prophets who charges them with the work of righteousness and justice, love and compassion.

So in Genesis, the most universal of the Mosaic books, and the one in which the people outside the Abrahamic covenant are most prominent, the two names are evenly matched: *Hashem* appears 165 times, *Elokim* 188. But in Leviticus, the book of priesthood and holiness, *Hashem* appears 311 times, *Elokim* a mere 5. In the prophetic books from Isaiah to Malachi, *Hashem* appears 1,991 times, *Elokim* a mere 61.

So the universal/particular dichotomy that runs through Judaism finds an echo in the names of God. The God of creation, *Elokim,* is universal. The God of revelation, *Hashem,* is particular.

Torah and Wisdom

So we have a dual ontology, two modes of being. But Judaism also recognises a dual epistemology. There are two ways of *knowing.* One is called *chokhmah,* 'wisdom', the other is *Torah,* 'teaching, instruction, law, guidance'. The difference was stated clearly by the sages: 'If you are told that there is wisdom among the nations, believe it. If you are told there is Torah among the nations, do not believe it.'

Wisdom is important because it is a biblical category. The word appears some 341 times in various inflections. There are entire books dedicated to *chokhmah,* known generically as the 'Wisdom literature'. The three classic examples are Proverbs, Ecclesiastes and Job. In Proverbs, the word appears 103 times, in Ecclesiastes 53 times, and in Job 31 times—between them, more than half the occurrences of 'wisdom' in the entire Hebrew Bible.

Wisdom is universal. We see this in many ways. Scholars point out that the Wisdom literature of the Hebrew Bible is closer to its counterparts in other ancient cultures, Ugaritic, Egyptian and Babylonian, than are the other biblical works. Nor is this surprising, since wisdom is the (albeit inspired) product of observation, experience and insight, unlike the prophetic literature, which is about the Divine word and revelation.

We can also see this by examining where the concept of wisdom appears in the Mosaic books. In Genesis it appears solely in connection with Egypt. When Pharaoh dreams his dreams and wants to know what they mean, he summons his 'wise men'. Joseph uses the word when speaking to Pharaoh, as does Pharaoh in describing Joseph ('there is no one as understanding and *wise* as you in all Egypt'). It also appears in the description of Bezalel, the man who made the appurtenances of the Sanctuary. As Maimonides notes in the last chapter of *The Guide for the Perplexed,* one of the senses of *chokhmah* is craftsmanship, a cultural universal. When Moses speaks of the universal significance of Torah he says, 'This is your *wisdom* and understanding in the eyes of the nations' (Deut. 4:6).

Consistently, in Psalms, Proverbs and Job, wisdom is associated with creation:

> How many are your works, O Lord! In *wisdom* you made them all; the earth is full of your creations. (Ps. 104:24)

> The Lord brought me *[wisdom]* forth as the first of his works, before his deeds of old; I was appointed from eternity, from the beginning, before the world began. (Prov. 8:22)

> When [God] established the force of the wind and measured out the waters, when he made a decree for the rain and a path for the thunderstorm, then he looked at *wisdom* and appraised it; he confirmed it and tested it. (Job 28:23–7)

Rashi, explaining the phrase, 'Let us make man in our image, *after our likeness*', says that it means 'the ability to understand and discern'.[12] Wisdom, understanding, discernment: these are the universal heritage of humankind. We can all use language. We can distinguish one thing from another. We have had, since Adam, the power to name and classify. Through observation and inference we can begin to understand the nature of the created world. That is *chokhmah*.

Torah is quite different. Time and again the Bible emphasises that this is Israel's unique gift. 'What other nation is so great as to have such righteous decrees and laws as this Torah I am setting before you today?' (Deut. 4:8) 'Moses commanded us the Torah, the heritage of the congregation of Jacob' (Deut. 33:4). 'He has revealed his word to Jacob, his laws and decrees to Israel. He has done this for no other nation' (Ps. 147:19–20). 'Moses received the Torah at Sinai and handed it on to Joshua, who handed it on to the elders, who handed it on to the prophets,' who handed it on to the sages, who handed it on to later generations.[13] Torah is the code of Jewish particularity, Israel's constitution as a nation under the sovereignty of God.

We can now state the difference between the two modes of knowledge. *Chokhmah* is the truth we discover; Torah is the truth we inherit. *Chokhmah* is the universal heritage of humankind; Torah is the specific heritage of Israel. *Chokhmah* is what we attain by being in the image of God; Torah is what guides Jews as the people of God. *Chokhmah* is acquired by seeing and reasoning; Torah is received by listening and responding. *Chokhmah* tells us what is; Torah tells us what ought to be. *Chokhmah* is about facts; Torah is about commands. *Chokhmah* yields descriptive, scientific laws; Torah yields prescriptive, behavioural laws. *Chokhmah* is about creation; Torah is about revelation.

We can now resolve the apparent contradiction between a famous saying of Maimonides and another by the sages. Maimonides declared, 'Accept the truth, whoever said it.'[14] The sages said, 'Whoever recites a teaching in the name of the one who said it, brings redemption to the world.'[15] Maimonides was interested in the truth of a proposition, not its author. For the sages, the reverse was true. Who said it is not irrelevant but essential.

Maimonides and the sages were talking about different kinds of truth. Truth as *chokhmah* has nothing to do with its author. Had Einstein not discovered the theory of relativity, eventually someone else would have. But when we speak of a revealed truth, it is vital to know the chain of transmission. Was the person who said it reliable? Was he part of the chain of tradition, from Moses across the generations? That is an essential difference between the truth we discover and the truth we inherit.

What is remarkable is the dignity the sages attached to *chokhmah*. They coined a special blessing to be said on seeing a non-Jewish sage: 'Blessed are you . . . who gave of his wisdom to mortals.'[16] Little short of astonishing is the fact that the sages prayed for the universal gifts of wisdom as the very first of the 'request blessings' of the daily prayer. This is the text:

> You grace humanity with knowledge and teach mortals understanding. Grace us with the knowledge, understanding and discernment that come from You. Blessed are You, Lord, who graciously grants knowledge.[17]

Although the prayer does not use the word *chokhmah*, it uses synonyms: 'knowledge, understanding and discernment'. But it is speaking about the universals of the human mind, not about Torah knowledge. That much is unmistakable, since the prayer is speaking about humanity *(adam)* and mortals *(enosh)* as a whole, not about Jews. Not until the next paragraph do we turn to the particular: 'Bring us back, our Father, to Your Torah.' This is yet another example of the basic structure of Jewish thought, which begins with the universal and only then proceeds to the particular.

We can now state the following: *chokhmah* has an honourable place within the Jewish worldview. It has religious dignity. It is the gift of God. It is available to everyone, because everyone is in the image of God. We can also hazard the following definition: *chokhmah* is what allows us to understand the world as God's work (science) and the human person as his image (the humanities).

The sages had harsh words for those able to study science who failed to do so:

> Rabbi Shimon bar Pazzi said in the name of R. Joshua ben Levi on the authority of Bar Kappara: One who knows how to calculate cycles and planetary courses but does not do so, of him Scripture says, 'But they have no regard for the deeds of the Lord, no respect for the work of his hands' (Isaiah 5:12). R. Shmuel bar Nahmani said in the name of R. Joshua, How do we know that it is a commandment to calculate cycles and planetary courses? Because it is written: 'This is your wisdom and understanding in the eyes of the nations.' What is wisdom and understanding in the eyes of the nations? It is the science of cycles and planetary courses.[18]

The passage brings together two different but equally striking propositions. The first is that neglect of science is tantamount to a religious failure to appreciate the greatness of the creator through his creation. The second is that a neglect of science among Jews means a diminution of Gentile respect for Judaism, and thus in a certain sense for God himself.

Maimonides put it more strongly still. Not in his philosophical work, but in his code of Jewish law, he ruled that study of natural science is the way to the love and fear of God: love by understanding the vastness and wisdom of creation, fear through contemplating the smallness of humankind in the scheme of things.

The Difference Between Wisdom and Culture

Yet it is here, at the climax of the argument, that we confront an apparently opposite phenomenon. The sages took a high view of *chokhmah*. It is part of the religious life. It is a *mitzvah*, a positive pursuit. They coined a blessing on seeing those who had achieved distinction in it. But there was one kind of wisdom of which they did not approve. They warned of its danger. And here they were specific. They called it *chokhmah Yevanit*, 'Greek wisdom'.[19] What was it, and why was it dangerous?

By *chokhmah Yevanit* the sages meant Greek culture in its broadest sense, its philosophy, ethics and religion. They sensed, rightly I believe, that it was subversive of Jewish faith. Greek philosophy left no space for revelation. Greek ethics was shot through with class distinctions. The idea that 'all men are created equal' would have sounded absurd to Plato and Aristotle, both of whom believed that some are born to rule, others to be ruled. As for Greek religion, it was pagan through and through. With this we come to the heart of the matter. Is wisdom universally wise?

If my analysis is correct, Judaism makes a distinction not made explicitly in the West until the eighteenth-century Scottish philosopher David Hume. There is, he said, a distinction between 'is' and 'ought', fact and value, description and prescription. The world as we perceive it through the senses is morally neutral. From how the world is, we cannot infer how it ought to be. For that we need another kind of knowledge entirely, knowledge that in Judaism is called Torah.

The Greeks did not believe this. They believed that nature is teleological, meaning that it carries within it its own purposes. The 'ought' is implicit within the 'is'. So it was natural to believe that just as the sun, the stars and the planets had their own hierarchy, so did human beings. Both were part of what came to be called the 'great chain of being'. Greek drama was built around the idea of tragedy, meaning roughly that there is such a thing as fate, divinely ordained, and the more we try to avoid it, the more we bring it about. Judaism, as I will argue in the final chapter, is incompatible with tragedy in the Greek sense.

So 'Greek wisdom' is not so much a form of wisdom as it is a mode of *culture*. The distinction between the two is hard to state but essential to understand. The sages and those who came before them lived in a world deeply hostile to Jewish values. Jews, under the Maccabees, had fought a battle against the imposition of Greek culture on Israel which at one point, under Antiochus IV, amounted to a public ban against the practice of Judaism.

The sages also knew—it was an insight that in the long run saved Judaism from extinction—that the military battle was ultimately less significant than the cultural battle. Within less than a century, Israel was again under foreign rule, this time that of Rome. The military victory lasted decades, the cultural victory has endured until today.

The essential question is, where does wisdom end and culture begin? The pursuit of wisdom has always had a hubris of its own. It has often overstepped its limits. It has laid claim to having discovered truths that apply in all times and places, only to find, a generation or more later, that those truths were not so much falsehoods as highly localised perceptions. That was how things seemed to those people at that time. Intellectually fashionable then, future generations ask themselves how intelligent individuals could possibly believe in such things. What passes as wisdom is rarely culturally neutral. It was a point made by Judah Halevi in the eleventh century. How can philosophy be absolute truth, he asked, when no two philosophers agree with one another?[20]

There were scientists at the end of the nineteenth century who believed that the future would contain no major new discoveries. What could be discovered had been discovered. That was before relativity theory, quantum physics, Heisenberg's uncertainty principle, Niels Bohr's complementarity theorem, the identification of DNA, the mapping of the human genome and PET scans of the human brain, discoveries that not only expanded the boundaries of science but also fundamentally changed our understanding of how the world works.

In the field of wisdom, the one thing of which we can be certain is that we cannot be certain. The more we know, the more we understand how little we know. Wisdom needs the kind of humility Newton expressed when he said, 'I seem to have been only like a boy playing on the seashore, and diverting myself in now and then finding a smoother pebble or a prettier shell than ordinary, whilst the great ocean of truth lay all undiscovered before me.' Newton, the greatest scientist of the age of science, was a deeply religious man.

To Change the World You Have to Understand the World

I have argued, not only in this chapter but throughout the book, that a basic duality runs through Judaism, shaping its view of the world. It honours both the universality of the human condition and the particularity of Jewish faith. So the Torah contains two stories, one from Adam to Noah, the other from Abraham to Moses. It contains two covenants, one with all humanity, the other with the people of Israel. There are two different names of God. There are two manifestations of God, one in creation, the other in revelation. And there are two forms of knowledge, *chokhmah* and Torah. Neither displaces or supersedes the other. To be a Jew is to be both. We are part of humanity and its story, and we are children of Abraham and Sarah and their story.

Without Torah we cannot understand the Jewish story. But without *chokhmah* we cannot understand the human story. As I put it above, there are three elements of Jewish faith: creation, revelation and redemption. Creation is God's relationship with the universe. Revelation is God's relationship with us. Redemption is what happens when we apply revelation to creation, when we apply God's word to God's world. *We cannot apply Torah to the world unless we understand the world.* Without an understanding of creation, we will fail to bring about redemption.

To apply Torah to the human mind, one must understand psychology and psychiatry. To apply it to society, we must understand sociology and anthropology. To cure poverty, we must understand economics. To avoid environmental catastrophe, we need to understand botany, biology, climatology and much else besides. All these things come under the general heading of 'wisdom', which I defined as the knowledge that helps us see the universe as God's work and the human person as God's image—in other words, the sciences and humanities broadly conceived.

There was a time when a purely instrumental reason was given for Jews pursuing secular studies. You needed it to get a job and earn a living. The sages gave another reason. It gave Jews, and by implication Judaism, respect in the eyes of the world. There was a deeper reason still. It allowed us to see the wisdom of God's creation. It led, said Maimonides, to the love and fear of God. Those who could study astronomy and failed to do so, said the sages, had 'no regard for the deeds of the Lord, no respect for the work of his hands'. I have argued that within the logic of Judaism as a whole, there is another reason. To redeem the world, you have to understand the world.

Throughout the whole of the first Gulf War, in 1991, my wife and I were in Israel. Thirty-nine times Saddam Hussein launched Scud missiles. Each time, we would retreat to our sealed room and put on gas masks, not knowing whether the next missile would contain chemical or biological weapons. Miraculously, there were almost no fatalities. But there was an unexpected casualty: family life. Israeli families were not used to spending prolonged periods together in a single room in situations of danger. The then mayor of Jerusalem, Teddy Kollek, set up a working group to deal with family stress. I received a phone call from his office asking if I would be the rabbinic member of the group. I laughed and said, 'I'm only a tourist here. Are there no other rabbis in Jerusalem?' The reply came back: 'We have many rabbis, but none expert in family psychology.' A rabbinate untrained in the wisdom of the world will find itself irrelevant to those immersed in the world.

A Judaism divorced from society will be a Judaism unable to influence society. It will live and thrive and flourish behind high walls within its own defensive space, but it will not speak to those who wrestle with the very realities—poverty, disease, injustice, inequality and other assaults on human dignity—to which Torah was directed in the first place. At best, those who engage with the world and are at the same time faithful to Judaism will be divided personalities, unable to integrate the two halves of their being because Torah and *chokhmah* are un-integrated in our time. They will suffer from the cerebral lesion I mentioned at the beginning of the chapter.

Creation and revelation have a single author. At the climax of Yom Kippur, in the last words of prayer, Jews say seven times: *Hashem hu ha-Elokim,* 'the God of revelation is the God of creation'. Judaism is a sustained call to heal the rift between creation and revelation, between the world as it is and the world as it ought to be. To do that requires both Torah and wisdom.

To be sure, the world of wisdom is a danger zone. All too rarely do scientists and humanists acknowledge the difference between fact and value, wisdom and culture. Perhaps, within the humanities, it is impossible to make a sharp separation between the two. Can we read Homer or Dante or Milton or T. S. Eliot without entering their mental world, their culture-saturated combination of fact and value, which may be incompatible with, subversive of or antagonistic towards the values to which Jews have been called?

Science can easily become scientism, the belief that what science measures is all there is. Materialism, determinism, behaviourism, Darwinism: these are all forms, not of science but of science-become-metaphor-and-myth, doctrines that lay claim to a truth far beyond the evidence on which they are based. So there is no risk-free encounter with wisdom. Even Maimonides, the greatest expert in Jewish law and life who ever entered the Elysian field of wisdom, was, in the view of many, too Platonic in his politics and too Aristotelian in his metaphysics.

But the demand for a life without risk is neither Jewish nor wise. The late Lubavitcher Rebbe, Rabbi Menahem Mendel Schneerson, said that the spies Moses sent to survey the land were not fainthearted individuals. Their reluctance to conquer the land was not because they feared defeat. They feared success. In the desert, they lived closely and continuously with God. He sent them manna from heaven, water from a rock, and surrounded them with clouds of glory. How could they be so directly in his presence if they had cities to build, fields to harvest, an economy to sustain and a land to defend? They wanted faith without risk. They failed to understand that faith is the courage to take a risk.

The idea of a risk-free life is an illusion. Segregating faith from the world means condemning faith to impotence within the world. Ultimately it means denying the connection between God and the world, which is a form of belief known as Gnosticism, not Judaism. John Milton wrote, 'I cannot praise a fugitive and cloistered virtue, unexercised and unbreathed, that never sallies out and sees her adversary, but slinks out of the race where that immortal garland is to be run for, not without dust and heat.'[21] Virtue, like faith, is tested in the real world with all its challenges and seductions.

There is such a thing as Judaic wisdom, Torah allied with *chokhmah,* however difficult this is to define or specify in advance. To give one example: by choosing to base his psychoanalytic theory on the Greek myth of Oedipus, Freud gave us an essentially tragic view of the human condition. Three figures since—Viktor Frankl, who gave people hope in Auschwitz; Aaron T. Beck, who developed cognitive therapy; and Martin Seligman, who pioneered in the field of positive psychology—produced a set of understandings of the human mind and its emotions far more in keeping with the spirit of Judaism. Nor is this a marginal phenomenon from a religious point of view. Maimonides called his ideal type, the sage, a *rofe nefashot,* a healer of souls: in a word, a psychotherapist.

I think in this context of Michael Walzer, Michael Sandel and the late Daniel Elazar, who advanced Jewish understandings of political theory; of the work of Leon Kass in bioethics, and Robert Winston's in the treatment of infertility. I think of Howard Gardner's insights into multiple intelligence, and Abraham Maslow's into the structures of human motivation. Isaiah Berlin taught us much about the nature of freedom: at his funeral I spoke of how his life's work was, intentionally or otherwise, an extended commentary on the book of Exodus. When I asked Jeffrey Sachs, perhaps the world's leading developmental economist, why he did what he did, he answered without hesitation: *tikkun olam* (repairing a fractured world).

Avivah Zornberg has shown how to combine a reading of Torah with a finely honed literary sensibility. The late David Daube, Regius Professor of Roman Law at Oxford, revealed the extent to which biblical narrative is suffused with legal ideas. Michael Fishbane's work on inner biblical exegesis has shown us how ancient is the Jewish instinct of midrash. There are countless other examples of how Torah can shed light on wisdom, and wisdom deepens our understanding of Torah. Rabbi Aharon Lichtenstein, himself an exemplar of this approach,[22] has written eloquently on the subject. That is the task of modern orthodoxy in our time.

Torah and *chokhmah* must be reunited if Judaism is to recover its ability to speak to the world without fear of the world, as was once done in philosophy by Maimonides, poetry by Judah Halevi and Ibn Gabirol, politics and statesmanship by Shmuel ha-Nagid and Abrabanel. But when it speaks to the world, what does it say? That, the final question of this book, is also the most fundamental. What is Judaism, and why?

11

Future Tense: The Voice of Hope in the Conversation of Humankind

The future for Jews and Judaism, in Israel and the Diaspora, is fraught with risk. That is one reason why I called this book *Future Tense*. But there is another and more fundamental reason. We will not understand Judaism, or the Jewish people, or the trajectory of Jewish history, until we ask: 'What made Jews different?' Everyone is different. Each culture has its characteristic voice, each faith its distinctive vision. Lose it, and the culture begins to fade, the faith begins to falter. What, then, is Judaism? What are Jews called on to do? And why, in the twenty-first century, does it matter? The answer, I will argue, has to do with the future tense. Judaism is supremely the religion of the *not-yet*. In this chapter I want to explain what that means and why it is important.

Judaism, I have argued, is not for Jews alone. If it were, it would make no sense. The God of Abraham is not a tribal God. He is the creator of heaven and earth. The God of Israel is not only the God of Israel. He made all human beings in his image. The God of the Hebrew Bible did not limit his blessings to one nation. After the Flood, he made a covenant with all humanity. Abraham and his descendants are not the only people in the Bible to encounter God. Abraham's family are not the only moral heroes. So is Pharaoh's daughter. So is Job. The Israelites are not the only people to whom God sends prophets. So were the people of Nineveh to whom God sent Jonah. 'Through you,' said God to Abraham, 'all the families on earth will be blessed.' How that will happen is not made clear in the Bible, yet the prophets were agreed that it would one day happen. Judaism is not for Jews alone.

What then did God, through the Jewish people, its laws, life and history, seek to say to the world? The answer, I believe, lies in four strange, highly distinctive features of Judaism as a faith.

The Great Mistranslation

The first occurs at the formative moment in the life of Moses, when the prophet encounters God at the burning bush. God summons him to lead the Israelites out of Egypt, but Moses is reluctant. 'Who am I,' he asks, 'to be worthy of such a task?' God reassures him, and then Moses asks, 'Who are you? When the Israelites ask, who has sent you, what shall I say?' God replies in a cryptic three-word phrase, *Ehyeh asher ehyeh* (Exod. 3:14).

It is fascinating to see how Christian Bibles translate this clause. The King James Version reads it as 'I am that I am.' Recent translations are variants of the same idea. Here are some examples:

I am who I am.
I am what I am.
I am—that is who I am.

These are all mistranslations, and the error is ancient. In Greek, *Ehyeh asher ehyeh* became *ego eimi ho on,* and in Latin, *ego sum qui sum:* 'I am he who is.' Augustine in the *Confessions* writes: 'Because he is *Is,* that is to say, God is being itself, *ipsum esse,* in its most absolute and full sense.' Centuries later, Aquinas explains that it means God is 'true being, that is being that is eternal, immutable, simple, self-sufficient, and the cause and principle of every creature'. And so it continued in German philosophy. God became Hegel's 'concrete universal', Schelling's 'transcendental ego', Gilson's 'God-is-Being' and Heidegger's 'onto-theology'.[1]

The mistake of all these translations is obvious to the merest beginner in Hebrew. The phrase means, 'I will be what I will be.' The verb *does not use the present tense.* Elsewhere, the Bible does. In the Ten Commandments, for example, the first verse reads, 'I am the Lord your God who brought you out of Egypt, out of the land of slavery.' Here the present tense ('I am') *is* used. But then, that verse does not speak of God's name. It speaks of his deeds. Here, however, Moses asked God for his name. God might have replied, as did the angel who wrestled with Jacob, with a rhetorical question, 'Why do you ask for my name?', implying that the very question is out of order. There are things human beings cannot know, mysteries they cannot fathom, matters that transcend the reach of human understanding.

But that is not what God says. He does answer Moses' question, but enigmatically, in a phrase that needs decoding. God tells Moses to say to the Israelites, ' "I will be" sent me to you.' It is as if God had said, 'My name is *the future tense*. If you seek to understand me, first you will have to understand the nature and significance of the future tense.'

'I am that I am' is a translation that owes everything to the philosophical tradition of ancient Greece and nothing to the thought of ancient Israel. The God of pure being, first cause, prime mover, necessary existence, is the god of the philosophers, not the God of the prophets.

What, then, is the meaning of 'I will be what I will be'? The name itself never recurs in the Hebrew Bible, but there is a later echo, in the great scene in which God appears to Moses on the mountain after the sin of the Golden Calf, in which he says, 'I will have mercy on whom I will have mercy, and I will have compassion on whom I will have compassion' (Exod. 33:19).

What this means is that God cannot be predicted or controlled. He cannot be confined to categories or known in advance. He is telling Moses, 'You cannot know how I will appear *until* I appear; how I will act *until* I act. My mercy, my compassion, my strategic interventions into history, cannot be controlled or foretold. I will be what, when and how I choose to be. I am the God of the radically unknowable future, the God of surprises. You will know me when you see me, but not before.'

To be sure, in one sense, the future is connected to the past. God keeps his promises. That is an essential element of Jewish faith. But this very fact reveals the difference between *predictability* on the one hand and *faithfulness* on the other. Objects fall, gas expands, particles combine: these things are predictable. But people freely honour obligations they have undertaken because they are faithful. That is the difference God never fails to teach Moses and the prophets.

God's name tells us that he is not an entity knowable by philosophy or science, deducible from the past. God awaits us in the unknown and unknowable future. That is the first stage of the argument: *the God of Israel is the God of the future tense.*

The Birth of History

The second is the Jewish sense of time. A remarkable range of scholars—historians like J. H. Plumb and Yosef Yerushalmi, the philosopher Ernst Cassirer, Harold Fisch the literary scholar, and Thomas Cahill, the popular historian—have pointed out that in the Hebrew Bible, a new concept of time was born.[2] Eric Voegelin, the historian of ideas, calls Israel 'a new genus of society' because, unlike all other ancient civilisations, it 'moved on the historical scene'.[3] Anthropologist Mircea Eliade says that 'the Hebrews were the first to discover the meaning of history as the epiphany of God'.[4] This was a world-changing event.

Time, for ancients, was cyclical, a matter of the slow revolving of the seasons and the generations, an endlessly repeated sequence of birth, growth, decline and death. Plato called time the 'moving image of eternity'. Nietzsche developed the theory of eternal recurrences. Since the permutations of possibility are finite while time is infinite, what happened once will happen again. According to Eliade, in all mythological cultures, events become real by imitating an archetype. Rituals symbolically replay acts that happened at the beginning of time and gave the world the shape it has. In myth, time is abolished. The participants in ritual are transported back to the primordial moment and become one with eternity. Mythic time is not historical but *anti*-historical time: time in which nothing really changes. Change is threatening. Therefore myth and ritual reassure the believer that change is an illusion, unreal. Until Israel appeared on the scene, all cultures were like that. Some still are.

Cyclical time is time as it appears in nature. All that lives, dies, but life itself lives on. Winds, storms, floods and drought wreak devastation, but nature recovers, homes are rebuilt, fields are replanted, and the cycle begins again. The dream of myth is order, and its perennial fear is chaos. Life is an ongoing struggle between these two opposites, which reflect the struggles of the gods, told in the endless stories of myth itself. The god of the sky fights the goddess of the sea. An inquisitive minor god steals one god's secret or another god's wife. The permutations are endless, but the basic plot is the same. First, there is order, then it is disturbed by a force of chaos: there is a battle and finally order is restored. So it was in ancient myth, and so it is today in its cinematic equivalents: *Star Wars, The Lord of the Rings* and the rest.

The Hebrew Bible is a radical break with this way of seeing things. God is to be found in history, not just in nature. Things do change. Human life is an arena of transformation. Abraham leaves the world of the Mesopotamian city-states to begin a new way of serving God. Moses and the Israelites leave Egypt to found a new social order. They are about to build a future unlike the past. That was the revolution. Without it, we would simply not have the key words we have come to accept as obvious, words like *progress, development, advance, creativity, originality.*[5] Until Abraham and Moses, no one thought of time as a journey in which where you are tomorrow will not be where you were yesterday. The concept of change as progress would have been equally incomprehensible. For the ancients, change was a challenge to the established order. That too exists in some cultures and individuals today.

To be sure, the prophets of Israel did not believe in 'progress' in the sense given by Europe in the seventeenth and eighteenth centuries. They did not believe all change is for the better. Some is for the worse. Nor did they believe that history is a story of continuous advance. Much of it is marked by regression. The proof is the story of the Israelites in the wilderness, a journey fraught with setbacks and delays. But time is nonetheless about transformation. The Moses who said, 'I am not a man of words,' is not the same as the man who forty years later delivered, in the book of Deuteronomy, some of the most gloriously eloquent speeches in history. The Israelites at the time of David are not the fractious group they were in the book of Numbers. The future is not a mere repetition of the past. Change, growth, development are all essential features of the human landscape. There are decisive moments that alter everything. God is not only present in eternity. He is also present in the here and now, in the process of change and transformation.

The literature of ancient Israel was the birth of history, though it is not the same as the history written by Greek historians such as Herodotus or Thucydides. The Greek historians wrote about what happened. The prophets and scribes of Israel believed that history was more than a series of happenings. It had meaning. It constitutes a narrative. J. H. Plumb wrote:

> The concept that within the history of mankind itself a process was at work which would mould his future, and lead man to situations totally different from his past, seems to have found its first expression among the Jews . . . The uniqueness of this concept lay in the idea of development. The past was no longer static, a mere store of information, example and event, but dynamic, an unfolding story.[6]

So the second point is that *in Judaism a new concept was born, of a future substantively different from the past.*

The Story Without an Ending

The third has to do with the nature of the Jewish narrative. Andrew Marr, we recall, said that Jews 'have always had stories for the rest of us'. The Hebrew Bible is a book of stories, quintessentially so. Whereas science and philosophy represent *truth as system,* Judaism represents *truth as story,* a sequence of events that must play themselves out in and through time.

Yet there is one aspect of the Hebrew Bible that has not had adequate attention. There are many types of story. Christopher Booker identifies seven basic plots: overcoming the Monster, rags to riches, the quest, the voyage and return, comedy, tragedy and rebirth.[7] There are many genres: epic, lyric, romance, satire and so on. But essential to them all, indeed what *makes* a story, is what Frank Kermode calls 'the sense of an ending'.[8] A narrative needs closure. The separated lovers reunite, or the once-united lovers part. The hero wins, or the hero dies. The wicked witch meets her end, or the noble figure falls from grace. Different genres call for different kinds of ending, but without an ending there is no closure, no resolution, no frame, no story.

Now consider the biblical narrative. David Clines, in his book *The Theme of the Pentateuch,* says that its theme is the promise of the land.[9] The story begins with God's call to Abraham to leave home and travel 'to the land which I will show you'. Seven times, God promises Abraham the land. He promises it again, once to Isaac and three times to Jacob. The logic of the narrative is unmistakable. The end, heralded at the beginning, will be the land. It will become Abraham's children's home. It is a story about a journey with a destination, a divine promise and its fulfilment. Abraham leaves one home to find another. The story begins with a departure and ends with an arrival.

Or so it should, but it doesn't. No sooner does Abraham arrive than a famine forces him to leave. He travels to Egypt, a journey that because of the attractiveness of Sarah, puts his life in danger.

He escapes the danger and returns, but again he has to leave, this time to rescue his nephew Lot. Again he returns, but a second time he has to leave because of famine, this time to Abimelech, king of Gerar. Again there is danger. Abraham survives and returns. But when Sarah dies he has nowhere to bury her, and he is forced to enter into lengthy negotiations with the Hittites to acquire even a burial plot for his wife. The story line is subverted time and again. And so it is with the life of Isaac, Jacob and Joseph. As Genesis draws to a close, the Israelites are in exile in Egypt, and the Promised Land is as distant as ever.

With exodus, the tragedy deepens. The Israelites have become slaves. The place of refuge has become the place of servitude. Then light dawns. God speaks to Moses at the burning bush, telling him to take the people out from Egypt and bring them to the land. Even so, there are seemingly inexplicable delays. Moses prevaricates, until God finally loses patience. He returns to Egypt, tells the people they are about to go free, and then delivers God's message to Pharaoh. But Pharaoh refuses. The Israelites think Moses has merely made matters worse. Moses, in turn, complains to God.

Moses delivers signs, God sends plagues, and each time Pharaoh maintains his refusal. When he seems finally about to change his mind, God hardens Pharaoh's heart. Eventually, after the tenth plague, Pharaoh says, 'Leave', but even then the way is not clear. God hardens Pharaoh's heart again, and Pharaoh and his army pursue the Israelites. They come up against the sea. They despair. A miracle happens. The sea divides. The Israelites pass through. Now at last they are beyond the reach of Pharaoh. They have left Egypt. They are on their way to the land. All that lies ahead of them is a journey of a few days.

But it turns out not to be so. At each difficulty, the Israelites want to give up and return to Egypt. Moses sends spies to get a glimpse of the land, but they come back with a devastating report. The land is good, but the people are giants, the cities well fortified, and an Israelite victory impossible. The people lose faith, and they are condemned to die in the desert. The arrival is delayed a further forty years.

Even then, the disappointments are not at an end. Moses himself, the man who led the people to freedom and the brink of the Promised Land, is told that he may not enter. In the final glimpse we have of him, he is standing on a mountain-top, seeing the land from afar. We are no nearer at the end of the story than Abraham was at the beginning.

Neither Genesis nor the Pentateuch as a whole, concludes with an ending. They are God's unfinished symphony. We are left in medias res, in liminal space midway between departure and arrival, tantalisingly close yet unmistakably distant. We have travelled through several centuries and generations on a journey with a destination that no one has yet reached.

So we expect that in the course of the other biblical books, we will find closure. By the end of the book of Joshua, the land has been conquered. Thirty-one battles have been fought. The nation has found a home. But as we read on, we discover that this is not a story in which people live happily ever after. Following Joshua, the rule of judges ends in anarchy: 'In those days there was no king in Israel; everyone did what they saw fit.'

The people choose monarchy, but this proves only a temporary unification. After the death of Solomon the kingdom splits in two. The northern kingdom is taken captive and disappears. The southern kingdom falls to the Babylonians. The Book of Books ends, at 2 Chronicles 36, with Cyrus, king of Persia, who has conquered Babylon, giving permission to the exiles to return. So we find ourselves—after thirty-nine books and more than a thousand years of history—back almost where the story began, in Babylon, not far from Ur of the Chaldees from where Abraham's family first set out.

There is no other story quite like this. It breaks all the rules of narrative form. It leads us to expectations that are never met in the way we anticipated them. The Hebrew Bible is *a story without an ending.* Yet there must be an end, for we have heard it since the beginning. It has three elements: a land, the blessing of many children—as many as the stars of the sky, the dust of the earth, the sand on the seashore—and the promise that 'Through you will all the families of the earth be blessed.' Yet the land is never secure. As for many children, Moses says at the end of his life, 'You are the smallest of all the peoples.' As for being a blessing to all the families on earth, by the end of the Bible we are still not quite sure what this might mean.

The Bible is one of the meta-narratives of Western civilisation, the Book of Books, the story of stories, yet Genesis and Deuteronomy and the Hebrew Bible all close with us, the readers, still awaiting the promised, predestined end. It is always just over the horizon, receding like a mirage in the distance. The Bible leaves us, in Harold Fisch's fine phrase, with 'the unappeased memory of a future yet to be fulfilled'.[10] So we arrive at a third proposition: *in Judaism we are always in the middle of a story whose ending lies in the future.*

The 'Not Yet' of History

Which brings us to the fourth of Judaism's unique ideas. It is the only civilisation whose golden age is in the future.

Judaism invented the messianic idea. It is a protean idea, taking different forms at different ages and in different imaginations. But it is present in all the prophets, from Isaiah to Jeremiah to Malachi. It may refer to nothing more than the restoration of Israelite sovereignty. It may mean a utopian end of war and the reign of peace. It may be more still: the righting of the wrongs of history, the rule of justice after the day of judgement. It may even be the death of death. It might be natural or supernatural, an event within historical time or 'the end of history'. Judaism knows all of these alternatives and more. Maimonides sensibly says that we will not know what it will be until it is. There is only one option mainstream Judaism does not entertain: the idea that the messiah has, in fact, come.

This was, of course, the parting of the ways between Judaism and Christianity. Judaism has had many putative messiahs. There were several in the first century. In the second century, Rabbi Akiva and others regarded Bar Kochba as a potential messiah. Maimonides in one of his epistles, *The Letter to Yemen,* recounts three such messiahs in his father's lifetime.[11] The most widely followed messianic figure was Shabbetai Zvi in the sixteenth century. Even afterwards there were several others. Reform thinkers in Germany and America saw emancipation as the dawn of the messianic age.

The baptised Karl Marx, whose grandfather was a rabbi, continued the tradition by formulating his own politicised, secularised version of the messianic idea. Many Jews believed that Theodor Herzl was a messiah—if not the 'son of David' then at least 'the messiah son of Joseph' who was his precursor. In our own time, some followers of the seventh Lubavitcher Rebbe, Rabbi Menachem Mendel Schneerson, thought that he was the messiah. Such is the pressure of messianic expectation among Jews. Yet in the final analysis, to be a Jew has always been to answer the question 'Has the messiah come?' with the reply 'Not yet'. Not while there is war and terror, hunger and injustice, disease and poverty, corruption and inequality. Hence the fourth conclusion: *in Judaism the golden age is always in the future.*

We have, then, in Judaism four remarkable, related ideas: a God whose name is in the future tense, a future-oriented concept of time, a literature whose stories always end in a future-not-yet-reached, and a golden age which belongs to the future.

The Risk of Freedom

The question is why. The answer lies in the radical Jewish belief in human freedom. We do what we choose to do. We are, within constraints, what we choose to be. Society is what we choose to make it. Judaism is supremely a religion of freedom.

Free will might seem obvious, but it is not. The ancients believed that fate lay in the lap of the gods or the configuration of the stars. The Greeks believed in blind fate, *ananke*. Spinoza thought all events, including human behaviour, were determined by natural necessity. Marx saw history as determined by economic interests. Freud thought human behaviour was governed by irrational, unconscious drives. Some neo-Darwinians see it as the result of genetic determinism. On all these views, freedom is an illusion.

Judaism argues otherwise, and it is important to understand why. If God is not within nature, but is himself the author of nature, then he is subject to no laws except those by which he chooses to bind himself. The very act of creation was a free divine choice. God is free to make or unmake, reward or punish, condemn or forgive. That explains the point with which we began. When God says to Moses, 'I will be what I will be,' and later, 'I will have mercy on whom I will have mercy,' he is saying that 'I, God, am free. What I do, how I appear, how I intervene: none of these things can be predicted or controlled. I am what I choose.' God is unknowable for the same reason that the future is unknowable: because of the nature of freedom.

If God is free and he bestows his image on us, then we too, within the limits set by our bodily existence, are free. That is the point of the Bible from the beginning. God gives Adam and Eve a command that they are free to obey or disobey. He gives Cain the freedom to control his negative impulses and the freedom to capitulate to them. The story of the Hebrew Bible is of God's gift of freedom to humankind.

It is a fateful choice, and one that brings God great grief. For we can use our freedom well or badly. We can use it to create or destroy. We can use it to deprive others of their freedom. That is the risk, but it is the risk God chooses to take. Much of the Bible is about how to construct relationships, marriages, families, communities and a society which will honour the freedom of others, so that my freedom is not purchased at the cost of yours. Much of the rest of the Bible is about how such relationships failed: about war and tyranny and the betrayal of freedom, about the corruption of kings, the weakness of priests, the exploitation of the poor by the rich, and the passionate but often unavailing protests of the prophets. It is, as Emmanuel Levinas put it, a difficult freedom.

In what does freedom consist? What makes Homo sapiens different? The answer lies in the fact that human beings have language. Other animals also have language. Primates do; so do dolphins; so even, by the dances they perform, do bees. Animals, especially the social animals that form groups, have ways of communicating. What makes human language unique is that *it contains the future tense.* We can speak of things that have not yet happened, and therein lies our freedom. Because we can speak of something that has not yet been, we can imagine it and therefore choose to act so as to bring it about. We are not held captive by the past.

Events that are not free have causes, and they lie in the past. Let go of an apple, and it falls. Put chemicals together, and they react. A cause always precedes its effect. That is what sciences study: universal relationships between causes and effects. Free human action stands outside the causal nexus. Only humans are capable of acting not just because of something that happened in the past but in order to bring about an imagined future. We go to university to get a degree. We work to earn a salary. We enter politics to win power. These are free acts because they are directed to a future we seek to bring about. The keyword of the first chapter of Genesis is *Yehi,* 'Let there be.' Creation, human or divine, means actualising what has not yet been.

We are free because we face an open future: open because it depends on us. We know the beginning of our story, but we do not yet know how it will end. That is the human condition, and it is why the Jewish story has a beginning but not an end. That is why God, about to lead his people from slavery to freedom, defines his name in terms of an open future: *Ehyeh asher ehyeh,* 'I will be what I choose to be'. That is why Jewish time is not cyclical time in which the future is a mere repetition of the past.

That is why in Judaism the golden age, the messianic destination, has not yet been. *The language of freedom is the future tense.* Judaism, the religion of freedom, is the religion of the future tense.

The Concept of Tragedy

A profound difference separates Judaism from the other great civilisation of the West, ancient Greece. The Greeks believed in a golden age that lay in the past. And they believed in fate, sometimes called *moira,* at others *ananke,* a future determined by the past. Therein lay the roots of one of Greece's greatest contributions to civilisation, the concept of tragedy.

The story of Oedipus, which Freud took as the emblematic human narrative, begins when the king and queen of Thebes, Laius and Jocasta, consult the Delphic oracle, Tiresias. He tells them that they will have a son who will kill Laius and marry Jocasta. To prevent this from happening, when the child is born, Laius has his feet bound together and pierced by a stake, and gives him to a herdsman whom he commands to kill him. The herdsman has pity on the child and gives him to a friend, who hands him over to Polybus, king of Corinth, who adopts him as his son and calls him Oedipus.

When Oedipus grows up, he visits the Delphic oracle, who tells him that he is destined to kill his father and marry his mother. To avoid this, he escapes from the people he thinks are his parents and goes to Thebes. There, he encounters a stranger at a crossroads with whom he has an argument, and eventually kills him. The stranger is of course Laius, Oedipus' unrecognised father. And so the story continues to its inevitable end. Everything Laius, Jocasta and Oedipus do to ensure that the oracle will not come true is a step towards bringing it about. That is an essential element of tragedy.

Tragedy means something more than misfortune, catastrophe or disaster. All human groups know disasters, but tragedy is a cultural artefact. It comes from a view of the world in which we believe we control fate but in fact fate controls us. There is a force, or a set of forces, operative in human destiny as in all else, that brings suffering regardless of what we do. Tragedy is powerful—Aristotle called it cathartic—because in it we enter a world in which even the greatest heroes fail and fall, because in the end, neither they nor we are masters of our fate. We are dust blown by the wind. We are tiny figures in a vast constellation of forces that are indifferent to our existence and can crush us without knowing we are there. Our dream of freedom—our belief that we can say, 'Let there be,' and there will be—is an illusion destined to be shattered on the rocks of reality. Tragedy, a coherent, profound view of the human situation, is the gift of the Greeks to the world.

Jews gave the world a different view, no less coherent and profound but deeply incompatible with a tragic view of life. It gave it the idea of hope. In a world of hope, we are not alone. We exist because someone, the One, created us in love. He knows we are here, hears our prayers, forgives our failures, lights our way through the wilderness of time, teaches us the paths of righteousness, speaks to us in the silence of the soul and takes our hand in the presence of fear, giving us the strength to resist despair. Hope is not mere longing, expectation, dream or desire, any more than tragedy is mere disaster. It is a culturally specific phenomenon, just as tragedy is, and the two cannot co-exist. If there is hope, there is no ultimate tragedy. If there is tragedy, there is no ultimate hope. The French playwright Jean Anouilh put the point forcefully in the words of the chorus at the beginning of his *Antigone:*

> Tragedy is clean, it is restful, it is flawless . . . In tragedy nothing is in doubt and everyone's destiny is known . . . There is a sort of fellow-feeling among characters in a tragedy: he who kills is as innocent as he who gets killed: it's all a matter of what part you are playing. Tragedy is restful; and the reason is that hope, that foul, deceitful thing, has no part in it.[12]

History without freedom equals tragedy. History plus freedom equals hope. With this we come finally to a definition of Judaism that explains not only what it has meant to Jews but what it has meant to the world. *Judaism is the voice of hope in the conversation of humankind.*

Agents of Hope

The prophets, even the most pessimistic, were all agents of hope. Jeremiah, one of the bleakest, bought a field in Jerusalem as a sign that he believed God would bring the people back from exile, which he did.

The nearest the Hebrew Bible comes to tragedy is the book of Job. Job is a good man who loses everything: his wealth, his health, his children. He rails against the injustice of his fate. His companions, conventional believers all, tell him that he is wrong. He must have committed some sin. Or God is sending him suffering to refine his soul. God's justice is inscrutable, therefore unchallengeable. Who are we to understand the infinite? But they are wrong. The book says so at the beginning and God says so at the end. Job has done nothing to deserve his fate.

For forty-two chapters of blazing poetry and prose, the book walks along the edge of the abyss. Yet Job is not a tragedy. What redeems the story is not the ending in which Job gets back his property and reputation, has other children, and lives to a good old age. Nor is it what God says to him when he finally speaks from out of the whirlwind. God gives Job no answers, only four chapters of rhetorical questions. It is the fact that God speaks to Job, and vindicates his challenge. Two facts shine through the book: Job refuses to lose faith in God and God refuses to lose faith in Job.

Job towards God is like Jacob wrestling with the angel, saying, 'I will not let you go until you bless me' (Gen. 32:26). At the end, God and man stand together in a momentous refusal to be parted. Job is not Lear or Hamlet or Othello, alone in an unfeeling world. The book of Job, paradoxically, is a love story, the love of a man for God and God for a man. Each is angry with the other, yet it is their meeting, not the answer to a question, that redeems fate from tragedy. By the end we begin to feel the full haunting significance of the phrase in Genesis 2: 'It is not good for man to be alone.'

God is the redemption of our solitude. Those who live in the presence of God are not immune to suffering, but they are able to say, 'Though I walk through the valley of the shadow of death I will fear no evil, for you are with me.' *Judaism is the principled defeat of tragedy in the name of hope.*

The Voice of the Not-Yet

That hope forms the substance and structure of Jewish practice. The Jewish festivals are all stories of hope. Passover tells us that a people enslaved, powerless and without rights can win their freedom. Pentecost tells us that a people unloved by their contemporaries can become the covenantal partner of God himself. Tabernacles tells us that even a homeless nation, living in temporary dwellings, is still on a journey to the Promised Land.

The New Year and Day of Atonement are festivals of a different kind of hope. The three pilgrimage festivals are about a nation and its history. The Days of Awe are about the individual and his or her destiny. They tell us that we are not prisoners of our past. We are not condemned forever to be haunted by the wrong we once did. We can repent and be forgiven; we can begin again. The liturgy on these holy days contains a line that in itself is the most explicit rejection of fate in the Greek sense. The Delphic oracle told of decrees that could not be averted, however hard people tried. On the high holy days Jews say to the contrary, 'Penitence, prayer and charity avert the evil decree.' In Judaism there is no such thing as a decree that cannot be averted. Therefore there is no future that is bereft of hope.

The social legislation of Judaism is a minutely articulated set of instructions for building a society of hope. No one is to be allowed to be destitute. The produce of the field and the wealth of the town must be shared. No one is condemned to a lifetime of slavery. One day in seven, all are free. No one is to be indebted forever. Every seven years, all debts are cancelled. No one is forced to sell his or her ancestral inheritance in such a way as to rob their children or grandchildren of their heritage. In the jubilee year, land returns to its original owners. The entire legislative structure is aimed at creating a culture of hope.

Even Judaism's ritual laws are based on this principle. *Tzitzit*, the command to make fringes with a thread of blue on the corners of garments, appears in the Bible immediately after the episode of the spies in which the people lost hope of inheriting the land. The cord of blue was to remind Jews of heaven, and the knowledge that in fighting their battles they were not alone. Even the apparently inscrutable rite of the Red Heifer, which purified people after contact with death, showed that there is no defilement that is permanent, no stain that cannot be removed.

Judaism's ethic of medicine, with its overwhelming emphasis on saving life, tells us that what can be cured need not be endured. Illness is not a divine decree that must be accepted. Not all, perhaps, but most of the commandments are either about creating hope, individually or through networks of support, or about behaviourally inculcating habits of hope.

So it is no accident that in the modern world many Jews became economists fighting poverty, or doctors combating disease, or lawyers contesting injustice, or teachers battling ignorance, or psychotherapists striving to defeat despair. The great Jewish thinkers, even those who had abandoned Judaism, were almost invariably utopians or revolutionaries, charting secular routes to hope.

That is why Jews were so often hated by reactionaries, defenders of the past, its prejudices and privileges. Jews refused to worship the established order when it was manifestly unjust. They refused to see the randomness of fate as inescapable, the result of fate or original sin or pre-ordained hierarchy, the will of the gods or the decree of history. If God is 'I will be what I will be', then humans too share that freedom, albeit within constraints. Each of us is challenged to become what we could become, and to make society what it might be. Judaism is a sustained protest against the world that was and is, in the name of the world that could be, should be, but is not yet. Judaism is the voice of the Not-Yet in human civilisation.

The Voice of Hope in the Conversation of Humankind

This was perhaps the greatest contribution of Judaism—via the Judaic roots of Christianity—to the West. The idea that time is an arena of change, and that freedom and creativity are God's gift to humanity, resulted in astonishing advances in science and our understanding of the world, technology and our ability to control the human environment, economics and our ability to lift people out of poverty and starvation, medicine and our ability to cure disease. It led to the abolition of slavery, the growth of a more egalitarian society, the enhanced position of women, and the emergence of democracy and liberalism. These were all consequences of 'the birth of the modern', set in motion by the Puritans, the Christians who came closest to the Hebrew Bible in their understanding of the world.

Jews never accepted that war, violence, injustice, exploitation, the corruptions of power and the seductions of success are written into the structure of the universe. They do not believe that tragedy is inevitable, that human aspiration is hubris to be punished by nemesis, that a blind fate governs all things, that the universe or the gods are at best indifferent, at worst actively hostile, to humankind. They do not believe that genetic determinism means that all our efforts to change are fruitless and unworthwhile. If God defines himself as 'I will be what I will be', then he is telling us that, created in his image, we too can be what we will be.

Within limits, to be sure. Judaism is not optimism. Jews do not believe in time as a story of unbroken progress. The tale of Adam and Eve is essentially about limits, about the things we can do but may not do. Jewish law is an assemblage of those limits. Without great care, the rich will exploit the poor, the strong will dominate and crush the weak. That was the burden of the prophetic message in ancient times. It should be so now.

To be a Jew is to be an agent of hope. Every ritual, every command, every syllable of the Jewish story is a protest against escapism, resignation and the blind acceptance of fate. Judaism, the religion of the free God, is a religion of freedom. Jewish faith is written in the future tense. It is belief in a future that is not yet but could be, if we heed God's call, obey his will and act together as a covenantal community. The name of the Jewish future is hope.

Somehow, in a way I find mysterious and moving, the Jewish people wrote a story of hope that has the power to inspire all who dare to believe that injustice and brutality are not the final word about the human condition, that faith can be more powerful than empires, that love given is not given in vain, that ideals are not illusions to give us comfort but candles to light our way along a winding road in the dark night without giving way to fear or losing a sense of direction.

The Jewish story is not for Jews alone. From the very beginning it was meant to be shared. When God said to Abraham, 'Through you all the families of earth will be blessed', when Moses said, 'This is your wisdom and understanding in the eyes of the nation', they were signalling that, improbably yet certainly, this journey across the wilderness of time in search of the Promised Land would be one from which all who believe in God, Jew and non-Jew alike, would draw courage. They too would walk it, each in their own way, towards their own field of dreams, their own destination of hope.

Was there ever a less likely hero than Abraham, a man who performed no miracles, led no nation, delivered no great sermon to be inscribed on the hearts of future generations, a man who was promised so much yet saw so little fulfilled in his lifetime? Was there ever a less likely candidate for immortality, or witness to the power of faith, than the people whose name, Israel, means 'One who wrestles with God and with men and yet survives'? For though Jews love humanity, they continue to wrestle with it, challenging the idols of the age, whichever the idols, whatever the age. And though Jews have loved God with an everlasting love, they have never stopped wrestling with him nor him with them. And still Jews survive.

And still Jewish faith survives, a difficult, austere yet honest faith that refuses to make its peace with the evil men do; a faith that sees God as a teacher and humanity his disciples, that believes in freedom and human responsibility and that, when asked, 'Has the Messiah come?' has consistently answered, 'Not yet.'

No faith has endowed the human person with more dignity, seeing us all, whatever our faith or lack of it, as the image and likeness of God, holding all human life sacred, believing that we all have within us the power to defeat the evil that lives in each of us, and insisting on the most improbable of all religious beliefs: that more than we have faith in God, God has faith in us and will never lose that faith.

Jews suffered for that faith, deeper, longer and in more lands than any other, yet they never lost their ability to challenge and argue and question, never sacrificed the critical edge of their intelligence. They did not define themselves as victims, nor did they lose hope or their sense of humour. And though many Jews, during and after the Holocaust, lost faith in God, they never lost their faith in life itself, here on earth with all its pain and loss.

The state of Israel is testimony to that faith. Which other people, exiled for so long, would retain the faith that one day they would return? Which other people would fight so defiantly against those who believe that Jews have no right to their own land where they can defend themselves against those who, throughout history, have sought to destroy them, often in the name of the very God to whom Jews dedicated their lives, knowledge of whom they first introduced to the world?

The world in the twenty-first century needs that faith. In an age of ecological devastation, it needs the Jewish reminder that we are placed on earth, as was Adam in the garden, to 'serve and conserve' it. In an age of economic inequalities, it needs the Jewish insistence on *tzedakah,* charity-as-justice. In an age of terror, it needs the Jewish insistence on the sanctity of life. In an age of religious extremism, it needs to hear the Jewish denial that you can win your place in heaven by murdering the innocent on earth. Martyrdom is the willingness to die for your faith, not the willingness to kill for your faith.

The world needs that difficult, often misunderstood and reviled, Jewish belief that though its religion is not the religion of all humanity, its God is the God of all humanity, so that the righteous of all faiths have a share in the world to come. For if we do not find a way for religions to live together peaceably and with mutual respect, we may yet betray God's image and destroy God's world.

Jews have turned inwards; they need to turn outwards. They are conscious of being different, but so is every member of a minority, and in a global age every group is a minority. Our uniqueness *is* our universality, and it is precisely by sharing our uniquenesses that we enlarge the heritage of humankind. Jews are not the only people to seek God, live lives of faith, work for the betterment of humanity or count themselves blessed by God's love. They are not alone. Jews have friends among many faiths, and among secular humanists, and they should cherish them all, making common cause with them in defence of freedom, human dignity and moral responsibility. They should not take every criticism as a form of antisemitism. They should rest secure in their unparalleled past and face the future with vigilance but without fear.

I have argued for a Judaism that has the courage to engage with the world and its challenges. Faith begets confidence, which creates courage. That is how Jews lived in the past and should live in the future. For they are the people of the journey to a distant destination, begun by Abraham, continued by a hundred generations of ancestors, and it still beckons. Judaism is faith in the future tense. Jews were and are still called on to be the voice of hope in the conversation of humankind.

Epilogue

It was the Holocaust survivors who taught me. I have read hundreds of books about the Shoa. I made a television programme from Auschwitz. To this day I cannot begin to imagine what they went through, how they survived the nightmare, and how they lived with the memories. Many did not. In my first career as a teacher of philosophy one of my academic colleagues committed suicide. I didn't know him well, but he seemed to me a quiet, gentle, loving man. It was only when he died that we discovered he was a Holocaust survivor. I knew, even from the Bible, what happened to Noah after the Flood, and Lot's wife when she turned back to look at the destruction. There are some memories that do not let you live.

But the survivors I came to know in the past twenty years were astonishing in their tenacious hold on life. Perhaps it's how they survived. Some believed in God, others didn't, but they all believed in life—not life as most of us understand it, something taken for granted, part of the background, but life as something to fight for, as a consciously articulated value, as something of whose fragility you are constantly aware. They had, in Paul Tillich's phrase, the courage to be. Slowly I began to think about a phrase, not one that exists in the traditional literature but one that was articulated in fateful circumstances and constituted a kind of turning point in modern Jewish history: *Kiddush hachayim,* the sanctification of life.

I had expected that trauma would turn the survivors inwards, making them suspicious of, even hostile to, the wider world. It didn't, at least not those I knew, and by the time I came to know them. Many of them had undertaken, fifty or more years after the event, to visit schools, talking to children, especially non-Jewish children. What amazed me as I listened to them telling their stories was what they wanted to say. Cherish freedom. Understand what a gift it is to be able to walk in the open, to see a flower, open a window, breathe free air. Love others. Never hate. Practise tolerance. Stand up for others if they are being picked on, bullied, ostracised. Live each day as if it might be your last. They taught the children to have faith in life. The children loved these elderly strangers from another world. I read some of their letters to them; they made me cry. Their courage kept me going through tough times. I count myself blessed to have known them.

Viktor Frankl was a survivor of Auschwitz who spent his time there helping people to find the strength to live. On the basis of his experiences in the death camps, he created a new school of psychotherapy, logotherapy, based on 'man's search for meaning'. He used to say, in the name of Kierkegaard, that the door to happiness opens outwards. By that he meant that the best cure for psychic pain was to care more about other people's pain. That too I learned from the survivors.

Many had lost their families in those years, so they became a kind of extended family to one another, supporting each other through the bad nights and haunted days. And somehow—I found this the most awesome fact about them—they were still capable of joy. In one of my books I had written about the Italian film director Roberto Benigni, who had made a comedy about the Holocaust and called it *Life Is Beautiful*. I said that though I understood the thesis of the film I could not agree with it. In essence it argued that humour kept you sane. Humour may have kept people sane, I said, but sanity was not enough to keep you alive.

'You are wrong,' one of the survivors said to me. Then he told me his story. He and another prisoner, about his age, were in Auschwitz, and they had reached the conclusion that unless they were able to laugh, eventually they would lose the will to live.

So they made an agreement. Each of them would look out, every day, for something about which they could laugh. Each night they would share their findings and laugh together. 'A sense of humour,' said the survivor, looking me in the eyes, 'kept me alive.' That night I wept at the thought of this man who had entered the gates of hell and not lost his humour or humanity.

Then I took out the book that contained the speech from which I had learned the phrase *Kiddush hachayim,* the sanctification of life. It was made by a rabbi, Yitzhak Nissenbaum, at the beginning of the Warsaw ghetto uprising in 1943. That was a turning point in history, one of the first moments since the failure of the Bar Kochba rebellion more than eighteen centuries earlier, when Jews fought back, refusing to die quietly on the altar of other people's hatred. It was a physical revolution, but it was a spiritual one as well. Rabbi Nissenbaum reminded his listeners that for centuries Jews had been faithful to the call of *Kiddush Hashem,* the sanctification of God's name. They were willing to die rather than give up their faith. *Kiddush Hashem* was the Jewish name for martyrdom.

That concept, he said, was no longer adequate. In all other persecutions, Jews had faced a choice: convert or die. In choosing to die, Jews gave witness to their faithfulness to God. The Nazis were different. They did not offer Jews a choice. So the Jewish response had to be different too. They had to fight back. They had to refuse to die. These were his words:

> This is a time for *Kiddush hachayim,* the sanctification of life, and not for *Kiddush Hashem,* the holiness of martyrdom. Previously the Jew's enemy sought his soul and the Jew sanctified his body in martyrdom. Now the oppressor demands the Jew's body, and the Jew is obliged therefore to defend it.[1]

Facing almost certain death, the fighters of the Warsaw ghetto made a momentous affirmation of life. That same spirit moved the builders and defenders of the land of Israel. 'I will not die, but I will live,' says the psalm, and continues, 'and I will declare the works of God.' Sometimes the refusal to die, the insistence on the holiness of life, is itself the work of God.

The time has come to summarise the argument of this book. Jews today face clear and present dangers. Antisemitism has returned in a fourth mutation, using the new media to globalise hate. The state of Israel faces relentless hostility on the part of its enemies, not to this policy or that but to its very existence as a non-Islamic, liberal democratic state. Neither of these phenomena is as yet a mass movement; they are confined to small groups of extremists. But the extremists have learned how to use the new media to inspire widespread fear, and that is what Jews feel today.

At the same time the Jewish people are internally weakened, by assimilation and outmarriage on the one hand, divisions and factionalism on the other. It is hard not to feel the weight of history bearing down on contemporary Jewry, for our people have been here before. Assimilation and factionalism marked Jewry in the late Second Temple period, as well as in Europe in the nineteenth and early twentieth centuries. Antisemitism has been a recurring feature of Jewish history. Jews are no strangers to danger.

But Judaism is a religion of history and freedom: history so that we can learn from it, freedom so that we can act differently next time. History is not inevitability: if it were, Judaism would be false and the tragic vision of the Greeks would be true. My argument has been that something must change in Jewish hearts and minds: the sense of isolation, sometimes proud, sometimes fearful, that comes from seeing yourself as 'the people that dwells alone'. That highly ambivalent phrase, uttered by one of Israel's enemies, the pagan prophet Balaam, should be called into question. It is not necessarily a blessing. It may be a curse. As a self-definition, it will become a self-fulfilling prophecy. Jews will find themselves alone.

The truths of Judaism were not meant for Jews alone. They were meant to inspire others. They do inspire others. They admire the strength of Jewish families and communities. They respect Judaism's commitment to education, argument and the life of the mind. They value its practice of *tzedakah,* charity-as-justice, and the idea of *tikkun olam,* healing a fractured world. They appreciate the clarity of Jewish thought as it applies to the ethical dilemmas of our time. Most of all they respect the fact that Jews do not try to convert anyone. In Judaism, you don't have to be Jewish to be good, to relate to God or to have a share in the world to come.

That delicate counterpoint between the particular and the universal is the music of the Jewish soul. But it also represents a human reality. George Orwell described it well when he differentiated between patriotism and nationalism.[2] Patriotism, he said, is 'devotion to a particular place and a particular way of life, which one believes to be the best in the world but has no wish to force on other people'. Nationalism, by contrast, 'is inseparable from the desire for power'. The abiding purpose of every nationalist, he said, 'is to secure more power and more prestige, *not* for himself but for the nation or other unit in which he has chosen to sink his own individuality'. Judaism is patriotism, not nationalism.

So it must be for every faith and civilisation if we are to safely negotiate the twenty-first century. The problems faced by Jews today are faced by everyone who believes in freedom, democracy and the dignity of the individual. The idea that Jews alone are threatened by terror, hate and the attrition of identity is simply misplaced. In the battles that lie ahead they have allies, but only if they seek them and are willing to work with them, with humility and a sense of global responsibility.

Nietzsche, as I argued in the first chapter, was right: *either* the will to power *or* the will to life. Nationalism was the twentieth-century expression of the will to power. Today it is more likely to be religiously based holy war. No one—no nation, culture or religion—is immune to the temptations of the desire for power. But these temptations must be resisted if humanity is to survive and build societies based on respect for difference and the integrity of the other. Jews have historically been cast in the role of the archetypal other. Therefore they must join with other others, wherever they see minorities persecuted, or populations reduced to poverty, wherever and whenever they hear the cry of the oppressed. Jews must learn to universalise their particularity.

The will to life is not easy or automatic. The human heart is weak and easily frightened into fear, aggression and demonisation. That is especially true in ages, such as the present, when humanity feels itself dragged, against its will, into a vortex of change. That is when people, fearing chaos, begin to divide the world into the children of light and the children of darkness and prepare themselves to fight holy wars in the name of this god or that, 'Jihad versus McWorld' as Benjamin Barber characterises one of the central conflicts of our time.[3] At such historic junctures, in Yeats' famous words, 'the best lack all conviction, while the worst are full of passionate intensity'.

I came to know the late Sir Isaiah Berlin towards the end of his long and distinguished life. He was one of the twentieth century's greatest defenders of freedom, but there was one thing on which we disagreed. At the end of his most famous essay, 'Two Concepts of Liberty', he quoted Joseph Schumpeter: 'To realise the relative validity of one's convictions and yet stand for them unflinchingly, is what distinguishes a civilised man from a barbarian.'[4] Together with others I asked: if one's convictions are only relative, why stand for them unflinchingly? If no truths are absolute, why choose to be civilised at all, rather than a barbarian? Barbarians, 'full of passionate intensity', tend to win the battle when their opponents' convictions are merely relative.

In Judaism, freedom is not a relative value. It is the gift of God who created the world in freedom. Jews believe, with the late John F. Kennedy, that 'the rights of man come not from the generosity of the state, but from the hand of God'. Life is holy.

So is liberty, the value Jews celebrate on Passover as they tell the story of the journey across the wilderness to the Promised Land that, as we saw in the first chapter, inspired George Eliot and Martin Luther King Jr. Jews must join with others in what will be in the twenty-first century, as it was in the twentieth, the defining struggle of our time: on the side of the will to life against the will to power.

That will mean engaging with the world, not disengaging from it. Wherever I see strong commitment in Jewry today—in Israel, in orthodoxy, in religious Zionism—I see an inward turn. Wherever I see an outward turn—among secular or non-Orthodox Jews—I see a weakening of identity and an abandonment of the classic terms of Jewish faith and life. I see, in other words, a continuation of the rift that began two centuries ago, between the particularists and universalists. It weakened Jewry then and is no less dysfunctional now.

Jews have lost touch with their soul. When Jews are in the news today it is almost invariably because of antisemitism, or some Holocaust-related issue, or the politics of the Middle East. I want to say to my fellow Jews with all the passion I can muster: Judaism is bigger than this. A people that has survived, its identity intact, for four thousand years, that reaffirmed life after the Holocaust, that rebuilt its ancestral home after two thousand years of exile and oppression, has more to say to the world than that it has enemies. Everyone has enemies. It has more to its identity than ethnicity. Everyone has ethnicity. Judaism is the sustained attempt to make real in life the transformative power of hope. And the world, in the twenty-first century, needs hope.

Judaism is, to use Nietzsche's phrase, a sustained transvaluation of values. It is the code of a nation that would be called, through its history, to show that civilisations survive not through strength but through the care they show for the weak; not by wealth but because of the help they give to the poor. Nations become invulnerable by caring for the vulnerable. These are deeply paradoxical propositions, and the only thing that can be said in their favour is that they are true. The people of the covenant were never numerous. The Holy Land was never large. The Israelites, later known as the Jews, were attacked by the greatest empires ever to have bestrode the narrow world like a colossus, and they outlived them all. The superpowers of history disappeared into the pages of history, while Jews continue to sing *Am Yisrael Chai,* 'the Jewish people lives'. None of this, I believe, was for the sake of Jews alone, or Judaism alone, but to give hope to the hopeless, dignity to humanity, and moral meaning and purpose to the human story.

Jews staked their existence on the will to life, the sanctity of life, and the transcending beauty of a life lit by hope. And yes, they had faults and doubts, they were obstinate, they had arguments they couldn't resolve and conflicts they couldn't contain, and they fell short time and again. Jews still do. The state of Israel still does. But a people driven by an ideal carries within it the renewable energy of self-criticism and rebirth. Strength fails, wealth diminishes over time, but ideals remain. The stars burn no less brightly because we have not yet reached them.

Jews had faith that the few can defeat the many and the weak outlive the strong if they are moralised and driven by high ideals. The 'war of all against all' exists. Hobbes called it the 'state of nature' in which life is 'solitary, poor, nasty, brutish, and short', the condition of many parts of the world today. Societies can transcend the state of nature by way of *covenant*—a supremely biblical idea. Covenant creates civil society, the perennial alternative to the tyrannical, totalitarian or theocratic state.

And that is the eternal choice, as salient now as at any other time in history: Nietzsche or Abraham? Al Qaeda or Isaiah? *Which will prevail, the will to power or the will to life?* That is a battle in which, in strange ways, Jews have often found themselves on the front line. It will continue to be so in the twenty-first century.

So there is work to do, work that begins within the Jewish soul. For something has changed. A people that can survive the

Holocaust can face the future without fear. So can Israel, having survived every assault by its enemies and given back to the Jewish people a space within which it can defend itself and begin to create the kind of society Jews were commanded to create. The Jewish people today should not doubt its strength. Nor should it doubt the courage it gives to others, or the hope it kindles in vulnerable nations and communities who feel themselves threatened and outnumbered. Now, when every instinct is telling Jews to turn inwards, to fear and be defensive, is the time to do precisely the opposite.

Jews should have enough faith not to fear, enough strength of mind to fight for the rights of oppressed minorities wherever we happen to be. They should be at the forefront of fighting poverty and disease in Africa, and among the leading campaigners for environmental responsibility. They should do so not to win friends or the admiration of others, but because that is what a people of God is supposed to do. Israel must prevail over its fears and not see every criticism as a form of antisemitism or Jewish self-hatred. Jews must stop seeing themselves as victims. They should remember that the word *chosen* means that Jews are called on to be self-critical, never forgetting the tasks they have been set and have not yet completed.

Religious Jews should have enough faith not to fear a confrontation with the world's wisdom, for if it is false they will not be led astray by it, and if it is true they will be enlarged by it. They should have enough self-confidence not to brand every novel thought a heresy, every question a danger, and every Jew who does not believe as we do an enemy. Judaism is stronger than some of its defenders have allowed it to be.

Once, after having spoken about some of these ideas, someone came up to me and said, 'I appreciated your words. But don't you think you are fighting a losing battle?' It was a good question. When I see the isolation of Israel, and the demonisation it suffers, and the return of antisemitism especially to university campuses; when I saw people marching in London under the banner of 'We're all Hizbollah Now'; when I see how little people learn from history, making the same mistakes time and again, I am almost tempted to agree, yes, perhaps this is a losing battle.

What I replied, though, was this: 'Yes, the Jewish fight is a losing battle. It always was. Moses lost. Joshua lost. Jeremiah lost. We have striven for ideals just beyond our reach, hoped for a gracious society just beyond the possible, believed in a messianic age just over the furthest horizon, wrestled with the angel and emerged limping. And in the meanwhile those who won have disappeared, and we are still here, still young, still full of vigor, still fighting the losing battle, never accepting defeat, refusing to resign ourselves to cynicism, or to give up hope of peace with those who, today as in the past, seek our destruction. That kind of losing battle is worth fighting, more so than any easy victory, any premature consolation.'

I do not believe that Jews have a monopoly on wisdom. Yet I was born a Jew, and I cannot betray the hundred generations of my ancestors who lived as Jews and were prepared to die as Jews, who handed their values on to their children, and they to theirs, so that one day their descendants might be free to live their faith without fear and be a source of inspiration to others, not because Jews are any better than anyone else but because that is our story, our heritage, our task, to be a source of hope against a world of despair.

I find it moving that in all the centuries when they were considered pariahs by others, Jews never internalised that perception. They were, they believed, a people loved by God, and though that knowledge could sometimes make them think themselves superior to others, at least it spared them from the worst excesses of self-hatred, that peculiarly modern Jewish affliction. On the festivals they remembered the past and hoped for the future. On Shabbat, however poor they were, they sat at the Sabbath table like free men and women, and sang. And though they could be wracked by poverty, still they built houses of study and sat learning

Talmud and cultivated the life of the mind. And though they were poor they knew there were others poorer than themselves, and they gave them aid, and invited them to their festive meals, and considered themselves bound by a covenant of mutual responsibility.

To have come through the Holocaust and still believe in life, to live through what Israel has lived through and still strive for peace, to have experienced the degree of hate poured out against them by some of Europe's greatest minds and remain undefiled: that is a people of which I am proud to be a part.

I know that not every Jew is Orthodox, and not all believe in God, and some find aspects of our faith unintelligible at best, and many find fault with Israel, and others with Diaspora Jewish life, and we give ourselves great heartache, and we can sometimes be, to others and to God, an exasperating people. Yet every Jew who stays loyal to her or his people, and contributes to it in some way, thereby adds something to the story of the Jewish people, and becomes an agent of hope in the world, God's partner in redemption.

Even if no victory is final, and for each of us there is a Jordan we will not cross, yet this small, otherwise insignificant people has, with surprising consistency, been a blessing to the families of the earth. And though it has fought a losing battle for four thousand years, it still lives and breathes and sings, refusing to despair, still bearing witness, without always knowing it, to the power of God within the human heart to lift us to achievements we could not have reached alone or without the faith of our ancestors. Jews are a small people. Every one of them counts. And the Jewish task remains: to be the voice of hope in an age of fear, the countervoice in the conversation of humankind.

Notes

Prologue

1 Paul Johnson, *A History of the Jews,* London, Weidenfeld and Nicolson, 1987, p. 586.

Chapter 1: Story of the People, People of the Story

1 I am indebted for this account to Gertrude Himmelfarb, *The Jewish Odyssey of George Eliot,* New York, Encounter Books, forthcoming.
2 Martin Luther King Jr, *I Have a Dream,* San Francisco, HarperSanFrancisco Faith, 1992, pp. 193–203.
3 Thomas Paine, *Political Writings,* Cambridge, Cambridge University Press, 1989, p. 41.
4 Emil Fackenheim, *The Jewish Return into History,* New York, Schocken, 1978, pp. 19–24.
5 Joseph B. Soloveitchik, *The Lonely Man of Faith,* New York, Doubleday, 1992.
6 Carl Schmitt, *The Concept of the Political,* Chicago, University of Chicago Press, 2007.
7 David Buss, *The Murderer Next Door,* New York, Penguin, 2006.
8 Aaron T. Beck, *Prisoners of Hate,* New York, HarperCollins, 1999.
9 See Michael Howard, *The Invention of Peace,* London, Profile, 2000.
10 Friedrich Nietzsche, *Twilight of the Idols and The Anti-Christ,* Harmondsworth, Penguin, 1968, p. 134.

Chapter 2: Is There Still a Jewish People?

1 Philologos, 'Peoplehood from the Jews?', *Jewish Daily Forward,* 11 June 2004.
2 David Vital, *The Future of the Jews,* Cambridge, Mass., Harvard University Press, 1990, p. 147.

3 See Michael Wyschogrod, *The Body of Faith: Judaism as Corporeal Election,* New York, Seabury Press, 1983, p. 239.
4 Jonathan Sacks, *One People?: Tradition, Modernity, and Jewish Unity,* London, Littman Library of Jewish Civilization, 1993.
5 *Tosefta Hagigah* 2:9; *Sotah* 14:9.
6 Josephus, *The Jewish War,* trans. G. A. Williamson, Harmondsworth, Penguin, 1959, p. 265.
7 Ibid., p. 264.
8 *Mishnah Avot* 3:2.
9 Saadia Gaon, *Emunot ve-Deot,* III:7; English translation: Saadia Gaon, *The Book of Beliefs and Opinions,* trans. Samuel Rosenblatt, Newhaven, Yale University Press, 1948, p. 158.
10 The manuscript is to be found in the public library at Neuchâtel (Cahiers de brouillons, notes et extraits, no. 7843).
11 *Babylonian Talmud, Yevamot* 47a.
12 Joseph B. Soloveitchik, *Listen—My Beloved Knocks,* trans. Z. Gordon, Jersey City, N.J., KTAV Publishing House, 2006.
13 See also Michael Wyschogrod, *The Body of Faith.*
14 See Jonathan Sacks, *Community of Faith,* London, Peter Halban, 1995.
15 *Leviticus Rabbah,* 4:6.
16 *Mekhilta de-Rabbi Shimon bar Yohai* to Exod. 19:6.
17 *Sifra, Behukotai* 2:7; *Babylonian Talmud, Sanhedrin* 27b; *Shevuot* 39a; *Numbers Rabbah* 10:5; *Song of Songs Rabbah* 7:1; *Yalkut Shimoni, Yitro* 290, 294; *Behukotai* 675.
18 *Sifra, Behukotai* 2:7.
19 Lev. 26:14–46; Deut. 28:15–68.
20 Arthur Koestler, *Promise and Fulfilment: Palestine, 1917–1949*, New York, Macmillan, 1949, p. 335.
21 Maimonides, *Mishneh Torah, Hilkhot Teshuvah,* 3:11.

Chapter 3: Jewish Continuity and How to Achieve It

1 For a fuller account see Jonathan Sacks, *Arguments for the Sake of Heaven: Emerging Trends in Traditional Judaism,* Northvale, N.J., Aronson, 1991; and *Will We Have Jewish Grandchildren?: Jewish Continuity and How to Achieve It,* London, Vallentine Mitchell, 1994.
2 Bernard Wasserstein, *Vanishing Diaspora: The Jews in Europe Since*

1945, Cambridge, Mass., Harvard University Press, 1996; Alan Dershowitz, *The Vanishing American Jew: In Search of Jewish Identity for the Next Century*, Boston, Little, Brown, c. 1997; Jonathan Sacks, *Will We Have Jewish Grandchildren?*

3 *Daily Telegraph*, 25 November 2006, see http://www.telegraph.co.uk/news/uknews/1535182/Is-this-the-last-generation-of-British-Jews.html.

4 Daniel Elazar, *People and Polity: The Organizational Dynamics of World Jewry*, Detroit, Wayne State University Press, 1989, pp. 329–33.

5 http://news.bbc.co.uk/1/hi/uk/7411877.stm.

6 I am indebted in this section to Shmuel Feiner, 'Moses Mendelssohn's Dreams and Nightmares', in Michael Brenner and Lauren B. Strauss (eds.), *Mediating Modernity: Challenges and Trends in the Jewish Encounter with the Modern World—Essays in Honor of Michael A. Meyer*, Detroit, Wayne State University Press, 2008. The classic work is Alexander Altmann, *Moses Mendelssohn: A Biographical Study*, University of Alabama Press, 1973.

7 Feiner, 'Moses Mendelssohn's Dreams and Nightmares', p. 268.

8 Moses Mendelssohn, *Jerusalem, or, On Religious Power and Judaism*, trans. Allan Arkush, Hanover, University Press of New England, 1983, p. 133.

9 Jean-Paul Sartre, *Anti-Semite and Jew*, trans. George J. Becker, New York, Schocken, 1995.

10 Emil L. Fackenheim, *The Jewish Return into History: Reflections in the Age of Auschwitz and a New Jerusalem*, New York, Schocken, 1978, pp. 19–24.

11 Andrew Marr, *Observer*, Sunday 14 May 2000.

12 Arthur Koestler, *The Thirteenth Tribe: The Khazar Empire and Its Heritage*, London, Hutchinson, 1976.

13 James Hider, 'A Tragic Misunderstanding', *The Times*, 13 January 2009.

14 Ruth Wisse, 'The Hebrew Imperative', *Commentary*, June 1990.

15 See also Jack Wertheimer, Charles Liebman and Steven M. Cohen, 'How to Save American Jews', *Commentary*, January 1996, pp. 47–51.

16 See Leon Festinger and James M. Carlsmith, 'Cognitive Consequences of Forced Compliance', *Journal of Abnormal and Social Psychology*, 58, pp. 203–10.

17 Alex and Brett Harris, *Do Hard Things: A Teenage Rebellion Against Low Expectations*, Colorado Springs, Multnomah Books, 2008.

Chapter 4: The Other: Judaism, Christianity and Islam

1 Amy Chua, *World on Fire,* New York, Anchor Books, 2004.

2 René Girard, *Violence and the Sacred,* Baltimore, Johns Hopkins University Press, 1977.

3 A key work is Rosemary Radford Ruether, *Faith and Fratricide: The Theological Roots of Anti-Semitism,* New York, Seabury Press, 1974. See also John G. Gager, *The Origins of Anti-Semitism: Attitudes Toward Judaism in Pagan and Christian Antiquity,* New York, Oxford University Press, 1983; Susannah Heschel, *The Aryan Jesus: Christian Theologians and the Bible in Nazi Germany,* Princeton, Princeton University Press, 2008.

4 Jewish isolationism is at the heart of the several critiques of Jews and Judaism in the era of ancient Greece and Rome. As I explain in chapter 5, I do not see this as antisemitism. It is something similar but different: xenophobia. But the singularity of Judaism was a scandal to Hellenistic universalism.

5 R. Naftali Zvi Yehudah Berlin, *Ha'amek Davar* to Gen. 11:1–9.

6 See, for example, Norman Gottwald, *The Tribes of Yahweh: A Sociology of the Religion of Liberated Israel, 1250–1050 BCE,* Maryknoll, N.Y., Orbis, 1979.

7 *Mishnah Sanhedrin* 4:5. The text of the Mishnah as we have it in printed editions states, 'One life in Israel.' However, as E. E. Urbach (*The Sages,* 1979) points out, the original text reads 'One life' without qualification. Indeed, the Mishnaic passage as a whole, about the sanctity of life, not of Jewish life, is unintelligible otherwise.

8 Samson Raphael Hirsch, *Commentary* to Gen. 9:14.

9 Aristotle, *Politics,* Book II, 1261, 'So that we ought not to attain this greatest unity even if we could, for it would be the destruction of the state.' Karl Popper, *The Open Society and Its Enemies,* Volume I, London, Routledge & Kegan Paul, 1966.

10 Jonathan Sacks, *The Dignity of Difference: How to Avoid the Clash of Civilizations,* London, Continuum, 2002. See also Colin E. Gunton, *The One, the Three, and the Many: God, Creation, and the Culture of Modernity,* Cambridge, Cambridge University Press, 1993.

Chapter 5: Antisemitism: The Fourth Mutation

1 Bernard Lewis, *Semites and Anti-Semites: An Inquiry into Conflict and Prejudice,* New York, Norton, 1986. Robert S. Wistrich (ed.), *Anti-Zionism and Antisemitism in the Contemporary World,* Basingstoke, Macmillan in association with the Institute of Jewish Affairs, 1990. Robert S. Wistrich, *Antisemitism: The Longest Hatred,* New York, Pantheon Books, 1991. Robert S. Wistrich, *Between Redemption and Perdition: Modern Anti-Semitism and Jewish Identity,* London, Routledge, 1990.

2 Ruth R. Wisse, *If I Am Not for Myself: The Liberal Betrayal of the Jews,* New York, Free Press, 1992.

3 See, for example, Rosemary Radford Ruether, *Faith and Fratricide: The Theological Roots of Anti-Semitism,* New York, Seabury Press, 1974; William Nicholls, *Christian Antisemitism: A History of Hate,* Northvale, NJ, Aronson, 1993; Jules Isaac, *The Teaching of Contempt: Christian Roots of Anti-Semitism,* trans. Helen Weaver, New York, Holt, Rinehart and Winston, 1964.

4 On this, see Amy Levine, *The Misunderstood Jew: The Church and the Scandal of the Jewish Jesus,* New York, HarperOne, 2007.

5 See Joshua Trachtenberg, *The Devil and the Jews: The Medieval Conception of the Jew and Its Relation to Modern Antisemitism,* New Haven, Yale University Press, 1943.

6 R. I. Moore, *The Formation of a Persecuting Society: Authority and Deviance in Western Europe, 950–1250,* Malden, Mass., Blackwell, 2007.

7 Raul Hilberg, *The Destruction of the European Jews,* Chicago, Quadrangle, 1961.

8 On philosophical antisemitism, see Nathan Rotenstreich, *Jews and German Philosophy: The Polemics of Emancipation,* New York, Schocken, 1984; Paul Lawrence Rose, *German Question / Jewish Question: Revolutionary Antisemitism from Kant to Wagner,* Princeton, N.J., Princeton University Press, 1992; Michael Mack, *German Idealism and the Jew: The Inner Anti-Semitism of Philosophy and German Jewish Responses,* Chicago, University of Chicago Press, 2003. On Heidegger, see Jonathan Glover, *Humanity: A Moral History of the Twentieth Century,* London, Cape, 1999, pp. 367–76.

9 Available online at http://www.european-forum-on-antisemitism.org/working-definition-of-antisemitism/.

10 See, for example, Joel Kotek, *Cartoons and Extremism: Israel and the Jews in Arab and Western Media,* London, Vallentine Mitchell, 2009; Manfred Gerstenfeld, *Academics Against Israel and the Jews,* Jerusalem Center for Public Affairs, 2007; Manfred Gerstenfeld, *Behind the Humanitarian Mask,* Jerusalem Center for Public Affairs, 2008; and the Middle East Media Research Institute website, which monitors the Middle East media.

11 Walter J. Ong, *Orality and Literacy: The Technologizing of the Word,* London, Routledge, 2002.

12 Benedict Anderson, *Imagined Communities: Reflections on the Origin and Spread of Nationalism,* Verso, 2006.

13 Jonathan Sacks, *The Home We Build Together: Recreating Society,* London, Continuum, 2007.

14 For a more negative evaluation, see See Bat Ye'or, *The Decline of Eastern Christianity Under Islam: From Jihad to Dhimmitude: Seventh–Twentieth Century,* trans. Miriam Kochan and David Littman, Madison, N.J., Fairleigh Dickinson University Press, 1996; *Islam and Dhimmitude: Where Civilizations Collide,* trans. Miriam Kochan and David Littman, Madison, N.J., Fairleigh Dickinson University Press, 2002.

15 Bernard Lewis, 'The New Anti-Semitism', *The American Scholar,* Volume 75, No. 1, Winter 2006, pp. 25–36.

16 Accounts can be found in R. Po-chia Hsia, *The Myth of Ritual Murder: Jews and Magic in Reformation Germany,* New Haven, Yale University Press, 1988; Hermann Strack, *The Jew and Human Sacrifice; Human Blood and Jewish Ritual, an Historical and Sociological Inquiry,* trans. Henry Blanchamp, New York, Blom, 1971; Joshua Trachtenberg, *The Devil and the Jews;* Alan Dundes (ed.), *The Blood Libel Legend: A Casebook in Anti-Semitic Folklore,* Madison, University of Wisconsin Press, 1991; Ronald Florence, *Blood Libel: The Damascus Affair of 1840,* Madison, University of Wisconsin Press, 2004.

17 The classic historical account is Norman Cohn, *Warrant for Genocide,* London, Eyre and Spottiswoode, 1967. See also Hadassa Ben-Itto, *The Lie That Wouldn't Die: The Protocols of the Elders of Zion,* London, Vallentine Mitchell, 2005.

18 They include a work by a French cleric, Abbé Barruel, blaming the

French Revolution on the Order of Templars; a second written by a German, E. E. Eckert, about Freemasons; and the third, a fictional dialogue between Montesquieu and Machiavelli written by Maurice Joly in 1864.

A survey of reactions can be found in MEMRI *Inquiry and Analysis Series—No. 114*, 'Arab Press Debates Antisemitic Egyptian Series "Knight Without a Horse"—Part III', 10 December 2002.

19 MEMRI *Inquiry and Analysis Series—No. 610*, 18 November 2003.

20 María Rosa Menocal, *The Ornament of the World: How Muslims, Jews, and Christians Created a Culture of Tolerance in Medieval Spain*, Boston, Little, Brown, 2002.

21 Hannah Arendt, *Antisemitism: Part One of the Origins of Totalitarianism*, New York, Harvest, 1958, pp. 4–5.

Chapter 6: A People That Dwells Alone?

1 'This brings me to the lamentable resolution adopted by the General Assembly in 1975, equating Zionism with racism and racial discrimination. That was, perhaps, the low point in our relations; its negative resonance even today is difficult to overestimate.' Kofi Annan, *Address to the Israel Foreign Relations Council and the United Nations Association of Israel*, Jerusalem, 25 March 1998.

2 Mary Robinson, former president of Ireland, by then the United Nations human rights commissioner and the person responsible for the gathering, had asked me to help. She knew in advance what was going to happen; she requested that Prince Hassan of Jordan and I (we were both members of the Eminent Persons Group) redraft some of the motions to be presented at Durban so as to address the concerns of the Palestinians and their supporters without an attack on Israel. We did, at a three-day session in Kings College London, organised by the group Rights and Humanity. When our proposals were rejected by the conference steering committee, I resigned from the group.

3 One distinguished instance was the late Yaakov Herzog, whose posthumously published essays were titled *A People That Dwells Alone*, London, Weidenfeld and Nicolson, 1975.

4 Jonathan Sacks, 'Alienation and Faith', reprinted in my *Tradition in an Untraditional Age: Essays on Modern Jewish Thought*, London, Vallentine Mitchell, 1990, pp. 219–44.

5 *Babylonian Talmud Taanit* 20a.

6 *Babylonian Talmud Sanhedrin* 105b.

7 See Arthur Hertzberg, *The French Enlightenment and the Jews: The Origins of Modern Anti-Semitism,* New York, Columbia University Press, 1990; Paul R. Mendes-Flohr and Jehuda Reinharz (eds.), *The Jew in the Modern World: A Documentary History,* New York, Oxford University Press, 1980; Jonathan Sacks, *Arguments for the Sake of Heaven: Emerging Trends in Traditional Judaism,* Northvale, NJ, Aronson, 1991.

8 Elon Founder, *Founder: A Portrait of the First Rothschild and His Time,* New York, Viking, 1996.

9 J. L. Talmon, *Israel Among the Nations,* London, Weidenfeld & Nicolson, 1970, p. 9.

10 Ibid., p. 18.

11 Quoted in Robert Liberles, *Religious Conflict in Social Context: The Resurgence of Orthodox Judaism in Frankfurt am Main, 1838–1877,* Westport, Conn.: Greenwood Press, 1985, pp. 46–7.

12 *Encyclopedia Judaica,* vol. 14, p. 26.

13 Moses Hess, *Rome and Jerusalem,* trans. Maurice J. Bloom, Fourth Letter, pp. 25–7.

14 Sander Gilman, *Jewish Self-Hatred,* Baltimore, Johns Hopkins University Press, 1986, pp. 188–208.

15 Talmon, *Israel Among the Nations,* pp. 36–8.

16 Ibid., pp. 43–5.

17 Jakob Klatzkin, 'Boundaries [1914–1921]', in Arthur Hertzberg (ed.), *The Zionist Idea: A Historical Analysis and Reader,* Philadelphia, Jewish Publication Society, 1997, p. 241.

18 Quoted in Amnon Rubinstein, *The Zionist Dream Revisited,* New York, Schocken, 1984, p. 20.

19 Ibid., pp. 23–4.

20 Ibid., p. 25.

21 To be sure, throughout the medieval rabbinic literature of lament, there is anguish at the isolation of Israel: 'Look down from heaven and see how we have become an object of scorn and derision among the nations,' goes one prayer. 'We are regarded as sheep led to the slaughter, to be killed, destroyed, beaten and humiliated.' But that is circumstance, not destiny. Rabbinic texts often cited to show that the rabbis thought antisemitism inevitable, on closer examination say nothing of the kind. The first person to suggest that antisemitism

was incurable was Leon Pinsker in 1882. We have here a prime example of what Eric Hobsbawm calls 'the invention of tradition'.

22 Mark Roseman, *The Villa, the Lake, the Meeting: Wannsee and the Final Solution*, London, Penguin, 2003.

Chapter 7: Israel: Gateway of Hope

1 Spinoza, *A Theologico-Political Treatise*, trans. R. H. M. Elwes, Mineola, NY, Dover, 2004, p. 46.

2 Jared Diamond, *Guns, Germs, and Steel: The Fates of Human Societies*, New York, Norton, 2005, p. 74.

3 *Babylonian Talmud, Ketubot* 110b.

4 Nachmanides, *Commentary* to Leviticus 18:25.

5 There were at least two proposals in the early twentieth century that separated the idea of self-government from that of the land of Israel: Herzl's Uganda scheme and Dubnow's argument for Jewish autonomy within the Pale of Settlement in Eastern Europe. Neither attracted significant support.

6 Edwin Hodder, *The Life and Work of the Seventh Earl of Shaftesbury*, London, 1886, II, p. 478 (italics in original). See Adam Garfinkle, 'On the Origin . . .', and Diana Muir, 'A Land Without a People for a People Without a Land', *Middle East Quarterly*, Spring 2008. Citations from Gertrude Himmelfarb, *The Jewish Odyssey of George Eliot*, New York, Encounter Books, forthcoming.

7 Raphael Mahler, *A History of Modern Jewry 1780–1815*, New York, Schocken Books, 1971, p. 621.

8 Moses Hess, *Rome and Jerusalem*, trans. Maurice J. Bloom, New York, Philosophical Library, 1958.

9 In Arthur Hertzberg, *The Zionist Idea: A Historical Analysis and Reader*, Philadelphia, Jewish Publication Society, 1997, pp. 178–98.

10 In ibid., pp. 200–25.

11 Martin Gilbert, *Israel: A History*, London, Doubleday, 1998, pp. 402–12.

12 Dennis Ross, *The Missing Peace: The Inside Story of the Fight for Middle East Peace*, New York, Farrar, Straus and Giroux, 2005, p. 748.

13 Ibid., pp. 766, 776.

14 Efraim Karsh, *Islamic Imperialism: A History*, New Haven, Yale University Press, 2007, p. 141.

15 Maimonides, *Mishneh Torah, Laws of Kings* 12:4.

16 For a recent evaluation, see Tamar Harman, 'Most Israelis Support

Negotiations with the Palestinian Authority and Favour the Two-State Solution', 9 March 2009, israelpolicyforum.ngphost.com/blog/most-israelis-support-negotiations-palestinian-authority-and-favor-two-state-solution.

17 www.adherents.com/adh_predom.html.

18 www.oic-oci.org.

Chapter 8: A New Zionism

1 See bibliography for the key works on the subject, especially those by Robert Bellah, Perry Miller and Daniel Elazar.

2 Brian MacArthur, *The Penguin Book of Historic Speeches,* London, Penguin, 1998, pp. 65–6.

3 A complete version of American Presidential Inaugural Addresses can be found at http://www.bartleby.com.

4 Text at http://www.chiefrabbi.org/speeches/European_Parliament_191108.pdf.

5 Text at http://www.nytimes.com/2009/01/20/us/politics/20text-obama.html.

6 Zvi Hirsch Chajes, *Torat Ha-Neviim,* Jerusalem, 1958, pp. 43–9.

7 Thomas Hobbes, *Leviathan,* ed. Richard Tuck, Cambridge, Cambridge University Press, 1991.

8 I Kings 21.

9 Rabbi Abraham Isaac HaCohen Kook, *Responsa Mishpat Cohen,* Jerusalem, Mossad HaRav Kook, 1966, pp. 305–60.

10 Sifra to Lev. 26:37.

11 The phrase 'consent of the governed' is, of course, from the American Declaration of Independence.

12 Thomas Paine, *Political Writings,* ed. Bruce Kuklick, Cambridge, Cambridge University Press, 2000, p. 3.

13 Alexis de Tocqueville, *Democracy in America,* abridged with an introd. by Thomas Bender, New York, Modern Library, 1981.

14 Charles S. Liebman and Eliezer Don-Yehiya, *Civil Religion in Israel: Traditional Judaism and Political Culture in the Jewish State,* Berkeley, University of California Press, 1983, pp. 81–122.

15 Orit Ichilov, 'Youth Movements in Israel as Agents for Transitions to Adulthood', *Jewish Journal of Sociology,* 19, June 1977, p. 25.

16 Liebman and Don-Yehiya, *Civil Religion in Israel,* p. 93.

17 Ibid., p. 91.
18 Lyrics at http://www.richardsilverstein.com/tikun_olam/2004/08/16/david-grossmans/.
19 John Schaar, *Legitimacy and the Modern State,* New Brunswick, N.J., Transaction, 1981, p. 291.
20 Paul Goldberger, *New York Times,* 13 August 1995.
21 Text at http://www.bartleby.com/124/pres67.html.
22 Alexis de Tocqueville, *Democracy in America,* pp. 179–88.

Chapter 9: The Jeish Conversation

1 Ruth R. Wisse, *Jews and Power,* New York, Nextbook & Schocken, 2007, p. xii.
2 Franz Rosenzweig, *Philosophical and Theological Writings,* trans. Paul W. Franks and Michael L. Morgan, Indianapolis, Ind., Hackett, 2000, p. 126.
3 *Targum Onkelos* to Gen. 2:7.
4 *Talmud Yerushalmi, Peah,* 1:1.
5 George H. Mead, *Mind, Self, and Society from the Standpoint of a Social Behaviorist,* ed. Charles W. Morris, Chicago, University of Chicago Press, 1934; Peter L. Berger and Thomas Luckmann, *The Social Construction of Reality: A Treatise in the Sociology of Knowledge,* New York, Irvington Publishers, 1980; Ludwig Wittgenstein, *Philosophical Investigations,* trans. G. E. M. Anscombe, New York, Macmillan, 1958; Charles Taylor, *Sources of the Self: The Making of the Modern Identity,* Cambridge, Mass., Harvard University Press, 1989.
6 *Babylonian Talmud, Berakhot* 26b.
7 Jonathan Eybeschutz, *Tiferet Yehonatan* to Gen. 37:4.
8 Maimonides, *Mishneh Torah, Deot 6:6.*
9 Heinrich Graetz, 'Judaism Can Only Be Understood Through Its History', in Michael Meyer (ed.), *Ideas of Jewish History,* New York, Behrman House, 1974, p. 223.
10 David Cohen, *Kol HaNevuah,* Jerusalem, Mossad HaRav Kook, 1979.
11 See Stuart Hampshire, *Justice Is Conflict,* Princeton, N.J., Princeton University Press, 2000.
12 *Mishnah Avot* 5:17.
13 *Babylonian Talmud Eruvin* 13b.

14 *Babylonian Talmud Baba Metzia* 84a.
15 Albert O. Hirschman, *Exit, Voice, and Loyalty: Responses to Decline in Firms, Organizations, and States,* Cambridge, Mass., Harvard University Press, 1970.
16 Moshe Avigdor Amiel, *Ethics and Legality in Jewish Law,* vol. 1, Jerusalem, 1992.
17 Ibid., p. 71.
18 Ibid., p. 79.
19 *Babylonian Talmud Kiddushin* 30b.
20 Alasdair MacIntyre, *After Virtue,* London, Duckworth, 1981, p. 206.
21 Samuel Freedman, *Jew Versus Jew: The Struggle for the Soul of American Jewry,* Simon and Schuster, 2007. Noah Efron, *Real Jews: Secular Versus Ultra-Orthodox: The Struggle for Jewish Identity in Israel,* New York, Basic Books, 2003. Milton Viorst, *What Shall I Do with This People?: Jews and the Fractious Politics of Judaism,* New York, Free Press, 2002.

Chapter 10: Torah and Wisdom: Judaism and the World

1 See Paul R. Mendes-Flohr and Jehuda Reinharz (eds.), *The Jew in the Modern World: A Documentary History,* New York, Oxford University Press, 1980, pp. 252–3.
2 William Rees-Mogg, *The Reigning Error: The Crisis of World Inflation,* London, Hamilton, 1974, p. 11.
3 Thorstein Veblen, 'The intellectual preeminence of Jews in modern Europe', *Political Science Quarterly,* vol. 34, no. 1, March 1919, pp. 33–42.
4 Yirmiyahu Yovel, *Spinoza and Other Heretics,* Princeton, NJ, Princeton University Press, 1989.
5 See Alasdair MacIntyre, *Against the Self-Images of the Age: Essays on Ideology and Philosophy,* Notre Dame, Ind., University of Notre Dame Press, 1971.
6 J. J. Schachter, 'Haskalah, Secular Studies and the Close of the Yeshiva in Volozhin in 1892', *The Torah u-Madda Journal,* vol. 2, 1990, pp. 200–76.
7 Cecil Roth, *The Jewish Contribution to Civilization,* London, Macmillan, 1938.
8 *Mishnah Avot* 3:14.
9 Judah Halevi, *Sefer ha-Kuzari,* Book IV, 1, 16; *Book of Kuzari,*

trans. Hartwig Hirschfeld, New York, Pardes Publishing House, 1946, pp. 199–201, 223.

10 Among traditional commentators, Abrabanel and Samuel David Luzzato believed that the midwives were Egyptian.

11 See Menahem Kellner, *Dogma in Medieval Jewish Thought: From Maimonides to Abravanel,* Oxford, Oxford University Press, 1986. Franz Rosenzweig, *The Star of Redemption,* trans. William W. Hallo, Notre Dame, Ind., Notre Dame Press, 1971.

12 Rashi, *Commentary* to Gen. 1:26.

13 *Mishnah, Avot* 1:1.

14 *Maimonides, Commentary to the Mishnah, Avot,* Introduction.

15 *Mishnah Avot* 6:6; *Kallah Rabbati* 2:15.

16 *Authorised Daily Prayer Book,* trans. Jonathan Sacks, London, Collins, 2006, p. 782.

17 Ibid., p. 80.

18 *Babylonian Talmud, Shabbat* 75a.

19 *Babylonian Talmud, Menachot* 99b.

20 Halevi, *Kuzari,* Book 1:13; Hirschfeld, p. 45.

21 John Milton, *Areopagitica,* available online at: http://74.125.77.132/search?q=cache:oV4MooqmAu8J:www.uoregon.edu/~rbear/areopagitica.html+milton+areopagitica&hl=en&ct=clnk&cd=2&gl=uk.

22 For a beautiful example, R. Lichtenstein's reading of a poem by Robert Frost, see: http://vbm-torah.org/archive/chag69/TuBishvat69.htm.

Chapter 11: Future Tense: The Voice of Hope in the Conversation of Humankind

1 See Richard Kearney, *The God Who May Be: A Hermeneutics of Religion,* Bloomington, Indiana University Press, 2001, pp. 20–38.

2 J. H. Plumb, *The Death of the Past,* London, Macmillan, 1969. Yosef Hayim Yerushalmi, *Zakhor: Jewish History and Jewish Memory,* New York, Schocken, 1982. Ernst Cassirer, *The Philosophy of Symbolic Forms,* trans. Ralph Manheim, New Haven, Yale University Press, 1953–96. Harold Fisch, *A Remembered Future: A Study in Literary Mythology,* Bloomington, Indiana University Press, 1984. Thomas Cahill, *The Gifts of the Jews: How a Tribe of Desert Nomads Changed the Way Everyone Thinks and Feels,* New York, Nan A. Talese, 1998.

3 Eric Voegelin, *Order and History, Volume 1, Israel and Revelation,* Baton Rouge, Louisiana State University Press, 1956, p. 113.
4 Mircea Eliade, *Cosmos and History; The Myth of the Eternal Return,* trans. Willard R. Trask, New York, Harper, 1959, p. 104.
5 Thomas Cahill, *The Gifts of the Jews,* is particularly good on this.
6 J. H. Plumb, *The Death of the Past,* pp. 56–7.
7 Christopher Booker, *The Seven Basic Plots: Why We Tell Stories,* London, Continuum, 2004.
8 Frank Kermode, *The Sense of an Ending: Studies in the Theory of Fiction,* Oxford, Oxford University Press, 2000.
9 David J. A. Clines, *The Theme of the Pentateuch,* Sheffield, University of Sheffield, 1978.
10 Harold Fisch, *A Remembered Future,* p. 19.
11 *Epistles of Maimonides: Crisis and Leadership,* trans. Abraham Halkin with discussions by David Hartman, Philadelphia, Jewish Publication Society, 1993.
12 Quoted in J. A. Cuddon, *The Penguin Dictionary of Literary Terms and Literary Theory,* London, Penguin, 1991, p. 985.

Epilogue

1 Quoted in Emil Fackenheim, *To Mend the World: Foundations of Future Jewish Thought,* New York, Schocken Books, 1982, p. 223.
2 George Orwell, 'Notes on Nationalism', in *The Penguin Essays of George Orwell,* Harmondsworth, Penguin, 1984, pp. 306–17.
3 Benjamin Barber, *Jihad vs. McWorld,* New York, Ballantine Books, 1996.
4 Isaiah Berlin, *Four Essays on Liberty,* Oxford, Oxford University Press, 1969, p. 172.

For Further Reading

I have not attempted a comprehensive bibliography: the literature on many subjects touched on in the book is vast; on others, almost non-existent. The works listed here will take you further into the argument. Some are standard texts; others are included for their insights into contemporary realities. Each helped me in thinking through the complex issues of identity, difference and human conflict.

Chapter 1: Story of the People, People of the Story

NARRATIVE AND COLLECTIVE IDENTITY:

Anderson, Benedict, *Imagined Communities: Reflections on the Origin and Spread of Nationalism,* Verso, 2006.

Cherry, Conrad (ed.), *God's New Israel: Religious Interpretations of American Destiny,* University of North Carolina Press, 1998.

Goff, Jacques Le, *History and Memory,* Columbia University Press, 1996.

Halbwachs, Maurice, *On Collective Memory,* trans. Lewis A. Coser, Chicago, University of Chicago Press, 1992.

Ignatieff, Michael, *Blood and Belonging: Journeys into the New Nationalism,* New York, Farrar, Straus and Giroux, 1994.

Kohn, Hans, *The Idea of Nationalism: A Study in Its Origins and Background,* New Brunswick, N.J., Transaction, 2005.

Long, V. Philips (ed.), *Israel's Past in Present Research: Essays on Ancient Israelite Historiography,* Winona Lake, Ind., Eisenbrauns, 1999.

Sacks, Jonathan, *The Home We Build Together: Recreating Society,* London, Continuum, 2007.

Smith, Anthony D., *Chosen Peoples: Sacred Sources of National Identity,* New York, Oxford University Press, 2004.

Smith, Anthony D., *The Cultural Foundations of Nations: Hierarchy, Covenant and Republic,* Malden, Mass., Blackwell, 2008.

Smith, Anthony D., *Myths and Memories of the Nation*, New York, Oxford University Press, 1999.

Smith, Rogers M., *Stories of Peoplehood: The Politics and Morals of Political Membership*, New York, Cambridge University Press, 2003.

Zerubavel, Eviatar, *Time Maps: Collective Memory and the Social Shape of the Past*, University of Chicago Press, 2004.

NIETZSCHE, THE WILL TO POWER AND THE JEWS:

Nietzsche, Friedrich, *Basic Writings of Nietzsche*, trans. Walter Kaufmann, New York, Modern Library, 1992.

Nietzsche, Friedrich, *Beyond Good and Evil: Prelude to a Philosophy of the Future*, trans. Judith Norman, Cambridge, Cambridge University Press, 2002.

Nietzsche, Friedrich, *On the Genealogy of Morals*, trans. Douglas Smith, Oxford, Oxford University Press, 1996.

Nietzsche, Friedrich, *Twilight of the Idols and The Anti-Christ*, trans. R. J. Hollingdale, Harmondsworth, Penguin, 1968.

Nietzsche, Friedrich, *The Will to Power*, trans. Walter Kaufmann and R. J. Hollingdale, London, Weidenfeld & Nicolson, 1968.

Mandel, Siegfried, *Nietzsche and the Jews: Exaltation and Denigration*, Amherst, N.Y., Prometheus, 1998.

Yovel, Yirmiyahu, *Dark Riddle: Hegel, Nietzsche, and the Jews*, Pennsylvania State University Press, 1998.

Chapter 2: Is There Still a Jewish People?

Friedmann, Georges, *The End of the Jewish People?*, trans. Eric Mosbacher, London, Hutchinson, 1967.

Koestler, Arthur, *Promise and Fulfilment; Palestine, 1917–1949*, New York, Macmillan, 1949.

Konner, Melvin, *Unsettled: An Anthropology of the Jews*, New York, Penguin, 2004.

Liebman, Charles S., Steven M. Cohen, *Two Worlds of Judaism: The Israeli and American Experiences*, New Haven, Yale University Press, 1990.

Sacks, Jonathan, *Crisis and Covenant: Jewish Thought After the Holocaust*, Manchester, Manchester University Press, 1992.

Sacks, Jonathan, *One People?: Tradition, Modernity, and Jewish Unity*, London, Littman Library of Jewish Civilization, 1993.

Soloveitchik, Joseph B., *Listen—My Beloved Knocks,* trans. Z. Gordon, Jersey City, N.J., KTAV Publishing House, 2006.

Vital, David, *The Future of the Jews,* Cambridge, Mass., Harvard University Press, 1990.

Wyschogrod, Michael, *The Body of Faith: Judaism as Corporeal Election,* New York, Seabury Press, 1983.

Chapter 3: Jewish Continuity and How to Achieve It

Abrams, Elliott, *Faith or Fear: How Jews Can Survive in a Christian America,* New York, Free Press, 1997.

Cohen, Steven M., *American Assimilation or Jewish Revival?,* Bloomington, Indiana University Press, 1988.

Cohen, Steven M., *American Modernity and Jewish Identity,* New York, Tavistock Publications, 1983.

Cohen, Steven M., Arnold M. Eisen, *The Jew Within: Self, Family, and Community in America,* Bloomington, Indiana University Press, 2000.

Cohen, Steven M., *Religious Stability and Ethnic Decline: Emerging Patterns of Jewish Identity in the United States: A National Survey of American Jews,* New York, Florence G. Heller—Jewish Community Centers Association Research Center, 1998.

Cohen, Steven M., *A Tale of Two Jewries: The 'Inconvenient Truth' for American Jews,* New York, Jewish Life Network/Steinhardt Foundation, 2006.

Cohen, Steven M., and Charles S. Liebman, *The Quality of American Jewish Life: Two Views,* New York, American Jewish Committee, 1987.

Dershowitz, Alan, *The Vanishing American Jew: In Search of Jewish Identity for the Next Century,* Boston, Little, Brown, 1997.

Farber, Roberta Rosenberg, Chaim I. Waxman (eds.), *Jews in America: A Contemporary Reader,* Hanover, University Press of New England, 1999.

Heilman, Samuel C., *Portrait of American Jews: The Last Half of the Twentieth Century,* Seattle, University of Washington Press, 1995.

Hertzberg, Arthur, *The Jews in America: Four Centuries of an Uneasy Encounter,* New York, Columbia University Press, 1997.

Hertzberg, Arthur, and Aron Hirt-Manheimer, *Jews: The Essence and Character of a People,* San Francisco, HarperSanFrancisco, 1998.

Liebman, Charles S., *The Ambivalent American Jew; Politics, Religion and*

Family in American Jewish Life, Philadelphia, Jewish Publication Society of America, 1973.

Liebman, Charles S., *Aspects of the Religious Behavior of American Jews,* New York, KTAV Publishing House, 1974.

Sacks, Jonathan, *Will We Have Jewish Grandchildren?: Jewish Continuity and How to Achieve It,* London, Vallentine Mitchell, 1994.

Susser, Bernard, and Charles S. Liebman, *Choosing Survival: Strategies for a Jewish Future,* New York, Oxford University Press, 1999.

Wasserstein, Bernard, *Vanishing Diaspora: The Jews in Europe Since 1945,* Cambridge, Mass., Harvard University Press, 1996.

Chapter 4: The Other: Judaism, Christianity and Islam

JUDAISM AND CHRISTIANITY:

Bellis, Alice Ogden, Joel S. Kaminsky (eds.), *Jews, Christians, and the Theology of the Hebrew Scriptures,* Atlanta, Society of Biblical Literature, 2000.

Carroll, James, *Constantine's Sword: The Church and the Jews, a History,* Boston, Houghton Mifflin, 2001.

Greenberg, Irving, *For the Sake of Heaven and Earth: The New Encounter between Judaism and Christianity,* Philadelphia, Jewish Publication Society, 2004.

Heschel, Susannah, *The Aryan Jesus: Christian Theologians and the Bible in Nazi Germany,* Princeton, Princeton University Press, 2008.

Isaac, Jules, *Has Anti-Semitism Roots in Christianity?,* trans. Dorothy and James Parkes, New York, National Conference of Christians and Jews, 1961.

Isaac, Jules, *Jesus and Israel,* trans. Sally Gran, New York, Holt, Rinehart and Winston, 1971.

Isaac, Jules, *The Teaching of Contempt; Christian Roots of Anti-Semitism,* trans. Helen Weaver, New York, Holt, Rinehart and Winston, 1964.

Maccoby, Hyam, *Judaism on Trial: Jewish-Christian Disputations in the Middle Ages,* London, Associated University Presses, 1982.

Maccoby, Hyam, *Judas Iscariot and the Myth of Jewish Evil,* New York, Free Press, 1992.

Maccoby, Hyam, *The Mythmaker: Paul and the Invention of Christianity,* New York, Harper & Row, 1986.

Maccoby, Hyam, *Paul and Hellenism,* London, SCM Press, 1991.

Maccoby, Hyam, *The Sacred Executioner: Human Sacrifice and the Legacy of Guilt,* London, Thames and Hudson, 1982.

Moore, R. I., *The Formation of a Persecuting Society: Authority and Deviance in Western Europe, 950–1250*, Malden, Mass.: Blackwell, 2007.

Neusner, Jacob, *A Rabbi Talks with Jesus*, Montreal, McGill-Queen's University Press, 2000.

Novak, David, *Jewish–Christian Dialogue: A Jewish Justification*, New York, Oxford University Press, 1989.

Novak, David, *Jewish–Christian Relations in a Secular Age*, San Francisco, Calif., Swig Judaic Studies Program at the University of San Francisco, 1998.

Novak, David, *Talking with Christians: Musings of a Jewish Theologian*, Grand Rapids, Mich., William B. Eerdmans Publishing Co., c. 2005.

Ruether, Rosemary Radford, *Faith and Fratricide: The Theological Roots of Anti-Semitism*, New York, Seabury Press, 1974.

Wyschogrod, Michael, *Abraham's Promise: Judaism and Jewish–Christian Relations*, Grand Rapids, Mich., William B. Eerdmans, 2004.

JUDAISM AND ISLAM:

Brown, Arthur, *Noah's Other Son: Bridging the Gap between the Bible and the Qur'an*, New York, Continuum, 2007.

Firestone, Reuven, *An Introduction to Islam for Jews*, Philadelphia, Jewish Publication Society, 2008.

Firestone, Reuven, *Who Are the Real Chosen People?: The Meaning of Chosenness in Judaism, Christianity, and Islam*, Woodstock, Vt., SkyLight Paths, 2008.

Katsh, Abraham I., *Judaism in Islām: Biblical and Talmudic Backgrounds of the Koran and Its Commentaries*, New York, Sepher-Hermon Press, 1980.

Lewis, Bernard, 'The New Anti-Semitism', *The American Scholar*, Vol. 75, No. 1, Winter 2006, pp. 25–36.

Lewis, Bernard, 'The Roots of Muslim Rage', *Atlantic*, September 1990.

Lewis, Bernard, *Semites and Antisemites*, New York, Norton, 1986.

Rosenthal, Erwin, *Judaism and Islam*, London, T. Yoseloff, 1961.

JEWS AND THE OTHER:

Biale, David, Michael Galchinsky, Susannah Heschel (eds.), *Insider/Outsider: American Jews and Multiculturalism*, Berkeley, University of California Press, 1998.

Gilman, Sander L., *Multiculturalism and the Jews*, New York, Routledge, 2006.

Sacks, Jonathan, *The Home We Build Together: Recreating Society,* London, Continuum, 2007.

Chapter 5: Antisemitism: The Fourth Mutation

Arendt, Hannah, *Antisemitism: Part One of the Origins of Totalitarianism,* New York, Harvest, 1958.

Berenbaum, Michael (ed.), *Not Your Father's Antisemitism: Hatred of the Jews in the 21st Century,* St Paul, Minn., Paragon House, 2008.

Berger, David, *From Crusades to Blood Libels to Expulsions: Some New Approaches to Medieval Antisemitism,* New York, Touro, 1997.

Chesler, Phyllis, *The New Anti-Semitism: The Current Crisis and What We Must Do About It,* San Francisco, Jossey-Bass, 2003.

Cohn-Sherbok, Dan, *Anti-Semitism: A History,* Thrupp, Stroud, Gloucestershire, Sutton, 2002.

Fineberg, Michael, Shimon Samuels, Mark Weitzman (eds.), *Antisemitism: The Generic Hatred: Essays in Memory of Simon Wiesenthal,* London, Vallentine Mitchell, 2007.

Gager, John G., *The Origins of Anti-Semitism: Attitudes Toward Judaism in Pagan and Christian Antiquity,* New York, Oxford University Press, 1983.

Gerstenfeld, Manfred, *Academics Against Israel and the Jews,* Jerusalem, Jerusalem Centre for Public Affairs, 2007.

Harrison, Bernard, *The Resurgence of Anti-Semitism: Jews, Israel, and Liberal Opinion,* Lanham, Rowman & Littlefield, 2006.

Iganski, Paul, Barry Kosmin (eds.), *The New Antisemitism?: Debating Judeophobia in 21st-century Britain,* London, Profile, 2003.

Katz, Jacob, *From Prejudice to Destruction: Anti-Semitism, 1700–1933,* Cambridge, Mass., Harvard University Press, 1980.

Kuntzel, Matthias, *Jihad and Jew-Hatred: Islamism, Nazism and the Roots of 9/11,* New York, Telos Press, 2007.

Laqueur, Walter, *The Changing Face of Anti-Semitism: From Ancient Times to the Present Day,* Oxford, Oxford University Press, 2006.

Lewis, Bernard, *Semites and Anti-Semites: An Inquiry into Conflict and Prejudice,* New York, Norton, 1986.

Maccoby, Hyam, *A Pariah People: The Anthropology of Antisemitism,* London, Constable, 1996.

MacShane, Denis, *Globalising Hatred: The New Antisemitism,* London, Weidenfeld and Nicolson, 2008.

Nicholls, William, *Christian Antisemitism: A History of Hate,* Northvale, N.J., Aronson, 1993.

Ozick, Cynthia, and Ron Rosenbaum (eds.), *Those Who Forget the Past: The Question of Anti-Semitism,* New York, Random House, 2004.

Perry, Marvin, and Frederick M. Schweitzer (eds.), *Antisemitic Myths: A Historical and Contemporary Anthology,* Bloomington, Indiana University Press, 2008.

Poliakov, Leon, *The History of Anti-Semitism,* 4 volumes, Philadelphia, University of Pennsylvania Press, 2003.

Rose, Paul Lawrence, *Revolutionary Antisemitism in Germany from Kant to Wagner,* Princeton, N.J., Princeton University Press, 1990.

Sartre, Jean-Paul, *Anti-Semite and Jew: An Exploration of the Etiology of Hate,* New York, Schocken, 1995.

Schoenfeld, Gabriel, *The Return of Anti-Semitism,* San Francisco, Encounter Books, 2004.

Trachtenberg, Joshua, *The Devil and the Jews: The Medieval Conception of the Jew and Its Relation to Modern Anti-Semitism,* Philadelphia, Jewish Publication Society, 1993.

Wistrich, Robert S., *Antisemitism: The Longest Hatred,* New York, Schocken, 1991.

Wistrich, Robert S., *Anti-Semitism and Multiculturalism: The Uneasy Connection,* Jerusalem, Hebrew University, 2007.

Wistrich, Robert S., *Between Redemption and Perdition: Modern Anti-Semitism and Jewish Identity,* London, Routledge, 1990.

Wistrich, Robert S., *Muslim Anti-Semitism: A Clear and Present Danger,* New York, American Jewish Committee, 2002.

Wistrich, Robert S. (ed.), *Anti-Zionism and Antisemitism in the Contemporary World,* New York, New York University Press, 1990.

Chapter 6: A People That Dwells Alone?

Gilman, Sander L., *Jewish Self-Hatred: Anti-Semitism and the Hidden Language of the Jews,* Baltimore, Johns Hopkins University Press, 1986.

Herzog, Yaacov, *A People That Dwells Alone: Speeches and Writings,* ed. Misha Louvish, London, Weidenfeld and Nicolson, 1975.

Kaminsky, *Yet I Loved Jacob: Reclaiming the Biblical Concept of Election,* Nashville, Abingdon Press, 2007.

Novak, David, *The Election of Israel: The Idea of the Chosen People,* Cambridge, Cambridge University Press, 1995.

Novak, David, *The Image of the Non-Jew in Judaism: An Historical and Constructive Study of the Noahide Laws,* New York, E. Mellen Press, 1983.

Novak, David, *Maimonides on Judaism and Other Religions,* Cincinnati, Hebrew Union College Press, 1997.

Novak, David, *Natural Law in Judaism,* Cambridge, Cambridge University Press, 1998.

Rubinstein, Amnon, *The Zionist Dream Revisited: From Herzl to Gush Emunim and Back,* New York, Schocken, 1984.

Sacks, Jonathan, *The Dignity of Difference: How to Avoid the Clash of Civilizations,* London, Continuum, 2002.

Sacks, Jonathan, *Radical Then, Radical Now,* London, HarperCollins, 2000 (published in USA as *A Letter in the Scroll,* New York, Free Press, 2000).

Sharansky, Natan, with Shira Wolosky Weiss, *Defending Identity: Its Indispensable Role in Protecting Democracy,* London, Perseus, 2008.

Talmon, J. L., *Israel Among the Nations,* London, Weidenfeld and Nicolson, 1970.

Talmon, J. L., *The Unique and the Universal,* New York, G. Braziller, 1966.

Walzer, Michael, *Interpretation and Social Criticism,* Cambridge, Mass., Harvard University Press, 1987.

Walzer, Michael, *Spheres of Justice: A Defense of Pluralism and Equality,* New York, Basic Books, 1983.

Walzer, Michael, *Thick and Thin: Moral Argument at Home and Abroad,* Notre Dame, Ind., University of Notre Dame Press, 1994.

Chapter 7: Israel, Gateway of Hope

Bard, Mitchell G., *Will Israel Survive?,* New York, Palgrave Macmillan, 2006.

Clinton, Bill, *My Life,* New York, Knopf, 2004.

Dershowitz, Alan, *The Case Against Israel's Enemies,* Hoboken, N.J., John Wiley & Sons, 2008.

Dershowitz, Alan, *The Case for Israel,* Hoboken, N.J., John Wiley & Sons, 2003.

Dershowitz, Alan, *The Case for Peace: How the Arab–Israeli Conflict Can Be Resolved,* Hoboken, N.J., John Wiley & Sons, 2005.

Gans, Chaim, *A Just Zionism: On the Morality of the Jewish State,* New York, Oxford University Press, 2008.

Gilbert, Martin, *Israel: A History*, McNally & Loftin, 2008.

Gordis, Daniel, *Coming Together, Coming Apart: A Memoir of Heartbreak and Promise in Israel*, Hoboken, N.J., John Wiley & Sons, 2006.

Gordis, Daniel, *If a Place Can Make You Cry: Dispatches from an Anxious State*, New York, Crown Publishers, 2002.

Gordis, Daniel, *Saving Israel: How the Jewish State Can Win a War That May Never End*, Hoboken, N.J., John Wiley & Sons, 2009.

Hertzberg, Arthur, *The Zionist Idea: A Historical Analysis and Reader*, Philadelphia, Jewish Publication Society, 1997.

Horovitz, David, *Still Life with Bombers: Israel in the Age of Terrorism*, New York, Alfred A. Knopf, 2004.

Laqueur, Walter, *A History of Zionism: From the French Revolution to the Establishment of the State of Israel*, New York, Schocken, 2003.

Laqueur, Walter, and Barry Rubin (eds.), *The Israel–Arab Reader: A Documentary History of the Middle East Conflict*, New York, Penguin Books, 1984.

Lochery, Neill, *The View from the Fence: The Arab–Israeli Conflict from the Present to Its Roots*, London, Continuum, 2007.

Lochery, Neill, *Why Blame Israel?*, Cambridge, Icon, 2004.

Lozowick, Yaacov, *Right to Exist: A Moral Defense of Israel's Wars*, New York, Doubleday, 2003.

O'Brien, Conor Cruise, *The Siege: The Saga of Israel and Zionism*, New York, Simon and Schuster, 1986.

Oren, Michael B., *Six Days of War: June 1967 and the Making of the Modern Middle East*, New York, Ballantine, 2003.

Ravitzky, Aviezer, *Messianism, Zionism, and Jewish Religious Radicalism*, Chicago, University of Chicago Press, 1996.

Ross, Dennis, *The Missing Peace: The Inside Story of the Fight for Middle East Peace*, New York, Farrar, Straus and Giroux, 2004.

Sachar, Howard M., *A History of Israel: From the Rise of Zionism to Our Time*, New York, Knopf, 2007.

Shindler, Colin, *A History of Modern Israel*, Cambridge, Cambridge University Press, 2008.

Vital, David, *The Origins of Zionism*, Oxford, Clarendon Press, 1975.

Vital, David, *Zionism: The Crucial Phase*, Oxford, Clarendon Press, 1987.

Vital, David, *Zionism, The Formative Years*, Oxford, Clarendon Press, 1982.

Chapter 8: A New Zionism

POLITICS, SOCIETY, IDENTITY AND CIVIL SOCIETY IN ISRAEL:

Almog, Oz, *The Sabra: The Creation of the New Jew,* Berkeley, University of California Press, 2000.

Ben-Yehuda, Nachman, *Masada Myth: Collective Memory and Mythmaking in Israel,* Madison, Wis., University of Wisconsin Press, 1995.

Cohen, Asher, and Bernard Susser, *Israel and the Politics of Jewish Identity: The Secular-Religious Impasse,* Baltimore, Johns Hopkins University Press, 2000.

Deshen, Shlomo, Charles S. Liebman and Moshe Skokeid (eds.), *Israeli Judaism: The Sociology of Religion in Israel,* New Brunswick, N.J., Transaction, 1995.

Kimmerling, Baruch, *The Invention and Decline of Israeliness: State, Society, and the Military,* Berkeley, University of California Press, 2005.

Liebman, Charles S., *Religion, Democracy and Israeli Society,* Amsterdam, The Netherlands, Harwood Academic, 1997.

Liebman, Charles S. (ed.), *Religious and Secular: Conflict and Accommodation Between Jews in Israel,* Jerusalem, Keter, 1990.

Liebman, Charles S., and Eliezer Don-Yehiya, *Civil Religion in Israel: Traditional Judaism and Political Culture in the Jewish State,* Berkeley, University of California Press, 1983.

Liebman, Charles S., and Eliezer Don-Yehiya, *Religion and Politics in Israel,* Bloomington, Indiana University Press, 1984.

Liebman, Charles S., and Elihu Katz (eds.), *The Jewishness of Israelis: Responses to the Guttman Report,* Albany, State University of New York Press, 1997.

Silberstein, Laurence J., *The Postzionism Debates: Knowledge and Power in Israeli Culture,* London, Routledge, 1999.

Zerubavel, Yael, *Recovered Roots: Collective Memory and the Making of Israeli National Tradition,* Chicago, University of Chicago Press, 1997.

THE POLITICS OF COVENANT AND
THE JEWISH POLITICAL TRADITION:

Allen, Joseph L., *Love and Conflict: A Covenantal Model of Christian Ethics,* Lanham, University Press of America, 1995.

Bellah, Robert, *Beyond Belief: Essays on Religion in a Post-Traditional World,* Berkeley, University of California Press, 1991.

Bellah, Robert, *The Broken Covenant: American Civil Religion in Time of Trial,* Chicago, University of Chicago Press, 1992.

Cohen, Stuart A., *The Three Crowns: Structures of Communal Politics in Early Rabbinic Jewry,* Cambridge, Cambridge University Press, 2007.

Elazar, Daniel, *Covenant and Civil Society,* New Brunswick, N.J., Transaction, 1998.

Elazar, Daniel, *Covenant and Commonwealth,* New Brunswick, N.J., Transaction, 1996.

Elazar, Daniel, *Covenant and Constitutionalism,* New Brunswick, N.J., Transaction, 1998.

Elazar, Daniel, *Covenant and Polity in Biblical Israel,* New Brunswick, N.J., Transaction, 1995.

Elazar, Daniel, *People and Polity,* Detroit, Wayne State University Press, 1989.

Elazar, Daniel (ed.), *Kinship and Consent,* Brunswick, N.J., Transaction, 1997.

Elazar, Daniel, and Stuart A. Cohen, *The Jewish Polity: Jewish Political Organization from Biblical Times to the Present,* Bloomington, Indiana University Press, 1985.

Hillers, Delbert, *Covenant: The History of a Biblical Idea,* Baltimore, Johns Hopkins University Press, 1969.

Miller, Perry, *The New England Mind: The Seventeenth Century,* Cambridge, Mass., Harvard University Press, 1954.

Mittleman, Alan L., *The Scepter Shall Not Depart from Judah, Perspectives on the Persistence of the Political in Judaism,* Lanham, Lexington, 2000.

Novak, David, *Covenantal Rights: A Study in Jewish Political Theory,* Princeton, N.J., Princeton University Press, 2000.

Novak, David, *The Jewish Social Contract: An Essay in Political Theology,* Princeton, N.J., Princeton University Press, 2005.

Paine, Thomas, *Political Writings,* ed. Bruce Kuklick, Cambridge, Cambridge University Press, 2000.

Sacks, Jonathan, *The Home We Build Together: Recreating Society,* London, Continuum, 2007.

Sacks, Jonathan, *The Politics of Hope,* London, Vintage, 2000.

Sacks, Jonathan, *Radical Then, Radical Now,* London, HarperCollins, 2000 (published in USA as *A Letter in the Scroll,* New York, Free Press, 2000).

Selznick, Philip, *The Moral Commonwealth,* Berkeley, University of California Press, 1994.

Sicker, Martin, *The Judaic State: A Study in Rabbinic Political Theory,* New York, Praeger, 1988.

Sicker, Martin, *The Political Culture of Judaism,* Westport, Praeger, 2001.

Sicker, Martin, *What Judaism Says About Politics: The Political Theology of the Torah,* Northvale, N.J., J. Aronson, c. 1994.

Smith, Anthony D., *Chosen Peoples,* Oxford, Oxford University Press, 2003.

Tocqueville, Alexis de, *Democracy in America,* abridged with an introduction by Thomas Bender, New York, Modern Library, 1981.

Walzer, Michael, *Exodus and Revolution,* New York, Basic Books, 1985.

Walzer, Michael (ed.), *Law, Politics, and Morality in Judaism,* Princeton, N.J., Princeton University Press, 2006.

Walzer, Michael, Menachem Lorberbaum, Noam J. Zohar, Yair Lorberbaum (eds.), *The Jewish Political Tradition* (2 volumes), New Haven, Yale University Press, 2000–03.

Chapter 9: The Jewish Conversation

Amiel, Moshe Avigdor, *Ethics and Legality in Jewish Law,* Vol. 1, Jerusalem, 1992.

Efron, Noah, *Real Jews: Secular Versus Ultra-Orthodox: The Struggle for Jewish Identity in Israel,* New York, Basic Books, 2003.

Freedman, Samuel, *Jew vs Jew: The Struggle for the Soul of American Jewry,* New York, Simon and Schuster, 2007.

Gopin, Marc, *Between Eden and Armageddon: The Future of World Religions, Violence, and Peacemaking,* Oxford/New York, Oxford University Press, 2000.

Gopin, Marc, *Holy War, Holy Peace: How Religion Can Bring Peace to the Middle East,* New York, Oxford University Press, 2002.

Jewish Political Studies Review, Vol. 12, Nos. 3 and 4, Fall 2000 (issue devoted to Jewish approaches to conflict resolution).

Rosenzweig, Franz, *Philosophical and Theological Writings,* trans. Paul W. Franks and Michael L. Morgan, Indianapolis, Hackett, 2000.

Sacks, Jonathan, *Arguments for the Sake of Heaven: Emerging Trends in Traditional Judaism,* Northvale, N.J., Aronson, 1991.

Shils, Edward, *The Virtue of Civility,* Indianapolis, Liberty, 1997.

Viorst, Milton, *What Shall I Do with This People?: Jews and the Fractious Politics of Judaism,* New York, Free Press, 2002.

Wisse, Ruth, *Jews and Power,* New York, Nextbook, Schocken, 2007.

Chapter 10: Torah and Wisdom: Judaism and the World

Heilman, Samuel C., *Sliding to the Right: The Contest for the Future of American Jewish Orthodoxy,* Berkeley: University of California Press, c. 2006.

Hirsch, Samson Raphael, *The Collected Writings,* New York, Feldheim, 1984–95.

Hirsch, Samson Raphael, *Fundamentals of Judaism: Selections from the Works of Rabbi Samson Raphael Hirsch,* ed. Jacob Breuer, New York, Feldheim, 1969.

Hirsch, Samson Raphael, *Horeb: A Philosophy of Jewish Laws and Observations,* trans. I. Grunfeld, London, Soncino Press, 1962.

Hirsch, Samson Raphael, *The Nineteen Letters,* trans. Karin Paritzky, Jerusalem, Feldheim, 1995.

Kook, Abraham Isaac, *The Lights of Penitence, The Moral Principles, Lights of Holiness, Essays, Letters, and Poems,* trans. Ben Zion Bokser, New York, Paulist Press, 1978.

Kook, Abraham Isaac, *Rabbi Kook's Philosophy of Repentance: A Translation of 'Orot ha-teshuvah',* Alter B. Z. Metzger, New York, Yeshiva University Press, 1978.

Kook, Abraham Isaac, *Selected Letters,* trans. Tzvi Feldman, Ma'aleh Adumim, Israel, Ma'aliot, 1986.

Margolese, Faranak, *Off the Derech: Why Observant Jews Leave Judaism,* Jerusalem, Devora Pub., 2005.

Sacks, Jonathan, *Tradition in an Untraditional Age,* London, Vallentine Mitchell, 1990.

Schachter, J. J. (ed.), *Judaism's Encounter with Other Cultures,* Northvale, N.J., Jason Aronson, 1997.

Shapiro, Marc B., *Between the Yeshiva World and Modern Orthodoxy: The Life and Works of Rabbi Jehiel Jacob Weinberg, 1884–1966,* Portland, Littman Library, 1999.

Sokol, Moshe Z. (ed.), *Engaging Modernity: Rabbinic Leaders and the Challenge of the Twentieth Century,* Northvale, N.J., Aronson, 1997.

Soloveitchik, Joseph B., *And From There You Shall Seek,* trans. Naomi Goldblum, Jersey City, KTAV Publishing House, 2008.

Soloveitchik, Joseph B., *Halakhic Man,* trans. Lawrence Kaplan, Philadelphia, Jewish Publication Society of America, 1983.

Soloveitchik, Joseph B., *The Halakhic Mind: An Essay on Jewish Tradition and Modern Thought,* New York, Seth Press, 1986.

Soloveitchik, Joseph B., *The Lonely Man of Faith,* New York, Doubleday, 2006.

Chapter 11: Future Tense: The Voice of Hope in the Conversation of Humankind

Bloch, Ernst, *The Principle of Hope,* trans. Neville Plaice, Stephen Plaice, and Paul Knight, Cambridge, Mass., MIT Press, 1986.

Cahill, Thomas, *The Gifts of the Jews: How a Tribe of Desert Nomads Changed the Way Everyone Thinks and Feels,* New York, Nan A. Talese, 1998.

Eliade, Mircea, *Cosmos and History; The Myth of the Eternal Return,* trans. Willard R. Trask, New York, Harper, 1959.

Fisch, Harold, *A Remembered Future: A Study in Literary Mythology,* Bloomington, Indiana University Press, 1984.

Kearney, Richard, *The God Who May Be: A Hermeneutics of Religion,* Bloomington, Indiana University Press, 2001.

Plumb, J. H., *The Death of the Past,* London, Macmillan, 1969.

Sacks, Jonathan, *From Optimism to Hope,* London, Continuum, 2004.

Sacks, Jonathan, *The Politics of Hope,* London, Vintage, 2000.

Voegelin, Eric, *Order and History, Volume 1, Israel and Revelation,* Baton Rouge, Louisiana State University Press, 1956.

Yerushalmi, Yosef Hayim, *Zakhor, Jewish History and Jewish Memory,* New York, Schocken, 1982.